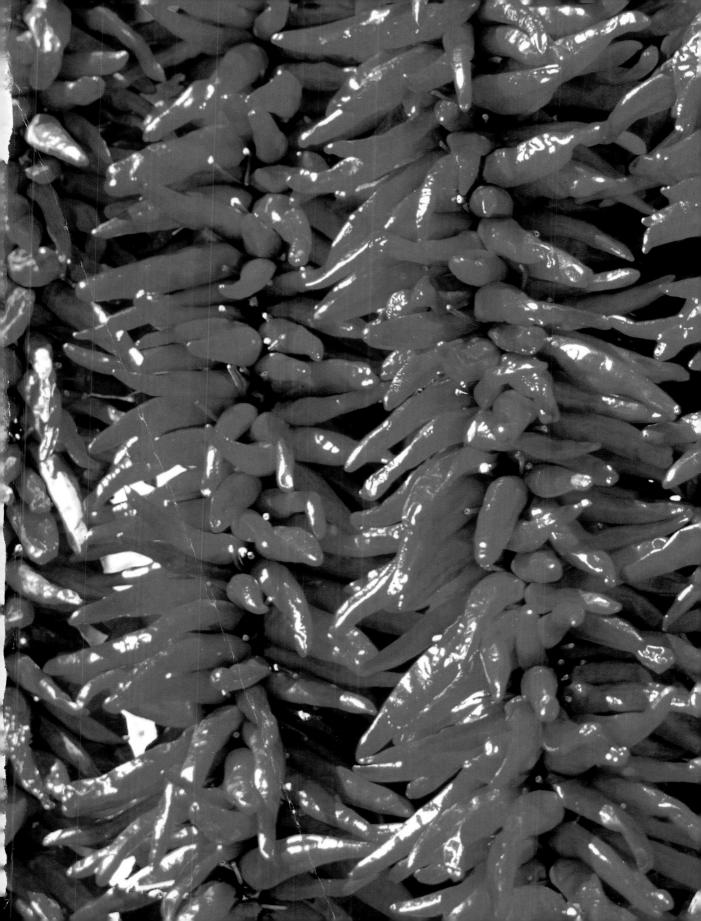

LEITH'S LATIN-AMERICAN COOKING

LATIN AMERICA

MEXICO

Gulf of Mexico

Mexico City

Acapulco

Belize
BELIZE

GUAT.
HOND.

Guatemala
SAL.
NICA.

Caribbean Sea

COSTA
RICA

PANAMA

Panama
Canal

Caracas

VENEZUELA

Georgetown
Paramaribo
Cayenne

Bogota

COLOMBIA

GUYANA
SURINAME
FRENCH GUIANA

Pacific
Ocean

Quito
EQUADOR

PERU

Manaus

Belém

Recife

BRAZIL

Salvador

Lima

Las Paz

BOLIVIA

Sucre

PARAGUAY

Rio de Janeiro

San Paulo

Anuncion

South
Atlantic
Ocean

North

URUGUAY

West

East

Valparaiso
Santiago

Rosario

Buenos Aires

Montevideo

Mar del Plata

South

CHILE

ARGENTINA

Scotia Sea

LEITH'S
LATIN-AMERICAN
COOKING

Valéria Vieira Sisti

Foreword by **Caroline Waldegrave**

Photographs by **Graham Kirk**

RUNNING PRESS
PHILADELPHIA · LONDON

9 8 7 6 5 4 3 2 1
Digit on the right indicates the number of this printing

Library of Congress Cataloging-in-Publication Number 98-65182
ISBN 0-7624-0357-8

PICTURE SOURCES—Robert Harding: pages 23, 27, 88, 139, 145 and 222;
Impact Photos: pages 8, 13, 73, 83 and 109; Lupe Cunha: pages 54, 101,
120, 127, 141 and 144; Panos Pictures: pages 36, 60, 80, 99, 103, 110, 130,
134, 147, 160, 164, 166, 172, 186, 202, 205, 213, 222, 230, 241, 246, 271
and 272; Pictor International: pages 1, 2, 4, 190 and 269; Telegraph Colour
Library: pages 41, 148 and 254.

This book may be ordered by mail from the publisher.
Please include $2.50 for postage and handling.
But try your bookstore first!

Running Press Book Publishers
125 South Twenty-second Street
Philadelphia, Pennsylvania 19103-4399

CONTENTS

Acknowledgements   10

Foreword   11

Introduction   12

A Brief History of Latin America and its Food   17

Catering Quantities   22

Soups   25

First Courses and Salads   37

Poultry   61

Meat   81

Seafood   111

Vegetable Dishes   131

Beans and Rice   149

Tortilla Dishes   161

Salsas, Sauces, and Stocks   173

Chiles   191

Desserts and Ice Creams   203

Cakes, Breads, Cookies, and Pastry   231

Drinks   255

Menu Suggestions   270

Glossary   274

Resources   283

Further Reading   284

Index   285

ACKNOWLEDGEMENTS

To write a cookbook has been a longtime dream of mine, but I was very naive to think that it would be a solitary task. A great many people helped me along the way, some in practical terms and others in supporting my ideas and plans. It is to thank them that I now write.

Caroline Waldegrave was the first to believe in the idea and her encouragement and help were invaluable. The staff of Leith's School were wonderfully eager to try all the recipes and their expert comments were a great help in adapting the recipes for a wider public. Special thanks go to Cherie Marshall and Emma Crowhurst for all their hard work and good humor when helping with the photography, and to Puff Fairclough for all her kind and expert advice.

Also thanks to Dodie Miller from the Cool Chile Company for all her help with the dried chiles, Elizabeth Morcom for the wine suggestions, and Elisabeth Lambert Ortiz for her support.

For this beautiful book I thank most heartily the photographer Graham Kirk who was assisted by David Barrett, the stylist Helen Payne, and David Palmer the designer. At Bloomsbury the enthusiasm of David Reynolds, Monica Macdonald, and everyone involved in the book made all my efforts worthwhile.

I would also like to thank Peter and Karin Thompson, Armand Sisti, and Lilian Armfield for their support during the time I was working on the book. Finally, a special thanks to my mother, Avzônea R. Vicira, for believing without seeing, and to my hustand, Richard, who put up with my changes of mood for months without ever failing to encourage me. To all of you my deepest gratitude and kindest thoughts.

FOREWORD

Working with Valéria has always been enjoyable and fascinating, and she has taught us all so much about Latin American food. Before the advent of Valeria we thought that there were two types of chile: green and red. How wrong we were!

All the recipes have now been tried and tested at the school, and the staff have enjoyed using them so much that many of the recipes have been incorporated into the full-time and evening class curriculum, and we will be running an annual course in Latin American Cookery. This book is, in fact, quite a departure for us, because we have always had strict rules on the Leith's way of cooking. In this book we have returned to the rustic roots of Latin American methods. The recipes here are all based on classic recipes, but Valéria has adapted them so that they can be cooked and enjoyed by us in the West.

I do hope that you enjoy cooking from this book.

Caroline Waldegrave
Co-owner and principal, Leith's School of Food and Wine

INTRODUCTION

All the nicest memories I have of my childhood are related to food. When I was about five years old, going to the baker to get the morning bread for my brothers and sisters for breakfast before they went to school was a real pleasure. Even though I did not go to school until I was seven, the errand made me take part in the morning eating ritual. Small, hot French bread was generously buttered and dipped into hot milky coffee or hot chocolate, making the bread soft and delicious.

From bread buyer I was promoted to popcorn maker, which was quite a feat considering my age and also that making popcorn for a family of twelve was no easy thing. I developed little sayings and dances to do around the popping pot, and firmly believed these voodoos were responsible for the perfect result every time, so I never dared not to do them. Even today, when it is difficult to find a corn that does not pop, I find myself going back to my routine to give it a better flavor, the sweet flavor of childhood.

I later progressed to making the much-loved crème caramel, always a favorite in any Latin American household, and was quick to learn that cooking has little to do with luck. All cooks know that crème caramel tastes better the next day, but try telling this to a house full of kids and their friends. I don't think a single one ever made it to the next day.

Almost without a sweet tooth myself, I always enjoyed making sweets, perhaps because of the popularity it won me with the family. I remember spending afternoons making coconut fondant sweets, milk pudding, chocolate fudge, and my particular favorite, ambrosia, which in Brazil is made with milk, sugar, and eggs and takes forever to do. I would persevere through intense heat, stirring the pan so the milk and sugar would not catch on the bottom. To make things even more difficult, I could not eat the finished dish until it was really cold because only then, when the sugar has lost its intensity, does it taste like the 'food of the gods.' My family was so large that we had an industrial four-door fridge in which it was easy to hide things, especially ambrosia, that I wanted to save for myself.

Another of my favorite occupations was to follow my mother to the market. She would buy fruit and vegetables for the whole week and we would go around the stalls looking, tasting, smelling, and touching the foods on display. Fresh produce was and still is seasonal in most Latin countries and we would wait anxiously for the right time of the year for our favorite produce. The mango, sweet corn, and guava seasons were much longed for, although I cannot say as much for the avocado. It was so abundant that we were sick of it by the end of the first week. Neighbors with avocado trees in their gardens would become very generous and send us baskets of them. Unfortunately, that did not happen with mangoes. There could never be enough of them, and we would start eating them while they were still green, too anxious to wait for them to ripen. Later in the season one of my greatest pleasures was to sit with friends under a mango or guava tree and eat as many of the ripe fruits as possible.

During the season for wild fruits, the whole family, including grandmother, relatives and friends, would go out for the day armed with picnic foods, drinks, hammocks, and ropes for making swings for the children. Once again, no fruit came back with us, as we ate everything we found on the spot. These idyllic days were before television arrived in our town: sadly, things are very different now. In my youth whole days were dedicated to cooking one single type of food, and usually one extra cook

would be hired for the occasion. Making compotes using fruits such as figs, green papaya, and jackfruit, to name but a few, involves an extraordinary amount of work, so enough was made to last quite a while. Similarly, baking was usually done in large batches on Saturdays and kept in tins for use during the following week. My mother used to keep these tins of delicious biscuits, breads, and brioches in her room, the only way she could make sure they lasted for more than one day.

Throughout my childhood and teenage years we always had a house cook, so it was difficult for me to use the kitchen while she was around. I used to wait until the middle of the afternoon, when everyone was resting, to do my cooking, and this is still my favorite time for it—when lunch has been taken care of and it is still too early to think about dinner.

In my late teens, parties were informal affairs. One of us would get a cook to make *galinhadas*, a dish of chicken, rice, and turmeric served with chili sauce and beans, and would invite all our friends to come around and eat it. Some cooks were famous locally for their *galinhadas* and could never keep up with the demand.

Years later, living in the United States, a whole new world of cooking possibilities opened up to me. For the first time I had Chinese and Mexican food, tasted frozen vegetables (I had been warned about them before I left home) and ate food out of cans. I can still remember my reaction when I was first offered an egg salad sandwich. I thought nothing could be less enticing and more bizarre than mashed-up boiled eggs between slices of soft white bread; fortunately, later in life I learned to be more tolerant about other people's taste in food.

While away from home at college, I virtually gave up cooking and didn't start again until I married a European and discovered that cooking could be a profession, not just a pastime. My professional training at Leith's School opened up a new world of possibilities for me and for many years I worked in the industry doing different jobs and learning about European cuisines. I have always been very interested in the history of food and finding out such things as where the different ingredients and techniques came from, who discovered them and how eating habits were formed. It is fascinating to learn how political and social history is determined by food.

Being a native of Brazil, it is only natural that I am also very interested in food from the Americas: it is a rich, complex, and fascinating subject and it has taken over two years to compile this book about it. Within these pages you will find recipes from the classic Latin American repertoire, as well as new recipes inspired by the ingredients or techniques of particular countries. To make the traditional recipes suitable for modern needs, the heavier ones have been revised to reflect healthier eating habits and the time-consuming ones have been simplified.

The more we know about food, the more it helps us understand different people and their cultures. The different cuisines of Latin America, so strongly rooted in the past, cannot be described using a single adjective. They are distinct, yet similar, just like the members of any family; studying the individuals throws light on the whole and vice versa.

A BRIEF HISTORY OF LATIN AMERICA AND ITS FOOD

In the 15th century the wealthy classes of Europe depended on the East to supply luxury items such as spices, silks, and porcelain. The trade was done through a chain of merchantmen, which started in Alexandria and Damascus and finished in Venice and Florence. By the time the goods reached their final destinations, their prices were so inflated by the profits of all the middlemen that finding new and less expensive ways of getting these goods was a constant preoccupation. As the main trade route to the East was dominated by the Ottoman Turks, a search also began for an alternative route.

The incentive was strong. During the Middle Ages, food—especially meat and game—was hardly palatable without strong seasoning. Meat was butchered in early November, salted to preserve it, and consumed throughout the winter. Salting was the only way of preserving food and tolerance for saltiness was amazingly high, as food historians found when they recreated medieval dishes from recipes of that time; the results were impossible to eat. Spices were used in large quantities, to mask the salt as well as the rotting of the meat. Sugar did not then exist, so all sweet foodstuffs were made with honey and, again, generously spiced. Such practices, however, were confined to wealthy households as spices were very expensive.

Spain and Portugal, the most powerful maritime nations at the end of the 15th century, were also looking for a new route to the Orient. The discovery of such a route would lead to a monopoly in the very lucrative spice trade, and could also be used as a vehicle for spreading the Christian faith. Both nations were deeply

Catholic, a fact that would play a significant role in the fate of the countries they "discovered."

Believing that the Earth was round, scholars thought that westward travel would eventually lead to the east. With that in mind, Christopher Columbus (1451–1506) set sail in August 1492 with the blessing and sponsorship of Queen Isabella of Spain. On October 12 he arrived in the Bahamas. Mistakenly believing that he had reached the Indies, he called the natives Indians. From this time forward Spain began its program of colonizing in earnest: expeditions went north towards Mexico and south towards the Andes. The men who went into these places in search of wealth and fame were called *conquistadores* (conquerors). The Conquest of the Aztecs in Mexico and the Incas in Peru is deeply controversial, mainly because of the atrocities perpetuated by the *conquistadores* in the name of their king and the Catholic Church.

The continents of North and South America became known to Europeans as the "New World," a term first used by Amerigo Vespucci (1451–1512), an Italian explorer. Ironically, it is he, rather than Columbus, who gave his name to the new continent.

The Mayas: *Central America and the Caribbean*
The areas now known as Honduras and Guatemala were once home to the Mayas, creators of the most advanced and sophisticated culture in pre-Conquest America. The Mayas flourished between the 4th and 10th centuries AD, and declined, it is believed, because of civil war, epidemics, and soil exhaustion. Temples and cities were abandoned to forest vegetation and people moved towards the

Yucatan peninsula, where descendants of the Mayas still live.

At its zenith the Mayan culture had amazingly rich and ornate religious architecture, and regular sacrifices were made to the gods in the hope of achieving a good harvest. When the Spaniards arrived, they found only vestiges of this ancient culture, but it endures none the less. Today, the people of the Yucatan peninsula still speak the Mayan language, have a cuisine distinct from the rest of Mexico, and physically look very much like their ancestors.

The Caribbean and Central America were abundant in fruit, wild birds, seafood, and vegetables, including sweet potatoes and cassava, which were unknown to the Spaniards. Maize was the main grain and more than 200 types were already developed by the time of the Conquest. It was eaten in a variety of forms, and its flour was made into a bread similar to the *tortilla* found in Mexico. Meat was very scarce in that tropical climate, but insects such as large spiders, worms, and giant ants were abundant and used in the local cooking. In fact, some types of worm are still regarded as a delicacy in Mexico. Chiles and annatto seed were, and still are, the most common ingredients used for flavoring.

The Aztecs: *Mexico*

The Aztec empire was relatively new when the Spanish explorer Hernando Cortes (1485–1547) arrived in Mexico in 1519. Its creation was made possible by an alliance between three rival tribes about 70 years before the arrival of the Spaniards. The first Aztec emperor, Montezuma I, started his reign in 1440 and expanded his

territory from the central plateau, where Mexico City is today, over 600 miles south to the border of modern Guatemala. When Montezuma II succeeded as the head of the empire in 1502, he started a campaign of conquering and absorbing new lands towards the south and the Pacific. Tenochtitlán, the Aztec capital, was the central point of the empire, receiving all the taxes collected from the conquered lands, and was also home to the major temples where human sacrifices were carried out.

The Aztec civilization was not as advanced and refined as that of the Mayas, but it was very organized none the less. Agriculture was all important and the land was owned by the community as a whole. Upon marriage, a young man would be granted a plot of land to provide for his family, and it would be given back to the community when he died.

Aztec society had a strict hierarchy, not unlike that found in European cultures. The emperor was at the top, followed by noble families, then priests, warriors, and peasants. Prisoners of war were treated as serfs or used for human sacrifice, which was considered an honor. It was very important to have enough warriors to be sacrificed, so additional grants of land were given to those who could secure prisoners during a war; sometimes wars were fought with the sole purpose of acquiring prisoners for sacrifice.

Religion ruled the life of the Aztecs and was the glue that held the empire together. Apart from the ruling élite, people had no personal wealth and no freedom of thought since intellectual and religious life were one and the same thing, closely guided by the priests towards war, human sacrifice, and successful harvests. Ceremonial cannibalism was also practiced by the Aztecs and it became the main excuse used by the Spaniards for the massacre of the Aztecs and the destruction of their cities.

The variety of ingredients and cooking techniques found in Mexico was a source of amazement to the Spaniards. Tomatoes, peppers, sweet potatoes, chiles, chocolate, and turkey were among the many novelties the *conquistadores* introduced to Europe. The more bizarre parts of the Aztec diet, such as frogs, worms, spiders, lizards, small dogs, and fungus-infested corn, were not exported.

The Incas: *Peru*

The Incas were the last in a series of great civilizations that existed in Peru. They arrived in the highlands of southern Peru in the 12th century AD and the city of Cuzco became their administrative and religious center. The empire expanded north to Ecuador and south to Bolivia, spreading into parts of Chile and Argentina. It was ruled by the king of the Incas, who had unlimited powers and was considered the embodiment of God on earth.

Although writing and the wheel were unknown in the Inca empire, it was a highly efficient organization that managed to keep areas of difficult access together under a single ruler. Like the Aztecs, Incas had no private ownership of land, but they worked along more socialist principles. Crops were divided into three, one-third being kept by the farmers, one-third going to sustain the priests and the bureaucracy, and the final third going to the government, who distributed it to widows, the aged, the debilitated, and nonproductive people. The government also had a policy of storing grain in warehouses for distribution in the event of bad harvests.

The Incas are famous for their irrigation systems, which harnessed water from the Andes and made it possible for the lower valleys near the coast to be cultivated. They also excelled at road building, having the whole empire linked by a complex system of roads and bridges—no mean feat considering the difficulties posed by the Andean mountains. Another of their skills was masonry, but many of their stone buildings were dismantled by the Spaniards and used in the construction of colonial buildings.

The Incas and the cultures that preceded them, such as the Paracas, Chimu, and Mochica, had highly skilled potters and weavers, and their surviving work testifies to their skill. Their highly crafted gold artifacts, however, were all melted down and sent to Spain.

With the conquest of Peru by the Spanish explorer Francisco Pizarro (1478–1541) and the breaking up of the Inca empire, the civilization fell apart. The complex irrigation systems were abandoned and the Incas who were not exterminated by European diseases or war retreated to the mountains.

The gold and emeralds that had attracted the Spanish to Peru were not the country's only wealth. It also had an abundance of fish and shellfish from the ocean and lakes, plus meat in the form of guinea pigs and dogs, among other foodstuffs. While important, maize would grow only in the lowlands, so it had fewer uses than in Mexico. It was mainly fresh ground and made into a type of porridge. In the Peruvian highlands, where corn did not grow, potatoes and quinoa were the main foods. Over a hundred different varieties of potatoes were grown, and the Incas even discovered a process of freeze-drying them. Potatoes would be left out at night in the freezing mountain air and in the morning they would be trodden on to extract all their moisture. The process was repeated for a few days until the potatoes were rock hard and free of liquid. The *chuño* or *papa gaca*, as they were known, were then stored and used in soups and casserole dishes, or grated to make flour. The very same technique is still used by the highland people of the Andes.

The Birth of Latin America

The term "Latin America" refers to the eighteen Spanish-speaking republics of the western hemisphere, together with Portuguese-speaking Brazil and French-speaking Haiti. The term "Meso-America" is sometimes used to denote the area covered by Central America and Mexico.

In the 400 years following the Conquest, the influence of the Portuguese in Brazil and the Spanish in the rest of Latin America led to a new race and a different cuisine being born. The introduction of cattle, pigs, wheat, sugar, citrus fruits, bananas, coconut, and rice transformed the cuisines of Mexico and South America, but those new ingredients did not supercede existing ones. Old and new techniques also co-existed; for example, many foods continued to be boiled, or steamed in banana leaves or corn husks. With the arrival of the pig, however, fat became widely available and frying became popular. Indeed, a large percentage of modern Latin American food is fried.

Wheat did not make a huge impact in Mexico, where corn tortillas are still as popular as they were 500 years ago, but it did gain a foothold in the northern region. Wheat became widely used outside Mexico for bread making, and Spanish- and Portuguese-style bread is very popular for breakfast.

Rice was immediately absorbed into the local cuisines and, together with potatoes and corn, quickly became a staple food. With cattle came dairy products, then unknown to the natives, while beef became the major food crop for the southern regions of South America.

The Spanish, having lived under Arab occupation for over 700 years, already had a rich and varied cuisine, and were the major influence on the Spanish-speaking countries throughout the colonial years. In fact, traces of Arab cuisine can still be found in many recipes. The Portuguese influence on Brazilian cooking can be seen in their love of sweets, cakes, and candies, a field in which Brazilian cooks excel. Brazil and the Caribbean share a unique Creole cuisine thanks to the African slaves who were brought into the New World to work on the sugar plantations. With them came a variety of ingredients and flavorings that distinguished their cooking from that found in the rest of Latin America.

The 19th century brought many other influences, including the arrival of Italian, German, Japanese, Chinese, Arab, and other immigrant groups. New foods were incorporated into the already rich local repertoire, creating a cuisine that is greater than the sum of its diverse parts.

CATERING QUANTITIES

Few people accurately weigh or measure quantities as a control-conscious chef must do, but when catering for large numbers it is useful to know how much food to allow per person. As a general rule, the more people you are catering for the less food per head you need to provide, e.g. 1/2 pound beef stew meat per head is essential for 4 people, but 1/3 pound per head would feed 60 people.

SOUP
Allow 1 cup soup per person, depending on the size of the bowl.

POULTRY
Chicken and turkey Allow 1 pound per person. An average bone-in chicken serves 4 people.
Duck A 6-pound bird will feed 3 to 4 people; a 4-pound bird will feed 2 people. A duck makes enough pâté for 6 people.

MEAT
LAMB
Cubed 2/3 pound per person (boneless, with fat trimmed away)
Roast leg 3 pounds for 3 to 4 people; 4 pounds for 4 to 5 people; 6 pounds for 7 to 8 people
Roast shoulder 4 pounds shoulder for 5 to 6 people; 6 pounds shoulder for 7 to 9 people
Roast breast 1 pound for 2 people
Grilled cutlets 3 to 4 per person
Grilled loin chops 2 per person

BEEF
Stew meat 1/2 pound boneless trimmed meat per person
Roast (boneless) 1/2 pound per person
Roast (bone-in) 3/4 pound per person
Roast whole tenderloin 4 pound piece for 10 people
Grilled steaks 1/2 pound per person depending on appetite

PORK
Cubed 1/3 pound per person
Roast loin or ham (boneless) 1/2 pound per person
Roast loin or ham (bone-in) 3/4 pound per person
2 average fillets will feed 3 to 4 people
Grilled 1/3 pound chop or cutlet per person

GROUND MEAT
1/3 pound per person for meatloaf, hamburgers, etc.
1/4 pound per person for steak tartare

FISH
Whole large fish (e.g. sea bass, salmon, whole haddock), weighed uncleaned, with head on: 3/4 to 1 pound per person
Cutlets and steaks 1/3 pound per person
Fillets (e.g. sole, lemon sole, plaice), 3 small fillets per person (total weight about 1/3 pound)
Whole small fish (e.g. trout, slip soles, small plaice, small mackerel, herring), 1/2 to 3/4 pound weighed with heads per person for main course; 1/3 pound per person for first course
SHELLFISH
Shrimp 2 to 3 ounces per person as a first course; 5 ounces per person as a main course
Mixed shellfish 2 to 3 ounces per person as a first course; 5 ounces per person as a main course

VEGETABLES

Weighed before preparation and cooking, and assuming 3 vegetables, including potatoes, served with a main course: 1/4 pound per person, except (per person):

Green beans 3 ounces
Peas 3 ounces
Spinach 3/4 pound
Potatoes 3 small (roast); 1/3 pound (mashed); 1 large or 2 small (baked); 1/4 pound (new).

RICE

Plain, boiled, or fried 1/4 cup (measured before cooking) or 1 cup (measured after cooking).
In risotto or pilaf 2 tablespoons per person (measured before cooking) for first course; 1/4 cup per person for main course.

SALADS

Obviously, the more salads served, the less guests will eat of any one salad. Allow 1 large portion of salad, in total, per head (e.g. if only one salad is served make sure there is enough for 1 serving each). Conversely if 100 guests are to choose from five different salads, allow a total of 150 portions) i.e. 30 portions of each salad).

Soups

SOUPS

A wide range of ingredients, flavors, and seasonings go into Latin America's favorite dishes. Typically soups top the list of the most popular dishes. Soups are widely eaten from Mexico to Argentina, and range from thin chicken or beef broths to creamy, stew-type potato and vegetable soups.

In Mexico, thinly sliced fried tortillas are added to a simple tomato and chili soup, then garnished with diced avocados and dollops of sour cream. The coastal areas, rich in seafood, provide a wide and exciting variety of soups flavored with chilies, limes, or coconut milk. The high Andean countries, namely Peru, Bolivia, Ecuador, Colombia, and Chile, with their huge selection of more than 100 varieties of potatoes, are known for their wonderful potato soups. In some recipes, more than five different varieties of potatoes are used, along with different vegetables and meats.

Colonial influences are still apparent in much Latin American cooking. Spanish gazpacho is a common dish in Mexico, while the Portuguese soup *caldo verde* is very popular in Brazil. Native tropical ingredients, such as avocado and hearts of palm, also play their part in the preparation of delicious cold soups. The most common thickenings or enriching agents are potatoes, nuts, seeds, and cornstarch; cream is very seldomly used in Latin American soups.

Some soups, like peanut soup, are common throughout Latin America, many offering different flavor variations. Starchy vegetables, such as sweet corn, sweet potatoes, and beans, are commonly used as thickening agents, while rice is often used to add body to both fish and chicken soups.

Peanut Soup

A popular dish throughout Latin America, this soup uses dried chipotle chilies, which have a delicious smoky flavor and quite a bit of heat. Start with one chili and add more to taste, if you dare.

Ingredients

2 tablespoons vegetable oil
2 medium onions, finely chopped
2 chipotle chilies, seeded and finely chopped
   (see page 198)
2 red bell peppers, seeded and chopped
1 can (14^1/$_2$ ounces) cut tomatoes,
   undrained
4 cups Beef Stock (see page 189)
1^1/$_3$ cups unsweetened peanut butter
Salt and freshly ground black pepper
3 tablespoons chopped fresh cilantro leaves

Method

1. Heat the oil in a large, heavy saucepan over medium-high heat. Add the onions; cook and stir until tender, about 10 minutes.

2. Add the chilies, peppers, tomatoes, and beef stock. Bring to a boil, reduce the heat to low, and simmer 25 minutes.

3. Add the peanut butter; stir until well blended. Transfer the soup to a blender or food processor, in batches, if necessary, and blend until smooth. Return to the rinsed-out pan. (The soup should have the thickness of heavy cream; if too thick, add additional stock or water.) Season with salt and pepper to taste. Just before serving, stir in the cilantro. Serve hot.

NOTE: Substitute red jalapeño peppers for the chipotle chilies.

WINE SUGGESTION: Verdelho madeira or dry amontillado sherry.

Avocado and Lime Soup with Cayenne Toasts

Here the low-fat yogurt balances the richness of the avocado in a delicious soup made for a hot summer's day. The Tabasco can be omitted or increased according to taste.

Ingredients

2 medium avocados, peeled, pitted, and diced
Juice of 4 limes
1 3/4 cups low-fat yogurt
Dash of Tabasco sauce
3 tablespoons coarsely chopped fresh cilantro
1 cup cold Chicken Stock (see page 188)
Salt and freshly ground white pepper

For the Cayenne Toasts:
1 French baguette
1/4 cup butter, melted
1 teaspoon cayenne pepper

For the garnish:
1 red bell pepper, seeded and finely diced

Method

1. In a blender or food processor, mix the avocado flesh and lime juice until smooth. Add the yogurt, Tabasco, and chopped cilantro and blend until completely smooth.

2. With the motor still running, gradually add the chicken stock and process until the soup is smooth but not too thick. Season with salt and pepper to taste. Refrigerate until well chilled, about 3 hours.

3. Preheat the oven to 400°F.

4. To prepare the cayenne toasts, slice the bread into 1-inch-thick rounds. In a small bowl, combine the butter and cayenne pepper. Brush both sides of the bread slices generously with the butter mixture and place on a baking sheet.

5. Bake for 10 minutes or until both sides are lightly browned, turning slices over after 5 minutes.

6. Garnish individual servings of the soup with the diced red pepper and serve with the cayenne toasts.

WINE SUGGESTION: Crisp, dry white.

Sweet Potato, Corn, and Green Chili Soup

This soup includes the two most-loved starchy foods in the Americas—potatoes and corn. Either Idaho or sweet potatoes can be used since both produce equally creamy results.

Ingredients

$^1/_4$ cup butter
1 medium onion, finely chopped
$1^3/_4$ pounds sweet potatoes (about 5 medium potatoes), peeled and chopped
4 cups Chicken Stock (see page 188)
2 cups fresh or frozen sweet corn
1 Fresno or Jalepeño chili pepper, seeded and finely diced (see page 194)
Salt and freshly ground black pepper

To serve: Cuban White Bread (see page 241)

Method

1. Melt the butter in a large saucepan over medium-high heat. Add the onion; cook and stir until tender, about 5 minutes. Add the sweet potatoes and stock and bring to a boil. Reduce the heat to low. Cover and simmer until the potatoes are tender, about 20 minutes.

2. Strain the soup, reserving the solids and liquid separately. Place the solids in a blender or food processor and blend until smooth. Return the stock to the rinsed-out pan and add the potato purée. Add the corn and chili pepper. Season with the salt and pepper to taste. Simmer an additional 10 minutes. If the soup is too thick, add additional chicken stock and simmer until thoroughly heated. Serve with the Cuban White Bread.

WINE SUGGESTION: Full-bodied white.

Sweet Corn Velouté

This creamy soup, with its subtle sweetness, is sure to become a favorite with the kids.

Ingredients

2 tablespoons butter
1 medium onion, chopped
2 tablespoons all-purpose flour
$^1/_2$ teaspoon cayenne pepper
$^1/_2$ teaspoon chili powder
Kernels from 3 large corn cobs, or 4 cups thawed frozen sweet corn
2 cups Chicken Stock (see page 188)
$1^3/_4$ cups milk
3 tablespoons finely chopped Italian parsley
Salt and freshly ground pepper

To serve: Cuban White Bread (see page 241)

Method

1. Melt the butter in a large saucepan over medium-high heat. Add the onion; cook and stir until tender, about 10 minutes. Add the flour, cayenne, and chili powder and cook an additional 3 minutes, stirring constantly.

2. Add the corn, chicken stock, and milk. Bring to a boil. Reduce the heat to low and simmer until the corn is very tender, about 20 minutes.

3. Remove the soup from the heat and place, in batches, if necessary, in a blender or food processor. Blend well. Strain the soup into the rinsed-out saucepan; discard the solids. Reheat the soup for 5 minutes, then add the chopped parsley. Season with the salt and fresh ground pepper to taste. Serve hot with Cuban White Bread.

WINE SUGGESTION: Chilled fino or manzanilla sherry.

Roast Pepper and Tomato Soup with Spicy Corn Muffins

Peppers, tomatoes, and potatoes—all ingredients native to Latin America—make up this delicious soup.

Ingredients

3 red bell peppers, quartered and deseeded
1 tablespoon butter
1 tablespoon olive oil
1 medium onion, chopped
1 teaspoon tomato purée
$^1/_2$ teaspoon fresh thyme leaves
$^1/_2$ teaspoon cayenne pepper
$^1/_2$ teaspoon ground cumin
Pinch of ground cinnamon
2 medium potatoes, peeled and coarsely
    chopped
1 can (14$^1/_2$ ounces) cut tomatoes, undrained
2 cups hot Chicken Stock (see page 188)
Salt and freshly ground pepper

For the garnish:
1 scallion, finely chopped

To serve: Spicy Corn Muffins (see page 240)

Method

1. Preheat the grill to high. Grill the peppers, skin side up, until they are blistered and blackened all over, about 15 minutes. Place the peppers inside a plastic bag until they are cool enough to handle. Remove and discard the skins and cut the peppers into strips.

2. Melt the butter with the oil in a large, heavy saucepan over medium-high heat. Add the onion and cook, stirring occasionally, until tender, about 10 minutes. Add the tomato purée, thyme, cayenne, cumin, and cinnamon; cook 2 minutes. Add the potatoes, tomatoes, and grilled pepper strips; mix well. Add the stock. Reduce the heat to low and simmer until the potatoes are tender, about 25 minutes.

3. Transfer the soup, in batches if necessary, to a blender or food processor; blend until smooth. Return to the rinsed-out pan. Season with salt and pepper to taste. Garnish with the scallions. Serve at once with the Spicy Corn Muffins.

WINE SUGGESTION: Dry rosé.

Green Soup with Hazelnuts

As in many dishes from Latin America, this recipe uses nuts as a thickening agent rather than cream. This is a substantial soup which can be served as a meal on its own.

Ingredients

2 tablespoons vegetable oil
2 medium onions, chopped
2 green Fresno or Kenyan chilies, seeded and finely chopped (see page 194)
2 slices white bread
4 ounces hazelnuts, roasted and peeled*
4 cups Chicken Stock (see page 188)
$1/2$ teaspoon cayenne pepper
Salt and freshly ground black pepper
1 pound fresh spinach leaves or 1 package (10 ounces) frozen leaf spinach, thawed and drained
8 ounces watercress, trimmed

*To roast the hazelnuts, soak them in cold water for 1 minute; drain. Place the nuts in a shallow baking pan and bake at 400°F until the skins begin to flake. Wrap a handful of the warm nuts in a clean towel; rub vigorously to remove most of the skins. Repeat with remaining nuts.

Method

1. Heat the oil in a large saucepan over medium-high heat. Add the onions and chilies; cook and stir until tender, about 15 minutes.

2. Trim the crusts from the bread and discard. Cut the bread into cubes and add to the onion mixture in the saucepan along with the hazelnuts. Reduce the heat to medium and cook until the nuts are golden brown, about 5 minutes. Add the chicken stock and cayenne. Season with the salt and pepper to taste. Reduce the heat to low, cover, and simmer for 10 minutes.

3. Meanwhile, prepare the fresh spinach by removing the stalks and any thick veins. Wash thoroughly in several changes of water and coarsely chop. Prepare the watercress by carefully picking over the leaves before washing thoroughly.

4. Add the spinach and the watercress stalks to the hot soup and cook for 5 minutes. Transfer the soup to a blender or food processor, in batches if necessary, and blend until smooth. Pour the soup back into the rinsed-out pan. Season with additional salt and pepper to taste. If too thick, add additional chicken stock.

NOTE: To keep the bright green color, do not reheat the soup more than once.

WINE SUGGESTION: Dry sherry.

Crab and Fish Soup

Found in abundance in the coastal areas of South America, crab is used in many Latin American recipes with delicious results.

Ingredients

2 dried pasilla or ancho chilies (see page 199)
$1/4$ cup butter
2 medium onions, thinly sliced
$1/4$ cup plus 2 tablespoons all-purpose flour
$3^1/2$ cups Fish Stock (see page 189)
1 bay leaf
8 ounces crabmeat
8 ounces haddock fillets, skinned and cut into
  2-inch strips
$2/3$ cup half-and-half
$2/3$ cup milk
Salt and freshly ground black pepper

For the garnish:
1 bunch fresh chives, finely chopped

Method

1. Remove the stems from the chilies; discard. Cut the chilies in half. Remove the seeds and membranes. Finely chop the peppers and place them in a small bowl. Add enough hot water to cover the peppers. Let stand 20 minutes. Drain the peppers and discard the soaking liquid.

2. In a large saucepan, melt the butter over medium-high heat. Add the onions and cook until tender, about 10 minutes. Stir in the flour and cook for 1 minute.

3. Add the soaked chilies, fish stock, bay leaf, half of the crabmeat, and all of the fish. Reduce the heat to low; simmer 20 minutes.

4. Remove the soup from the heat; transfer to a blender or food processor, in batches if necessary, and blend until smooth. Strain it through a sieve back into the rinsed-out pan. Add the remaining crabmeat, the half-and-half, and milk. Season with salt and pepper to taste. Continue cooking until heated through. If the soup is too thick, add a few more tablespoons fish stock.

5. Sprinkle with the chives just before serving.

WINE SUGGESTION: Dry white.

Chilled Hearts of Palm and Avocado Soup

Although chilled soups are not very common in Latin America, the combination of rich avocado and delicately tart hearts of palm makes this soup a success.

Ingredients

1³/₄ cups Chicken Stock (see page 188)
1¹/₃ cups half-and-half
1¹/₃ cups milk
1 can (14 ounces) hearts of palm, drained and coarsely chopped
1 avocado, peeled, pitted, and cubed
Juice of 2 limes
Pinch of cayenne pepper
Dash of Tabasco sauce
Salt and freshly ground white pepper

For the garnish:
1 tablespoon chopped fresh cilantro leaves

Method

1. In a blender or food processor, blend all of the ingredients except the salt and pepper together until smooth. Season with the salt and pepper to taste. Cover and refrigerate until chilled, about 3 hours. The mixture should have the consistency of heavy cream. If the soup is too thick, add a few more tablespoons chicken stock or water.

2. Serve well chilled, sprinkled with the chopped cilantro.

WINE SUGGESTION: Light summery white.

Tropical-style Rice Soup

The basis for this soup is a strong-flavored stock made from chicken, beef, or fish to which rice and coconut are added. Finely chopped vegetables can also be included for extra flavor and texture.

Ingredients

2³/₄ cups Chicken Stock (see page 188)
1 bouquet garni
1 green Thai or serrano chili, seeded and finely chopped (see page 194)
³/₄ cup long-grain white rice, uncooked
4 tablespoons butter
¹/₄ cup flaked coconut
Salt and freshly ground black pepper
2 tablespoons finely chopped fresh flat-leaf Italian parsley leaves

Method

1. In a large saucepan, bring the stock, bouquet garni, and green chili to a boil over medium-high heat. Add the rice. Reduce the heat to low and simmer for 20 minutes. Remove the bouquet garni. Stir in the butter and coconut; simmer 5 to 10 minutes. Season with salt and pepper to taste.

2. Add the chopped parsley just before serving. Serve hot.

NOTE: Leftover chicken, fish, or turkey can be added to this soup with delicious results.

WINE SUGGESTION: California chardonnay.

Shrimp and Fish Soup

Fish and shellfish soups are found in all the coastal areas of Latin America, with shrimp being the favorite shellfish. Places with a more profound African influence, such as the Caribbean and northeast Brazil, add coconut and a larger amount of chilies to their fish soups, but either way they are always delicious and easy to make.

Ingredients

2 tablespoons vegetable oil
4 small onions, finely chopped
4 garlic cloves, crushed
$1/2$ teaspoon chili powder
1 teaspoon minced fresh marjoram
1 can (8 ounces) cut tomatoes, undrained
1 green bell pepper, diced
1 red bell pepper, diced
5 cups Fish Stock (see page 189)
Salt and freshly ground black pepper
14 ounces cod or haddock fillets, skinned and
  cut into 2-inch chunks
12 ounces raw, medium shrimp, shelled and
  deveined (see page 277)

For the garnish:
2 tablespoons finely chopped fresh flat-leaf
  Italian parsley
1 bunch of fresh chives, finely chopped

To serve: crusty white bread

Method

1. In a large saucepan, heat the oil over medium-high heat. Add the onions; cook and stir until tender, about 10 minutes.

2. Stir in the garlic, chili powder, marjoram, tomatoes with their juice, and the bell peppers. Reduce the heat to low; simmer 5 minutes. Add the fish stock and season with salt and black pepper to taste. Increase the heat to high. Return the soup to a boil. Reduce the heat to low and add the fish and shrimp. Cover and simmer until the fish is cooked, about 5 minutes.

3. Season again with salt and pepper to taste. Stir in the parsley and chives. Serve at once with the white crusty bread.

NOTE: For a richer soup, add $3/4$ cup coconut milk along with the raw fish. Other types of shellfish can be used with equally good results.

WINE SUGGESTION: Crisp, dry white.

First Courses
and Salads

FIRST COURSES AND SALADS

A first course served as an individual separate dish is not usually found in Latin America. It is more common to serve a variety of appetizers, normally arranged on one plate and shared by all. The appetizers can vary from very light nibbles, such as grilled shrimp and chicken-heart kebabs, to more substantial *empanadas* or *tamales*, small baked or steamed pies filled with chicken, fish, or cheese.

Throughout Latin America there is a tradition of selling snack-type foods in the streets, markets, and cafés. They are basically finger foods eaten at odd hours and they vary from country to country. In Peru *antichudos* (spicy ox-heart brochettes) are very popular, and there are seafood equivalents along the coast. In central Brazil vendors fill huge vats of salted boiling water with corn on the cob, while street vendors offering ceviche are common in Lima and Quito.

The Portuguese and Spanish, who were themselves influenced by invading nations, introduced their love of fried food to South America when they arrived in 1492. Frying was then unknown in local cuisines, but has since become a favorite method of food preparation. A variety of fried food, from small potato dumplings with different fillings to light pastry snacks such as *pastelzitos*, filled with the same fillings as *empanadas* are found in many Latin countries.

Chile, Argentina, Brazil, and Uruguay all have shops where these savory snack foods, as well as sweets and cakes, coffee, tea, and soft drinks, are sold throughout the day to the delight of the locals and foreigners. These shops have different names in different countries but they can be easily spotted by the crowds that throng there around 11:00 in the morning and 4:00 in the afternoon.

Salads are usually simple and served with a meal. The most popular include a variety of steamed or boiled vegetables tossed in a light dressing. Pickled vegetables are also very popular, and glass jars containing beautifully arranged carrots, cauliflowers, onions, green beans, and baby corn can be found in many South American supermarkets. Again, what would be thought of as a salad or first course in the United States is an appetizer for Latin Americans.

One of the most unusual salads is found in Mexico, where *nopales*, the young and tender "paddles" of the prickly pear cactus, are eaten as a vegetable. When the spines are removed, the pads are thinly sliced and eaten raw in salads, or cooked until very tender and eaten as a vegetable. Canned *nopales* are called *nopalitos*.

Ceviches almost deserve a chapter on their own, being among the most widely known dishes from South America. Their birthplace is disputed between Peru and Ecuador, and as both countries have an amazing variety of fish and shellfish, they could easily have come from either. There are innumerable recipes and variations of ceviche, all with delicious results. It can be eaten as a first course or main dish, depending on the accompaniments served with it.

Hearts of Palm Flan with Herb Pastry

Hearts of palm have a delicate flavor and texture and are used very much like asparagus—in dressing on their own, in salads, or in pies and quiches. Fresh hearts of palm are very hard to find, even in South America, so canned ones are widely used.

Ingredients

1 recipe Fresh Herb Pastry (see page 251)
2 tablespoons butter
2 cans (14 ounces each) hearts of palm, drained and cut into 1-inch chunks
2 tablespoons finely chopped fresh Italian flat-leaf parsley leaves
1 teaspoon dried oregano
2 eggs
2 egg yolks
$^2/_3$ cup light cream
$^2/_3$ cup milk
Salt and freshly ground black pepper
3 tablespoons grated Parmesan cheese

To serve: Spicy Tomato Sauce (see page 181)

Method

1. Preheat the oven to 400°F.

2. On a floured surface, roll out the pastry to a 12-inch circle. Place in an 11-inch flan ring and chill well.

3. Melt the butter in a large skillet. Add the hearts of palm, parsley, and oregano and cook over medium heat for 5 minutes. Set aside to cool slightly.

4. Bake the chilled pastry blind: prick the bottom of the pastry to prevent it from puffing up while baking. Line the pastry with parchment paper and fill with dried beans. Bake in the center of the oven for 15 minutes, then remove the beans and paper and continue baking 5 minutes. Cool slightly. Reduce the oven temperature to 350°F.

5. Mix together the eggs, yolks, cream, and milk in a medium bowl; season with salt and pepper.

6. Spoon the hearts of palm mixture into the bottom of the flan; sprinkle with the cheese. Carefully pour the egg mixture on top. Bake in the center of the oven until golden and just set in the center, about 25 minutes.

7. Remove from the oven and allow to cool in the flan ring for 10 minutes before transferring to a serving dish. Serve warm with the Spicy Tomato Sauce.

NOTE: In addition to being easier to use, flan rings or loose-bottomed metal tart pans conduct the heat better, preventing the pastry from becoming soggy.

WINE SUGGESTION: Dry white.

Flaky Shrimp and Coconut Torte

Latin Americans are very fond of any sort of pie, torte, or turnover, and the filling will vary according to the region and the occasion. Seafood is usually reserved for special days, while chicken, beef, or cheese fillings are eaten more frequently.

Ingredients

1 recipe Puff Pastry (see page 252), or
   1 package (17¼ ounces) frozen puff pastry
   sheets, thawed
1 egg, beaten, for glazing

For the filling:
2 tablespoons butter
1 onion, finely chopped
1 garlic clove, crushed
1 green Thai chile, seeded and chopped (see
   page 194)
½ red bell pepper, seeded and diced
½ green bell pepper, seeded and diced
½ teaspoon cayenne pepper
3 large tomatoes, peeled, seeded, and chopped
3 scallions, coarsely chopped
3 tablespoons chopped fresh parsley leaves
1 pound large uncooked shrimp , shelled and
   deveined (see page 277)
½ cup liquid cream of coconut
Salt and freshly ground pepper

For the salad:
2 tablespoons vegetable oil
1 tablespoon lemon juice
Salt and freshly ground pepper
2 bunches watercress, trimmed and washed

For the garnish:
2 tablespoons sesame seeds, lightly toasted

Method

1. Preheat the oven to 425°F.

2. Make the filling: melt the butter in a large skillet. Add the onion, garlic, chile, and bell peppers; cook over medium heat until almost tender but not brown.

3. Add the cayenne, tomatoes, scallions, and parsley and cream of coconut. Bring to a boil; reduce the heat and cook uncovered for 20 minutes.

4. Add the shrimp and cook for 5 minutes, or until the shrimp turn opaque. Season with salt and pepper; transfer to a bowl to cool.

5. On a floured surface, roll out half of the pastry into a 12 x 8-inch rectangle. Transfer to a baking sheet and prick well all over. Chill for 10 minutes. Bake for 15 minutes or until light brown. Reduce the oven temperature to 400°F.

6. Roll out the remaining pastry until it is a little larger than the baked pastry base. Mound the filling in the center of the base and top with the remaining pastry, gently tucking it under the base. Brush with the beaten egg; chill for 15 to 20 minutes. Glaze again and score the top in a crisscross pattern.

7. Bake for 30 to 35 minutes, or until the pastry is golden brown. Remove from the oven; transfer to a serving plate and keep warm while making the salad.

8. In a large bowl, mix the oil, lemon juice, and salt and pepper. Just before serving, toss the watercress leaves in the dressing and sprinkle with the sesame seeds. Serve the torte warm with the watercress salad.

WINE SUGGESTION: Medium-dry white.

Potato and Cheese Cakes with Peanut Sauce

Ecuador has many wonderful recipes using potatoes and this is one of them. Although cheese is not used very often, it makes a delicious combination with the spicy peanut sauce.

Ingredients

2 pounds potatoes
2 tablespoons butter
2 medium onions, finely chopped
3/4 cup sweet corn
3 scallions, finely chopped
1 egg, beaten
1/2 teaspoon cayenne pepper
2 cups shredded Cheddar cheese
Salt and freshly ground pepper
All-purpose flour
2 eggs, beaten
Dry bread crumbs
Vegetable oil for frying

For the peanut sauce:
3 tablespoons vegetable oil
2 onions, finely chopped
1 green Fresno or Kenyan chile, seeded and
   chopped (see page 194)
2 garlic cloves, crushed
2 medium tomatoes, peeled, seeded, and
   chopped
2 tablespoons crunchy, natural peanut butter
Salt and freshly ground pepper

For the garnish:
1 small bunch watercress

Method

1. Peel, boil, drain, and mash the potatoes while still warm.

2. Melt the butter in a medium skillet. Add the onions and cook over low heat until almost tender, about 10 minutes. Mix in the corn and scallions; continue cooking for 2 minutes.

3. In a large bowl, mix the potatoes, 1 beaten egg, onion mixture, cayenne, and cheese. Season with salt and pepper.

4. With hands dipped in flour, shape the mixture into 12 balls, then flatten each ball into a patty. Dip each patty into the beaten eggs, then the bread crumbs. Refrigerate for at least 15 minutes.

5. Make the sauce: heat the oil in a large skillet. Add the onions and chile and cook over very low heat for about 10 minutes; do not let the onions turn brown. Add the garlic, tomatoes, and peanut butter; cook over low heat for 10 minutes. Season to taste with salt and pepper; set aside to cool.

6. Pour enough oil into a large skillet to reach halfway up the patties. Heat the oil until hot. Fry the patties a few at a time, turning once, until golden brown. Drain well on paper towels; keep warm until all the patties are fried.

7. To serve: put 3 cakes on each plate and garnish with the watercress. Pass the sauce separately or pour into small ramekins and place on each plate.

WINE SUGGESTION: California chardonnay.

Chick Pea Soufflé Cakes with Red Pepper Mayonnaise

Chickpeas arrived in the Americas with the Spanish, who were introduced to them by the Arabs. They are especially popular in Mexico. These soufflé cakes are quick and easy to make, and look and taste wonderful.

Ingredients

1 can (15 ounces) chickpeas
4 tablespoons vegetable oil
1 small onion, chopped
1 garlic clove, crushed
Pinch sugar
$1/2$ teaspoon paprika
$1/2$ teaspoon cayenne pepper
$1/2$ teaspoon ground cumin
1 teaspoon all-purpose flour
$1/4$ cup heavy cream
2 eggs, separated
Salt and freshly ground pepper

For the garnish:
Fresh cilantro leaves

To serve: Spicy Red Pepper Mayonnaise (see page 187)

Method

1. Drain the chickpeas and rinse well. Place in a blender or food processor and purée. Transfer to a large bowl and set aside.

2. Heat 2 tablespoons of the oil in a small skillet. Add the onion and cook over very low heat until almost tender, about 10 minutes. Add the garlic, sugar, paprika, cayenne, and cumin; cook, stirring for 1 minute.

3. Add the flour and cook for 1 minute. Mix in the cream and simmer for 1 minute. Add the cream sauce and egg yolks to the chickpea purée. Season to taste with salt and pepper.

4. Whisk the egg whites until stiff but not dry; gradually fold into the chickpea mixture.

5. Heat the remaining 2 tablespoons oil in a large skillet. Fry spoonfuls of the chickpea mixture, turning once when they are golden brown, about 2 minutes on each side. Drain on paper towels; keep warm until all the cakes are fried.

6. Garnish with the cilantro leaves and serve warm with the Spicy Red Pepper Mayonnaise.

WINE SUGGESTION: Light-acidity white.

Crab Gratin

Crab is found in abundance along the coasts of Latin America. Chile, Peru, and Ecuador have a great variety and quantity of shellfish, with shrimp , crab, and lobster being among the favorites.

Ingredients

12 ounces cooked crabmeat, well picked over
Juice of 1 lime
Salt and freshly ground pepper
2 tablespoons vegetable oil
1 medium onion, finely chopped
2 garlic cloves, crushed
2 scallions, white and green parts, chopped
3 tomatoes, peeled, seeded, and diced
$1/4$ cup chopped fresh cilantro leaves
1 cup fresh white bread crumbs
$1/3$ cup heavy cream
3 tablespoons grated Parmesan cheese

To serve: lemon and lime wedges

Method

1. Season the crabmeat with the lime juice, salt, and pepper.

2. Preheat the oven to 425°F.

3. Heat the oil in a sauté pan. Add the onion and cook over low heat for 8 minutes. Add the garlic, scallions, tomatoes, and half the cilantro; continue cooking 5 minutes over medium heat.

4. Put the onion mixture into a large bowl and add the crabmeat, the remaining cilantro, half the bread crumbs, the heavy cream, salt, and pepper; mix thoroughly. (The mixture should have the consistency of soft mashed potatoes. If the mixture is too wet, add some more bread crumbs. If too dry, add some more cream or milk.)

5. Brush a medium crab shell or scallop shells with oil, spread the mixture into it and sprinkle the top with some bread crumbs and the Parmesan. Place on a baking sheet and bake on the top rack of the oven until bubbly and golden brown, about 15 minutes. Serve hot with the lemon and lime wedges.

NOTE: *This recipe can also be baked in a well-buttered shallow gratin dish.*

WINE SUGGESTION: Dry white.

Spicy Shrimp and Crab Cake

Of all the shellfish found in Latin America, shrimp are the favorite, followed closely by crabs and lobsters.

Ingredients

For the batter:
1 1/4 cups all-purpose flour
1/2 teaspoon turmeric
1/3 cup vegetable oil
3/4 cup milk
2 teaspoons baking powder
3 eggs
Salt and freshly ground pepper

For the filling:
2 tablespoons vegetable oil
1 onion, finely chopped
1 red bell pepper, seeded and diced
1 red Fresno or Kenyan chile, seeded and diced
   (see page 194)
3 scallions, finely chopped
2 tomatoes, peeled, seeded, and diced
1/2 pound uncooked shrimp, shelled and
   deveined (see page 277), or 6 ounces
   cooked shrimp
6 ounces crabmeat, well picked over
3 tablespoons chopped fresh cilantro leaves

To serve: mixed green salad

Method

1. Preheat the oven to 400°F.

2. Mix all the batter ingredients together in a food processor or blender until smooth. Season well with salt and pepper; set aside while making the filling.

3. Heat the oil in a large skillet. Add the onion, bell pepper, and chile; cook over low heat until tender but not brown, about 10 minutes. Add the scallions and tomatoes; cook, uncovered, over medium heat for about 10 minutes or until there is very little liquid left. Add the shrimp and crabmeat; season with salt and pepper and cook for 5 minutes. Transfer to a plate to cool.

4. Lightly oil a 10-inch square baking dish and pour in half the batter mixture. Spread the shrimp mixture gently over the top, sprinkle with the cilantro and pour the remaining batter on top.

5. Bake for 25 minutes, then reduce the oven temperature to 350°F. Bake until a sharp knife or skewer inserted into the center comes out clean. Serve warm, cut into diamonds, with a mixed green salad.

NOTE: The shrimp and crab filling can be substituted by Picadillo (see page 92), shredded chicken or leftover Two-Bean Chili with Vegetables (see page 85).

WINE SUGGESTION: Full dry white.

Marinated Quail's Eggs

Quails' eggs are very popular, especially in Brazil, where they are hard boiled, peeled, and left overnight to marinate in an oil and vinegar dressing, then served with French bread as an appetizer.

Ingredients

24 quails' eggs

For the dressing:
1/3 cup olive oil
2 garlic cloves, sliced
1/4 cup white wine vinegar
1 Thai red chile, seeded and diced (see
   page 194)
1 (2-inch) cinnamon stick
Salt and freshly ground black pepper
Generous pinch cayenne pepper
2 tablespoons finely chopped fresh parsley
   leaves

Method

1. Cook the quails' eggs for 4 minutes in boiling salted water. Remove and plunge into a bowl of cold water to prevent further cooking. When cold, peel carefully and set aside.

2. Put all the dressing ingredients into a small saucepan and bring to a boil. Remove from the heat, add the eggs and set aside until cooled. When cooled, remove the sliced garlic and cinnamon stick. This can be prepared a day in advance; cover the marinated eggs and store in the refrigerator.

WINE SUGGESTION: Crisp, dry white.

Avocado and Red Pimiento Salad with Lime Chile Dressing

Avocado dishes in many different forms are served with almost any meal in Mexico. In this recipe the chile dressing balances a little of the avocado richness and the pimientos add a touch of sweetness.

Ingredients

1 can (14 ounces) whole red pimientos in water
  or 1 jar (12 ounces) roasted red peppers
3 tablespoons olive oil
2 tablespoons vegetable oil
1 garlic clove, sliced
$1/2$ teaspoon hot red pepper flakes
1 tablespoon white wine vinegar
Salt and freshly ground black pepper
2 ripe avocados, peeled and pitted
Juice of 1 lemon
Juice of 3 limes
2 tablespoons coarsely chopped fresh
  cilantro leaves

For the garnish:
2 tablespoons chopped fresh Italian flat-leaf
  parsley leaves

To serve: tortilla chips

Method

1. Drain the pimientos well and cut into $1/2$-inch strips.

2. In a small saucepan, mix the oils, garlic, pepper flakes, and vinegar; bring to a boil. Transfer to a medium heatproof bowl and season with salt and pepper. Add the pimiento strips to the hot dressing and set aside until cooled.

3. Cut the avocados into large cubes; toss in the lemon juice, then mound in the center of a serving plate. Remove the pimiento strips from the dressing and arrange them around the avocados.

4. Remove the garlic from the dressing and discard. Add the lime juice and cilantro and whisk with a fork until emulsified; season to taste with salt and pepper. Spoon over the avocados and pimientos. Sprinkle with the chopped parsley and serve with the tortilla chips.

WINE SUGGESTION: Rosé.

Tortilla Salad with Watercress and Chile Dressing

This is a good recipe for using up leftover tortillas and is a complete meal in itself.

Ingredients

1 red bell pepper, seeded and cut into
  $1/2$-inch strips
1 yellow bell pepper, seeded and cut into
  $1/2$-inch strips
$1/2$ large cucumber, seeded and cut into julienne
  strips
2 medium zucchini, cut into julienne strips
3 large tomatoes, peeled, seeded, and cut into
  thin strips
1 head iceberg lettuce
2 (6-inch) Wheat-Flour Tortillas (see page 166)

For the dressing:
$1/3$ cup vegetable oil
$1/3$ cup olive oil
$1/3$ cup lemon juice
1 red chile, seeded and finely chopped (see
  page 194)
1 small bunch watercress, leaves only
2 tablespoons chopped fresh Italian flat-leaf
  parsley leaves
Juice of 1 lime
Dash chili sauce (optional)
Salt and freshly ground pepper

For the garnish:
1 ounce double Gloucester cheese, coarsely
  grated

Method

1. Blanch the peppers, cucumber, and zucchini for a few seconds in boiling salted water. Run them under cold water, drain, and pat dry with paper towels.

2. Put all the dressing ingredients into a blender or food processor and process until smooth. Season to taste with salt and pepper.

3. Transfer the dressing to a bowl, add the peppers, cucumber, zucchini, and tomatoes; marinate for 30 minutes.

4. Cut the lettuce into $1/2$-inch strips; refrigerate until ready to assemble the salad.

5. Put one tortilla on top of the other and roll them up like a cigar. Cut crosswise at $1/2$-inch intervals to form strips.

6. When ready to serve, mix the lettuce and tortilla strips with the vegetables and toss well. Arrange on a serving plate and sprinkle the grated cheese on top. Serve at once.

WINE SUGGESTION: Rose.

Zucchini and Green Bean Salad

This delicious Mexican recipe has been adapted from *The Mexican Cookbook* by Sue Style.

Ingredients

$^3/_4$ pound green beans, trimmed and halved
$^3/_4$ pound zucchini, trimmed and cut lengthwise
   into 2-inch strips
1 avocado, peeled, pitted, and cubed
2 Granny Smith apples, cored and chopped

For the dressing:
1 egg
$^1/_2$ cup plain yogurt
Salt and freshly ground pepper
$^2/_3$ cup vegetable oil
Juice of 2 lemons
1 teaspoon honey
$^1/_2$ garlic clove, crushed

For the garnish:
Seeds from 1 pomegranate (optional)

Method

1. Cook the beans and zucchini in lightly salted boiling water until just tender. Run under cold water; drain well.

2. Place all the dressing ingredients in a blender or food processor and process until smooth. Pour half the dressing over the beans and zucchini and toss to coat.

3. Mix the avocado and apples gently into the salad. Garnish with the pomegranate seeds. Serve well chilled.

NOTE: The raw egg in the dressing can be substituted by 2 hard-cooked yolks.

WINE SUGGESTION: Crisp, dry white.

Warm Okra Salad with Couscous Timbales

Okra arrived in the Caribbean and Brazil with the African slaves and has been a favorite vegetable ever since. In this recipe the couscous, also from Africa, is colored with turmeric, a very popular food coloring in many Latin American countries.

Ingredients

$^1/_2$ pound fresh okra
3 tablespoons vegetable oil
2 garlic cloves, sliced
1 medium onion, thinly sliced
Juice of 1 lemon
Pinch sugar
$^1/_2$ teaspoon cayenne pepper
3 tablespoons cider vinegar
2 tablespoons olive oil
3 tomatoes, peeled, seeded, and cut into strips
Salt and freshly ground pepper

For the couscous:
$^2/_3$ cup Chicken Stock (see page 188)
$^1/_2$ teaspoon ground turmeric
$^3/_4$ cup couscous
1 tablespoon wine vinegar
1 tablespoon olive oil
Salt and freshly ground black pepper

For the garnish:
$^1/_2$ cup coarsely chopped salted peanuts

Method

1. Rinse the whole okra, drain well, and pat dry. Trim off and discard both ends of the okra pods. Set the okra aside.

2. Make the couscous: place the chicken stock and turmeric in a small saucepan and bring to a boil.

3. Put the couscous into a medium heatproof bowl; add the vinegar, olive oil, salt, and pepper and mix well. Pour in enough boiling stock just to cover the couscous.

Cover the bowl with plastic wrap. After 10 minutes, fluff the couscous with a fork, then cover with a plate or clean kitchen towel until ready to use.

4. In a large skillet or wok, heat the vegetable oil and garlic over medium heat. When the garlic begins to brown, remove and discard it. Add the onion and stir-fry for 2 minutes, being careful not to burn it.

5. Turn the heat to high, add the okra and quickly stir-fry them for 2 minutes. Add the lemon juice, sugar, and cayenne and toss the okra until it turns bright green. Add the vinegar, olive oil, and tomatoes and season with salt and pepper. Continue cooking for 2 minutes.

6. To serve, spoon the couscous into small, greased ramekins and press down firmly with the back of a spoon. Unmold the couscous onto warm plates, spoon the okra on the side and pour any remaining dressing around. Sprinkle the peanuts on top and serve at once.

WINE SUGGESTION: Medium-dry white.

Ceviche

Ceviche is eaten in great quantities in Peru and Ecuador, and the fish mostly used is corvina, which is found only on the Pacific coast of South America.

Ingredients

1 pound halibut or other firm white fish fillets
Juice of 3 limes
Juice of 2 lemons
2 red Thai chiles, seeded and finely diced (see page 194)
Salt
$^1/_4$ cup orange juice
3 tomatoes, peeled, seeded, and finely diced
3 tablespoons vegetable oil
3 tablespoons coarsely chopped fresh cilantro leaves
2 scallions, white and green parts, finely chopped
Pinch cayenne pepper
1 ripe avocado, peeled, pitted, and diced
Freshly ground black pepper

For the garnish:
Cured Onions (see page 144)

To serve: corn on the cob or boiled potatoes

Method

1. Cut the fish into $1^1/_2$-inch chunks. In a glass bowl, combine the fish, lime and lemon juices, the chiles, and salt; toss well. Cover and refrigerate for 2 hours, stirring occasionally.

2. Add the remaining ingredients and toss gently to blend all the flavors.

3. Garnish with the Cured Onions and serve with boiled potatoes or hot corn on the cob.

VARIATION: Mixed ceviche can be made using fresh salmon, mackerel, shrimp, and scallops.

WINE SUGGESTION: Spicy white.

Avocado, Papaya and Grapefruit Salad

This is a very simple, summery salad using native tropical Latin American ingredients in a light and refreshing way.

Ingredients

2 pink grapefruit, peeled and sectioned
1 ripe avocado, peeled, pitted, and thinly sliced
1 ripe papaya, quartered, seeded, peeled, and thinly sliced
5 tablespoons vegetable oil
3 tablespoons white wine vinegar
1 teaspoon hot red pepper flakes
Salt and freshly ground pepper

To serve: Cuban White Bread (see page 241)

Method

1. Mound the grapefruit sections in the center of a serving plate. Arrange the avocado slices around them. Finally, arrange the papaya slices around the avocados. Chill 10 minutes.

2. Whisk the oil, vinegar, and pepper flakes together. Season to taste with salt and pepper. Pour the dressing over the fruit and serve at once with thinly sliced Cuban White Bread.

VARIATION: Section the grapefruit over a plate to collect the juices and substitute for the vinegar in the dressing.

WINE SUGGESTION: Fruity, dry white.

Seafood, Avocado and Hearts of Palm Salad

A delicious summer dish that can be prepared in advance and mixed together just before serving.

Ingredients

For the dressing:
²/₃ cup sour cream
²/₃ cup crème fraîche
Juice of 2 limes
3 red Fresno or jalapeño chiles, seeded and
  finely chopped (see page 194)
1 tablespoon chopped fresh chives
Salt and freshly ground pepper

For the salad:
1 can (14 ounces) hearts of palm, drained and
  cut into 1-inch slices
3 large tomatoes, peeled, seeded, and diced
2 large avocados, peeled, pitted, and cut into
  1-inch cubes
1 pound mixed, cooked seafood

For the garnish:
1 small bunch watercress

Method

1. Mix all the dressing ingredients together in
    a small bowl. Season to taste with salt and
    pepper, cover and refrigerate.

2. In a medium bowl, combine the hearts of
    palm, tomatoes, avocados, and seafood; mix
    with enough dressing to coat lightly.

3. Arrange the salad on a serving plate, garnish
    with watercress and pass the remaining
    dressing.

*NOTE: If crème fraîche is unavailable, you can use
1¹/₃ cups sour cream.*

*NOTE: If using frozen seafood, put it into a
colander, add the juice of 1 lemon, sprinkle with
salt and let it thaw for 1 hour, or until thoroughly
defrosted.*

WINE SUGGESTION: Dry white.

Mixed Kidney Bean Salad

Beans are extremely popular in all Latin American countries, but, strangely enough, there are very few salad recipes that include them.

Ingredients

1 can (15 ounces) black beans
1 can (15 ounces) kidney beans
$^1/_2$ recipe Cured Onions (see page 144)
$^1/_4$ cup vegetable oil
1 garlic clove, crushed
3 tablespoons white wine vinegar
$^1/_2$ teaspoon chili powder
$^1/_2$ teaspoon ground cumin
$^1/_2$ teaspoon ground coriander
Salt and freshly ground pepper
$^1/_4$ cup finely chopped fresh Italian flat-leaf
    parsley leaves
1 teaspoon dried oregano

Method

1. Drain and rinse the black and kidney beans. Transfer to a heatproof bowl and add the Cured Onions.

2. In a small saucepan, mix the oil, garlic, vinegar, spices, and salt. Bring to a boil and pour the hot dressing over the beans; mix well to coat them. Add the parsley and oregano and season to taste with salt and pepper. Cover and allow the mixture to marinate at room temperature for at least 3 hours, or refrigerate overnight, tossing once or twice.

3. Serve cold or at room temperature.

NOTE: Any selection of beans can be used for this recipe (black-eyed, borlotti, pinto, etc.). It is also delicious made with chickpeas or lentils.

WINE SUGGESTION: Fruity red.

Marinated Vegetable Salad

Very popular in Brazil and other South American countries, this salad is delicious as an accompaniment to barbecued meats, or on its own.

Ingredients

$^1/_2$ pound green beans, ends trimmed
$^1/_2$ pound broccoli, cut into small florets
$^1/_2$ pound cauliflower, cut into small florets
$^1/_2$ pound new potatoes, scrubbed and halved
2 zucchini, cut into 1-inch rounds
1 bunch radishes, trimmed
1 red bell pepper, roasted, peeled, and cut into $^1/_2$-inch strips
1 yellow bell pepper, roasted, peeled, and cut into $^1/_2$-inch strips
1 can (8$^1/_2$ ounces) sweet corn, drained and rinsed

For the dressing:
$^2/_3$ cup vegetable oil
1 large onion, finely chopped
1 red Dutch chile, seeded and chopped (see page 194)
2 garlic cloves, crushed (optional)
1 teaspoon ground cumin
$^1/_4$ cup white wine vinegar
Juice of 2 limes
2 tablespoons chopped fresh oregano leaves
$^1/_4$ cup chopped fresh Italian flat-leaf parsley leaves
Salt and freshly ground pepper

Method

1. Cook the beans, broccoli, cauliflower, potatoes, zucchini, and radishes separately in boiling water until just tender. Drain and run under cold water until cooled. Drain thoroughly.

2. Make the dressing: heat the oil in a medium skillet; add the onion and chili and cook over very low heat until almost tender, about 10 minutes. Add the garlic and cumin and continue cooking for 2 minutes.

3. Transfer the onion mixture to a small bowl, add the vinegar, lime juice, herbs, and seasoning to taste.

4. Combine all the vegetables in a large bowl; pour the dressing over and mix gently but thoroughly. Cover and refrigerate for at least 1 hour, tossing the vegetables in the dressing once.

5. Remove the salad from the refrigerator 20 minutes before serving.

NOTE: Almost any vegetables can be used for this salad—snow peas, baby corn, etc. It is particularly good served with barbecued meat. To make it into a main dish, add a few hard-cooked quails' eggs.

WINE SUGGESTION: Dry rose.

Peruvian Quinoa Salad

Quinoa is a grain that has been popular in Peru since Inca times, when it was considered a holy grain and more highly regarded than the potato. It has a high nutritional value, is easy to prepare and digest, and is normally used in Peruvian soups, stews, and casseroles.

Ingredients

3 cups (1 pound) raw quinoa
2 quarts cold Chicken or Vegetable Stock (see page 188)
1 red bell pepper, roasted, peeled, and finely diced
1 green bell pepper, roasted, peeled, and finely diced
2 green Anaheim chiles, roasted, peeled, and finely diced (see page 194)
2 tomatoes, peeled, seeded, and diced
1 cup roasted peanuts, coarsely chopped

For the dressing:
1/4 cup peanut oil
Juice of 1 lime
1 tablespoon white rum
5 tablespoons coarsely chopped fresh cilantro leaves
Pinch ground turmeric
1 garlic clove, crushed (optional)
3 tablespoons coarsely chopped fresh Italian flat-leaf parsley leaves
Salt and freshly ground black pepper

Method

1. Rinse the quinoa thoroughly under cold water until the water runs clear. In a large saucepan, mix the quinoa and stock; bring to a boil and simmer for 8 to 10 minutes, or until the grains are translucent. Drain well and spread on a plate to cool.

2. In a large bowl, mix the peppers, chiles, tomatoes, and half the peanuts.

3. In a blender or food processor, process all the dressing ingredients until thoroughly combined.

4. Add the cooled quinoa and dressing to the peppers and mix well. Season to taste with salt and pepper, cover, and chill. Before serving, sprinkle with the remaining peanuts. Serve with barbecued meat, cold cuts, or on its own as a light meal.

NOTE: Quinoa is available at health food stores.

WINE SUGGESTION: Medium-dry white.

Poultry

POULTRY

One of the most popular foods brought to Europe from Mexico was turkey. It reached England around 1524 through Turkish merchants, so it became known as the "turkie cock," later just "turkey." In fact, the turkey has many different names, all wrongly attributing its origins to places like India and Peru. It slowly replaced the traditional festive birds used until then in England and France, such as swans and peacocks, and by the mid-17th century the turkey was already the established meat for Christmas dinner. Around the world it became the bird to use at large gatherings, especially in Latin America where families are usually large. The relatively low price of turkey meat made it accessible to everyone.

Migrating ducks, geese, and other wildfowl passing through Mexico and Central America were a source of game before 1500, and the Aztecs had already domesticated some types of duck, quail, and dove, as well as the turkey. To this day, there are many duck, pigeon, and even grouse recipes in Latin America.

Another bird quickly adopted by Latin Americans soon after the Conquest was the chicken. Together with the pig, the chicken is easily and cheaply raised on scraps, even by the poorest household, and it became the most popular poultry choice throughout the continent. Recipes using turkey or game were easily adapted to chicken, and new methods of cooking introduced by the Spaniards made it a complete and almost instant success. In the countryside, free-range chickens are bought alive in markets and killed at home, just before being cooked, but in city supermarkets the "battery" chicken is now all too common.

The following recipes have exotic and ancient influences: from the Mayan and Aztec cuisines comes the practice of using oily seeds to thicken and enrich sauces, while African slave cookery uses dried shrimp and okra. Chilies are often included and serve to unite all the ingredients and techniques of several very different cultures.

Roasting Tables

If using a fan (convection) oven, reduce the cooking times by 15 percent or reduce the oven temperature by 40° F.

Meat		Temperature	Cooking time
		°F	per lb
Beef	Brown	425	20 mins +
	Rare roast	325	15 mins
	Medium roast	325	20 mins
Pork	Roast	400	25 mins
Lamb	Brown	425	20 mins
	Roast	375	20 mins
Chicken		400	15–20 mins
Note: Few chickens, however small, will be cooked in much under an hour.			
Turkey	Small *(under 13 pounds)*	400	12 mins
	Large *(13 pounds and over)*	350	15 mins
Note: For more detailed timings see chart over. (Few turkeys, however small, will be cooked in under 2 hours.)			
Duck/goose	Small *(under 5 pounds)*	375	20 mins
	Large *(5 pounds and over)*	350	25 mins

Jointing a Chicken

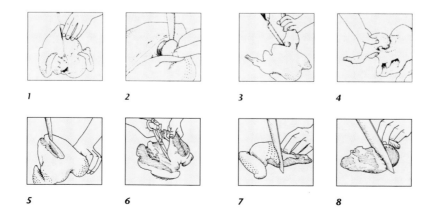

1 2 3 4

5 6 7 8

Garlic-roasted Chicken with Sweet Potatoes

Although this recipe uses a lot of garlic, the final result is quite mild in flavor. The slow and covered cooking process results in a deliciously tender and full-flavored chicken. While the covered pot allows the aromas to develop more slowly, it also results in a better flavor of the finished dish.

Ingredients

1 (4-pound) roasting chicken
4 tablespoons Chicken Stock (see page 188)
6 garlic cloves, crushed
Juice of 2 lemons
2 tablespoons butter, melted
1 green apple, cored and quartered
Salt and freshly ground pepper
2 tablespoons chopped fresh parsley
1 teaspoon chopped fresh thyme leaves
1^1/$_2$ pounds sweet potatoes, peeled and cut into
   rounds 1 inch thick
2 medium onions, thinly sliced
2 tablespoons olive oil

To serve: Mexican Rice (see page 158)

Method

1. Wipe the chicken inside and out with a damp paper towel.

2. In a small bowl, mix together the stock, half of the garlic, the lemon juice and melted butter; brush it all over the chicken.

3. Place the apple quarters inside the breast cavity of the chicken, season with salt and pepper, then place in an ovenproof casserole dish with a tight-fitting lid.

4. In a small bowl, mix together the parsley and thyme. Arrange layers of sweet potatoes, onions, and the remaining garlic around the chicken, scattering the herbs evenly over each layer. Season with additional salt and pepper. Drizzle the sweet potatoes with olive oil.

5. Cover the casserole dish tightly and place the chicken in a cold oven. Bake at 400°F for 1 hour. Check that the potatoes are not getting too dry; if they are, drizzle them with a few tablespoons of chicken stock. Continue baking, covered, an additional 30 minutes.

6. Remove the lid from the casserole dish and bake an additional 15 minutes or until the chicken is no longer pink in the center and the sweet potatoes are slightly browned. Serve in the baking dish for a rustic appearance, or transfer to a warm serving dish. Serve hot with the Mexican Rice.

WINE SUGGESTION: Zesty white.

Creamy Chicken Gratin

This is a very simple, homey dish which can be made using turkey as well as chicken.

Ingredients

1 (4-pound) chicken
1 carrot, cut into $^1/_2$-inch-thick slices
1 small onion, quartered
1 celery stalk, coarsely chopped
6 peppercorns
1 bay leaf

For the sauce:
2 tablespoons vegetable oil
1 large onion, finely chopped
2 garlic cloves, crushed
5 tomatoes, peeled, seeded, and chopped
1 tablespoon tomato purée
2 tablespoons chopped scallions
2 tablespoons finely chopped fresh parsley
$^1/_2$ teaspoon cayenne pepper
Salt and freshly ground pepper
$^2/_3$ cup heavy cream
2 cups (8 ounces) Mascarpone cheese
2 tablespoons fresh white bread crumbs

Method

1. Place the chicken in a large saucepan. Add the carrot, onion, celery, peppercorns, and bay leaf. Add enough water to cover. Bring to a boil over high heat. Reduce the heat to low and simmer, uncovered, for 1 hour or until the chicken is no longer pink in the center. Remove the chicken from the cooking liquid, let it cool, then remove the meat from the bones. Discard the bones and save the stock for later use.

2. In a large skillet, heat the oil over medium-high heat. Add the onion and cook until the onion is tender, about 10 minutes. Add the garlic, tomatoes, tomato purée, scallions, parsley, and cayenne. Season with the salt and pepper to taste. Reduce the heat to medium and cook for 10 minutes, stirring occasionally.

3. Preheat the oven to 400°F. Lightly grease a medium-sized gratin or shallow baking dish.

4. In a large bowl, combine half of the cream and the tomato sauce. Add the chicken pieces; mix lightly until the chicken is evenly coated. Spoon the chicken mixture into the gratin dish.

5. In a medium bowl, combine the Mascarpore cheese and the remaining cream; season with salt and pepper. Beat with a wooden spoon until well blended. Spread the cheese mixture over the chicken and sprinkle with the bread crumbs. Bake for about 20 minutes or until lightly browned and bubbly.

WINE SUGGESTION: Medium-dry white.

Chicken, Pepper, and Chile Sausages

Sausages are very popular throughout Latin America, from the Spanish *chorizo* and many variations of it, to the milder Portuguese *linquiça*. Pork sausages are the most common, but this chicken recipe, a favorite with children, is especially delicious for barbecues.

Ingredients

1/4 cup butter
3 tablespoons vegetable oil
1 large onion, minced
2 large garlic cloves, crushed
1 medium red bell pepper, seeded and finely diced
1 medium green bell pepper, seeded and finely diced
1 teaspoon ground cumin
1 tablespoon chopped fresh oregano leaves
1 teaspoon hot red pepper flakes
6 chicken thighs, skinned and boned
2 chicken breasts, skinned and boned
2 scallions, chopped
2 tablespoons finely chopped parsley
Salt and freshly ground black pepper
About 6 feet of sausage casing
Vegetable oil for frying

To serve: Sweet Potato Purée (see page 146)
Salsa Cruda (see page 176)

Method

1. In a large skillet, melt the butter with the oil. Add the onion and cook over medium heat until the onion is tender, about 10 minutes. Add the garlic, peppers, cumin, oregano, and red pepper flakes; cook 2 minutes.

2. Using a food processor, pound the chicken meat to a coarse purée. Transfer to a bowl and add the onion mixture, including the fat. Add the scallions and parsley and season with the salt and pepper.

3. Make the sausages: position a 1/2-inch plain nozzle in a piping bag and fill with the chicken mixture. Insert the nozzle into the sausage casing and hold it there with one hand while squeezing the mixture through the piping bag with the other. (Do not fill the skins too tightly or they will burst during cooking.) Tie into 4-inch sausages. Refrigerate, covered, for 1–2 hours.

4. Poach the sausages: bring a deep medium-sized saucepan of water to a boil over high heat. Carefully drop in the sausages. Reduce the heat to low and simmer for 10 minutes. Remove the sausages and pat dry with paper towels.

5. In a large skillet, heat 1 tablespoon oil over medium heat. Add the sausages and cook 10 minutes or until browned. Drain on paper towels. Serve with Sweet Potato Purée and Salsa cruda.

NOTE: This recipe makes 18 (4-inch) sausages. Whether barbecued or grilled, they make a delicious sandwich filling.

WINE SUGGESTION: Light, fruity red.

Chicken and Okra Casserole

This is a typical Brazilian dish, having distinct influences from Portugal (casserole dishes), Africa (use of okra), and native Indian cuisine (coloring).

Ingredients

3 tablespoons vegetable oil
1 (4-pound) chicken, cut into 8 pieces (see page 63)
1 1/3 cups hot Chicken Stock (see page 188)
2 medium onions, chopped
1 red Fresno or jalapeño chili, seeded and chopped (see page 194)
2 garlic cloves, crushed
1 teaspoon ground turmeric
1/2 teaspoon ground coriander
1/2 teaspoon ground cumin
1 can (14 1/2 ounces) chopped tomatoes, undrained
3 tablespoons finely chopped fresh parsley
1 bunch scallions, white and green parts, chopped
Salt and freshly ground pepper
1 pound okra
Juice of 1 lemon
2 tablespoons coarsely chopped fresh cilantro leaves

To serve: Polenta (see page 245)
Salsa Cruda (see page 176)

Method

1. Heat half of the oil in a large skillet over medium-high heat. Place the chicken pieces, skin sides down, in the skillet and cook until browned on all sides, about 15 minutes. Transfer the chicken to a large bowl. Add 2/3 cup of the chicken stock to the skillet. Bring to a boil, stirring well with a wooden spoon and scraping up any sediment from the bottom of the skillet. Pour the liquid over the chicken.

2. Heat the remaining oil in the deglazed pan. Add the onions and chili; cook and stir until tender, about 10 minutes. Add the garlic, turmeric, ground coriander, and cumin. Cook 1 minute, stirring constantly.

3. Add the tomatoes, parsley, half of the scallions, and the remaining chicken stock. Season with the salt and pepper. Return the chicken pieces to the pan. Reduce the heat to low, cover, and cook until the chicken is no longer pink in the center, about 35 minutes.

4. Wash and dry the okra well. Trim the ends and discard.

5. Just before serving, transfer the chicken pieces to a warm dish. Bring the sauce to a boil and add the okra. Stir in the lemon juice and cilantro; cook 5 minutes. Add the remaining scallions and season with salt and pepper to taste. Pour okra mixture over the chicken pieces and sprinkle with the remaining scallions. Serve with the Polenta and Salsa Cruda.

NOTE: If the okra is overcooked, it will become sticky, slimey, and lose its bright green color. If you prefer, the okra can be quickly stir-fried and served as a separate dish.

WINE SUGGESTION: Medium-bodied red.

Chicken Thighs in Pumpkin Seed Sauce

Nuts and seeds are frequently used to thicken and enrich classic Mexican sauces. Dairy products, such as cream, butter, and cheese, were introduced in the 16th century by the Spaniards, but the traditional recipes using nuts have survived almost unchanged even to the present day.

Ingredients

8 chicken thighs
Salt and freshly ground pepper
2 tablespoons peanut oil

For the sauce:
1 cup pumpkin seeds
2 teaspoons ground cumin
1/2 teaspoon paprika
2 green jalapeño or Fresno chilies, seeded and
    finely chopped (see page 194)
1 1/3 cups Chicken Stock (see page 188)
4 tablespoons chopped fresh parsley
4 tablespoons chopped fresh cilantro leaves
Salt and freshly ground pepper

For the garnish:
2 tomatoes, peeled, seeded, and finely diced
1 tablespoon chopped fresh parsley

Method

1. Season the chicken thighs with salt and pepper. Heat the oil in a large skillet over medium heat. Add the chicken and cook until browned on all sides, about 15 minutes. Remove the chicken from the skillet and drain on paper towels.

2. Make the sauce: drain off any excess fat from the skillet. Add the pumpkin seeds to the skillet and cook over medium heat 2 minutes or until lightly toasted, stirring frequently. Add the cumin, paprika, and chilies and cook, stirring constantly, 1 minute.

3. Add half of the chicken stock to the skillet and mix thoroughly, scraping up any sediment from the bottom of the pan. Transfer the sauce to a blender, process until smooth, then pour back into the pan. Add the remaining stock, parsley, and cilantro. Season with salt and pepper. Bring to a boil over high heat. Add the browned thighs, turning to coat well with the sauce. Reduce the heat to low, cover, and simmer until the chicken is no longer pink in the center, about 25 minutes.

4. Transfer the chicken to a serving plate and sprinkle with the tomatoes and parsley. Serve warm.

WINE SUGGESTION: Alsace white.

Chicken in Tomatillo and Nut Sauce

Pollo en mole verde, as this traditional Mexican dish is called, is made using tomatillos—small, ripe green tomatoes also known as husks or Mexican green tomatoes. *Moles* are thick sauces made with a combination of nuts, dried or fresh chilies, and other ingredients such as onions, tomatoes, and cilantro. They play an important part in Mexican cuisine and are the basis of many famous dishes, such as the festive Turkey in Chocolate and Chili Sauce (see page 75).

Ingredients

2 tablespoons vegetable oil
1 (4-pound) chicken, cut into 8 pieces (see page 63)

For the sauce:
2 tablespoons vegetable oil
$^1/_2$ cup pumpkin seeds
$^1/_4$ cup chopped walnuts
$^1/_2$ cup blanched slivered almonds
1 green bell pepper, skinned, seeded, and chopped
2 green Thai chilies, skinned, seeded, and chopped (see page 194)
1$^1/_3$ cups Chicken Stock (see page 188)
1 can (16 ounces) tomatillos, drained (see note)
1 large onion, chopped
3 tablespoons chopped fresh cilantro leaves
1 garlic clove, crushed
Salt and freshly ground black pepper

To serve: Baked Red Rice (see page 159)
Jalapeño and Lime Salsa (see page 177)

Method

1. In a large skillet, heat the oil over medium-high heat. Add the chicken, skin sides down, and cook until browned on all sides, about 15 minutes. Transfer the chicken to a large bowl and rinse the pan.

2. Make the sauce: heat the oil in a skillet. Add the pumpkin seeds, walnuts, and almonds. Reduce the heat to medium and cook, stirring frequently, until the nuts are lightly toasted, about 2 minutes.

3. Transfer the toasted nuts to a blender or food processor. Add the green pepper and chilies and process until smooth. Add the chicken stock, tomatillos, onion, cilantro, and garlic and process to a thick, smooth purée. If the sauce is too thick, add a few more tablespoons chicken stock.

4. Preheat the oven to 400°F.

5. Pour the nut purée back into the skillet and cook over medium heat about 5 minutes, stirring frequently. Season with salt and pepper to taste.

6. Pour the sauce over the chicken pieces and toss lightly to coat all pieces evenly. Arrange the chicken in a shallow baking dish. Cover with remaining sauce. Cover and bake for 35 minutes or until chicken is no longer pink in the center. Serve with the Baked Red Rice. Pass the Jalapeño and Lime Salsa separately.

NOTE: Green gooseberries can be used instead of the tomatillos. In the classic recipe, the chicken is poached gently in chicken stock before adding it to the sauce. Both versions give delicious results.

WINE SUGGESTION: Full-bodied white.

Spicy Chicken Wings

This finger food is especially delicious when served with cold beer on a hot summer's day. It can also be made substituting chicken hearts for the chicken wings. Thread the marinated hearts onto wet bamboo skewers and grill for 5 minutes on each side.

Ingredients

20 chicken wings
Vegetable oil for frying

For the marinade:
2 garlic cloves, crushed
2 tablespoons vegetable oil
Juice of 2 limes
1 teaspoon chili powder
2 teaspoons sugar
$1/2$ teaspoon salt
$1/2$ teaspoon paprika

For the garnish:
Lemon wedges

Method

1. Wipe the chicken wings with damp paper towels.

2. In a large bowl, combine all the marinade ingredients. Add the chicken wings and toss to coat. Cover and set aside for at least 30 minutes, turning the wings in the marinade once.

3. In a large skillet, heat the oil over medium-high heat. Add the chicken wings in batches of 5 and cook, turning once, until golden brown on the outside and no longer pink in the centers, about 10 minutes. Remove to paper towels to drain well.

4. Transfer the wings to a plate lined with paper towels. Sprinkle with the salt and serve immediately with the lemon wedges.

NOTE: Omit the oil. Prepare and marinate the chicken as directed. Place the chicken on skewers and grill over medium coals until no longer pink in the center, 10–15 minutes.

WINE SUGGESTION: Crisp, dry white.

Chunky Chicken Mousse

This is a very light and lemony chicken mousse—ideal for a buffet or summer lunch.

Ingredients

3 bone-in chicken breasts
5$\frac{1}{3}$ cups Chicken Stock (see page 188)
Juice of 1 lemon
2 teaspoons unflavored gelatin
2 tablespoons olive oil
1 medium onion, finely chopped
2 scallions, finely chopped
1 red bell pepper, seeded and finely diced
6 ounces cream cheese, softened
$\frac{2}{3}$ cup heavy cream
2 tomatoes, peeled, seeded, and finely diced
3 tablespoons finely chopped fresh parsley
   leaves
1 teaspoon Dijon mustard
Salt and freshly ground black pepper

For the garnish:
1 small bunch watercress
Lemon wedges

Method

1. Place the chicken breasts in a medium saucepan. Add the chicken stock; cover. Bring to a boil over high heat. Reduce the heat to low, simmer for 15 minutes or until chicken is no longer pink in the center. Remove the chicken from the stock; set aside to cool. Remove the meat from the bones, shred, and set aside.

2. Place the lemon juice in a small saucepan. Sprinkle with the gelatin and stir. Let stand 10 minutes.

3. Heat the olive oil in a large skillet over medium-high heat. Add the onion, scallions, and red pepper; cook and stir until tender, about 10 minutes.

4. In a large bowl, combine the cream cheese, cream, tomatoes, parsley, and mustard. Add the onion mixture; mix well. Season with salt and pepper to taste. Stir in the shredded chicken.

5. Place the saucepan with the gelatin over low heat and stir until dissolved, 2–3 minutes. Add to the chicken mixture; mix well.

6. Brush a 6-cup ring mold lightly with oil. Spoon the chicken mixture into the prepared mold; cover and refrigerate for at least 4 hours.

7. Remove the mold from the refrigerator 30 minutes before serving. Unmold onto a serving dish and garnish with the watercress and lemon wedges.

NOTE: The mousse can be made into individual servings using small ramekins.

WINE SUGGESTION: Light white.

Chicken with Shrimp and Peanut Sauce

This unusual dish is called *xinxim de galinha* in Brazil and is a good example of African cuisine incorporating native ingredients such as peanuts. The result is as unique and exciting as the cuisine of Bahia, where it comes from.

Ingredients

Juice of 3 limes
2 garlic cloves, crushed
Salt and freshly ground pepper
1 (4-pound) chicken, cut into 8 pieces (see page 63)
4 tablespoons vegetable oil
1 large onion, finely chopped
2 teaspoons paprika
4 ounces dried shrimps, ground (see page 277)
$^1/_2$ cup roasted peanuts, ground
2 red Thai or Indian chilies, seeded and finely chopped (see page 194)
$^2/_3$ cup Chicken Stock (see page 188)
3 tablespoons chopped fresh Italian flat-leaf parsley
3 tablespoons chopped fresh cilantro leaves

Method

1. In a large bowl, combine the lime juice, garlic, salt, and pepper. Add the chicken pieces; toss to coat. Cover and refrigerate at least 30 minutes.

2. In a large saucepan, heat 2 tablespoons of the oil over medium-high heat. Add the onion; cook and stir until tender, about 10 minutes. Add the paprika, shrimp, peanuts, and chilies; cook, stirring constantly, 2 minutes.

3. Heat the remaining oil in a large skillet over medium-high heat. Add the chicken pieces and cook until browned on all sides, about 15 minutes. Remove the chicken from the skillet and place on paper towels to drain.

4. Add the chicken stock to the onion mixture in the skillet; stir well. Bring to a boil over medium-high heat. Add the chicken pieces and season with salt and pepper. Reduce the heat to low, cover, and simmer until the chicken is no longer pink in the center, about 30 minutes, turning the chicken pieces once during cooking and adding a few tablespoons additional stock if necessary.

5. Just before serving, stir in the parsley and the cilantro. Season with additional salt and pepper to taste. (The sauce should be quite thick.)

VARIATION: This dish can also be made with duck which has been cut into 6 pieces and from which the excess fat has been removed.

WINE SUGGESTION: California white.

Lime-and-lemon-glazed Poussins

Lime is used extensively as a seasoning for poultry, pork, and fish in many Latin American countries. In this recipe, lemon juice is mixed with sugar syrup, giving the poussins a delicate yet tangy flavor.

Ingredients

4 small poussins or Rock Cornish hens
4 tablespoons olive oil
Salt and freshly ground black pepper
1 tablespoon coarsely chopped fresh thyme
  leaves
1 tablespoon coarsely chopped fresh rosemary
Juice of 2 lemons
2^1/$_2$ cups granulated sugar
4 cups water
2 limes
4 lemons

For the garnish:
1 small bunch watercress

To serve: Yellow Coconut Rice (see page 157)

Method

1. Preheat the oven to 400°F.

2. Place the poussins, breast sides up, in a shallow roasting pan. Brush with the olive oil and season with the salt and pepper. In a small bowl, combine the herbs with the juice of 2 lemons; pour over the poussins. Set aside to marinate for 20 minutes.

3. Place the sugar and water in a large saucepan; cook over low heat until the sugar has dissolved completely, about 10 minutes. Increase the heat to high and bring to a boil. Cook 10 minutes.

4. Pierce the limes and 4 lemons all over with a skewer, then add them to the sugar syrup. Boil until the syrup has thickened slightly and the fruits are soft with a glassy appearance, about 15 minutes.

5. Remove the fruits from the syrup with a slotted spoon and add them to the roasting pan with the poussins. Baste each poussin with about 2 tablespoons of the syrup. Bake for 30–35 minutes, basting once, or until the poussins are golden brown and no longer pink in the center.

6. Serve each poussin with one whole lemon and half a lime, and garnish with the watercress. (The inside of the lemon and lime can be scooped out and eaten.) Spoon a good portion of the juices over the top and serve with the yellow rice.

NOTE: The remaining lemon and lime syrup can be saved and used to make ice creams, served warm with cakes, or used to sweeten fresh fruit.

WINE SUGGESTION: White Graves.

Turkey in Chocolate and Chili Sauce

This is the national dish of Mexico. Since, like most national dishes, it is a little costly and requires extra time in the kitchen, it is reserved for special occasions and larger gatherings. Its Mexican name, *mole poblano de Guajelote*, indicates its origins. *Poblano* means "from Puebla," the capital of the state with the same name, which was founded in 1531 by the Spaniards and is one of the two cities with the most churches in Mexico. In colonial times, when illustrious visitors came to town, all the local convents tried to outdo each other in preparing unusual dishes. Legend has it that Sister Andrea de la Asunción, cook for the Santa Rosa convent, was walking in despair within the walls of the convent not knowing what to cook for the visiting viceroy, when an angel appeared and gave her this recipe. Neither the nun nor the angel can claim the recipe as their own, however, since a dish very similar was served to Hernando Cortes at the court of the Emperor Montezuma I and recorded in the chronicles around 1519.

Ingredients

1 (8-pound) turkey, cut up into 8–10 pieces (see page 63)
1 small bunch parsley, stalks and leaves
4 dried pasilla chilies (see page 199)
4 dried mulato or poblano chilies (see page 199)
6 dried ancho chilies (see page 199)
5 tablespoons vegetable oil
3 onions, finely chopped
3 garlic cloves, crushed
$1/2$ cup raisins
$1/2$ cup sesame seeds, lightly toasted (see note on page 76)
1 cup blanched almonds, lightly toasted (see note on page 76)
1 teaspoon ground cinnamon
$1/2$ teaspoon aniseed
$1/2$ teaspoon cumin seeds
$1/2$ teaspoon coriander seeds
$1/4$ teaspoon ground cloves
4 tomatoes, peeled, seeded, and chopped
$3/4$ cup cornmeal
$1 3/4$ cups Chicken Stock (see page 188)
2 ounces bittersweet chocolate, finely chopped or grated

For the garnish:
2 tablespoons toasted sesame seeds

To serve: Mexican Rice (see page 158)

Method

1. Place the turkey pieces in a Dutch oven or large saucepan; add the parsley and enough water to cover. Bring to a boil over high heat. Reduce the heat to low, cover, and simmer until the turkey is no longer pink in the center, about 2 hours. Drain the pieces well and reserve the cooking liquid. Rinse out the pan for later use.

2. Prepare the chilies: cut them in half, remove all the veins and seeds, and discard. Tear the chilies into small pieces and place in a small bowl. Add enough of the turkey cooking liquid to cover and set aside to soak for 40 minutes.

3. In a large skillet, heat 3 tablespoons of the oil over medium-high heat. Add the turkey pieces, a few at a time, and cook until browned on all sides, about 15 minutes. Cover and keep warm while preparing the sauce.

4. Add the remaining 2 tablespoons oil to the Dutch oven and heat over medium-high heat. Add the onions; cook and stir until tender, about 10 minutes. Add the garlic, raisins, toasted sesame seeds, almonds, cinnamon, aniseed, cumin, coriander, and

Recipe continued on next page

cloves; cook and stir until tender, about 10 minutes. Stir in the tomatoes.

5. Transfer the chilies and their cooking liquid to a blender or food processor; blend until the mixture forms a smooth purée. Return the purée to the pan, add the cornmeal and stock, and bring to a boil over high heat. Reduce the heat to low and simmer for 20 minutes, stirring occasionally.

6. Add the chocolate; stir until melted. Add the turkey pieces; simmer 30 minutes or until the turkey is no longer pink in the center.

7. To serve, transfer the turkey and sauce to a serving dish and sprinkle with the 2 tablespoons toasted sesame seeds.

NOTE: To toast the nuts, place them in a shallow baking pan. Bake at 375°F until golden brown, 10–12 minutes for the almonds, 4 minutes for the sesame seeds. Or, place the almonds in a small skillet over medium heat. Cook until almost done (about 8 minutes), add the sesame seeds and stir continuously until they start popping and turn light brown.

VARIATION: This dish can also be made with chicken.

WINE SUGGESTION: Full-bodied white.

Turkey Blanquette with Coconut Milk and Chilies

The mixing of chilies and coconut is always a happy one. The coconut milk counteracts the heat of the chilies while also adding a delicate flavor to the turkey.

Ingredients

3 garlic cloves, peeled
4 shallots, peeled
2$^2/_3$ cups coconut milk
Juice of 2 limes
1$^1/_2$ teaspoons ground ginger
1$^3/_4$ pounds turkey breast meat, cut into 1-inch pieces
Salt and freshly ground white pepper
4 small red serrano chilies or 2 small Thai chilies (see page 197)
1 teaspoon crushed coriander seeds

For the garnish:
2 tablespoons chopped fresh cilantro leaves

To serve: Green Rice (see page 156)

Method

1. In a blender or food processor, place the garlic and shallots and blend until puréed. Add $^2/_3$ cup of the coconut milk, the lime juice, and ground ginger; blend until smooth.

2. Pour the sauce into a large skillet; add the turkey in a single layer. Season with the salt and pepper. Bring to a boil over high heat. Reduce the heat to low, cover, and simmer for 5 minutes.

3. Stir in the remaining 2 cups coconut milk, the whole chilies, and the crushed coriander seeds. Cover and cook 20 minutes or until the turkey is no longer pink in the center, stirring occasionally.

4. When ready to serve, remove the turkey pieces with a slotted spoon to a serving bowl or platter, cover, and keep warm. Increase the heat to medium-high. Continue to simmer the sauce until it is reduced by half. Season with salt to taste, then pour over the turkey. Sprinkle with the cilantro and serve with Green Rice.

WINE SUGGESTION: California white.

Turkey Escalopes with Chili Cream Sauce

Although not native to Latin America, cilantro is hugely popular throughout the continent and used generously by every cook. For maximum flavor, add the freshly snipped leaves to any dish just before serving.

Ingredients

2 pounds turkey breast meat
3 tablespoons all-purpose flour
2 tablespoons vegetable oil

For the sauce:
3 green Fresno or jalapeño chilies, seeded and
  chopped (see page 194)
1 1/3 cups heavy cream
2 shallots, finely chopped
1/2 cup coarsely chopped fresh cilantro leaves
1 garlic clove, crushed
Salt and freshly ground pepper

For the garnish:
2 tomatoes, peeled, seeded, and finely diced

Method

1. Trim any fat from the turkey breast and discard. Cut the meat into 8 portions, place between sheets of waxed paper or plastic wrap, and flatten with a rolling pin or a meat mallet to a 1/2-inch thickness.

2. Coat the turkey lightly in flour, shaking off any excess. Cover and refrigerate while preparing the sauce.

3. In a heavy, medium saucepan, combine the chilies, cream, shallots, cilantro, and garlic. Bring to a boil over high heat. Reduce the heat to low and simmer for about 5 minutes or until the sauce has thickened slightly, stirring frequently. Transfer the sauce to a blender and blend until smooth. Return to the rinsed-out saucepan. Season with salt and pepper to taste and keep warm.

4. Heat the oil in a large skillet over medium-high heat. Add the turkey and cook until browned on both sides. Reduce the heat to low; cook 4 minutes or until the meat is no longer pink in the center.

5. Place 2 pieces of turkey on each plate. Top with the sauce and garnish with the tomatoes.

NOTE: The chili sauce can be made up to 1 day in advance. Cover and refrigerate until ready to serve. Heat thoroughly just before serving. This sauce is also very good served with grilled fish or chicken.

WINE SUGGESTION: Crisp, dry white.

Duck with Rice and Mint

The Spanish tradition of cooking poultry or meat with rice is also very strong in many Latin American countries. In Spain itself, various types of meat, fish, and shellfish are cooked with rice and flavored with saffron. Latin American recipes, on the other hand, tend to use only one type of meat, usually poultry, and the most common flavoring is turmeric, which imparts a bright yellow color and very subtle flavor to any dish.

Ingredients

1 duck, cut up into 8 pieces
1 tablespoon vegetable oil
2 onions, finely chopped
2 garlic cloves, crushed
1 1/2 cups long-grain white rice, washed and drained well
1 teaspoon crushed cumin seeds
1 teaspoon ground turmeric
2 tablespoons finely chopped fresh mint leaves
Salt and freshly ground black pepper
1/4 cup brandy
2 2/3 cups Chicken Stock (see page188)

To serve: Salsa Cruda (see page 176)

Method

1. Place some of the duck fat in a large saucepan and cook over medium heat until melted. Add the duck pieces, skin sides down, and cook until browned on all sides, 10–15 minutes. Transfer the browned pieces to a large bowl and drain all of the excess fat from the pan. If necessary, deglaze the pan with a few tablespoons water; pour the liquid over the duck.

2. Heat the oil in the deglazed pan over medium-high heat. Add the onions; cook and stir until tender, about 10 minutes. Add the garlic and rice. Reduce the heat to medium; cook, stirring occasionally, 5 minutes. Stir in the cumin and turmeric; cook 1 minute.

3. Add the mint and duck pieces to the pan; mix thoroughly with the rice. Season with salt and pepper. Add the brandy and enough chicken stock just to cover. Cover with a tight-fitting lid and cook 20 minutes.

4. Remove the lid from the pan to check if the rice and duck are both cooked. If not, add a few additional tablespoons of hot stock and simmer, covered, for another 5 minutes or until the rice is cooked and all the liquid is absorbed.

5. Serve in the cooking dish or transfer to a warm serving dish. Serve with the Salsa Cruda.

WINE SUGGESTION: Medium-bodied red.

Meat

MEAT

When the Spanish reached Mexico in 1519, they were amazed to see the variety of wild birds, game, and other sources of meat available to the Aztecs. The turkey was already domesticated and much appreciated, together with a species of small dog that was specially bred for cooking. Insects, lizards, young ducks, rabbits, hare, and deer were all relatively common parts of the diet, and a taste for the exotic continues to this day, with such things as snakes, armadillos, giant ants, and monkeys being eaten with great gusto by many people.

In Peru, the Incas raised llamas, vicuñas, and a type of guinea pig called *cuy* that, even today, still provides more than 50 percent of the animal protein eaten in Peru. The basis of the Inca and Aztec diet at the time of the Conquest was grains and potatoes; meat was reserved for the aristocracy and royalty.

The Spanish introduced chickens, pigs, cattle, sheep, and goats. The pig and chicken became very popular and slowly replaced animals like dogs and lizards on native tables. As with all the other ingredients brought by the *conquistadores*, the new meats were mixed into the local cuisine, adapted into old recipes and became an intrinsic part of the cuisine of Latin America.

Today, with the exception of Argentina and parts of Brazil and Uruguay, which are large producers of beef cattle, beef is still reserved for special occasions. Poultry and pork are the most commonly eaten meats in Latin American countries, and in Peru and Ecuador *cuy* is still the most popular.

The average Argentinian eats one pound of beef a day, and in the southern part of Brazil beef is consumed regularly in great quantities. Uruguay produces and eats large quantities of lamb and beef, and Uruguayans enjoy their meat as much as their Argentinian neighbors.

With the introduction of pork, Latin American cooking underwent something of a transformation. Until then, no fat or oil had been used and food was mostly steamed in corn husks or banana leaves. With the pig came fat, and thus began the love of fried food. Today, in almost all Latin American countries, a large percentage of the food is fried, and oil is used generously in most dishes.

The influences in meat recipes range far and wide. From the Arabs, via the Spaniards, came recipes for meat cooked with fruit, raisins, nuts, and spices like cinnamon. From the Portuguese in Brazil comes a tradition of rich, slow-cooked stews, as well as a love of fried food. Added to this pot of influences were the culinary traditions of African slaves.

Chilies were the major form of seasoning before the Conquest and remain so today, although in countries where there was a greater European influence, such as Argentina, Costa Rica, Chile, and Uruguay, the food tends to be milder.

Beef and Dried Fruit Stew

The Argentinian pampas (grasslands) produce wonderful beef, and although most of the time it is simply grilled or roasted, some unusual recipes do exist. Certainly brought to Argentina by the Spaniards, this recipe has Middle Eastern influence in the use of dried fruit.

Ingredients

$^1/_2$ pound mixed dried fruit, such as prunes and
  apricots
$1^1/_4$ cups Beef Stock, warmed (see page 189)
3 tablespoons vegetable oil
2 pounds chuck steak, trimmed and cut into
  1-inch cubes
$1^1/_4$ cups dry red wine
1 tablespoon butter
1 medium onion, finely chopped
1 garlic clove, crushed
1 carrot, peeled and coarsely chopped
Salt and freshly ground pepper

To serve: Fried Rice (see page 155)

Method

1. Put the mixed dried fruit into a medium bowl with the stock and let soak for 1 hour. Drain, reserving the soaking liquid; set the fruit aside.

2. In a dutch oven, heat the oil over medium-high heat and brown the meat, a few pieces at a time. Transfer the meat to a bowl. Deglaze the pan with some of the wine and add the pan juices to the meat.

3. Melt the butter in the deglazed pan. Add the onion and cook over very low heat until almost tender, about 10 minutes. Add the garlic and carrot, the remaining wine and reserved liquid from the dried fruit and bring to a boil. Reduce the heat to low, add the browned meat pieces and any accumulated juices and simmer, covered, for 2 hours or until the beef is tender.

4. Add the dried fruit and continue simmering for 20 minutes. If the sauce is too thick, add a little water. Season to taste with salt and pepper and serve with the Fried Rice.

WINE SUGGESTION: Fruity red.

Two-Bean Chili with Vegetables

Chili con carne was created in Texas during the 1870s as an interpretation of Mexican cuisine. Mexicans, however, deny any part in the creation of the dish, and anyone who has traveled in Mexico will testify to its nonexistence on restaurant menus. Nevertheless, this delicious culinary mistake is worth perpetuating.

Ingredients

2 tablespoons vegetable oil
2 large onions, chopped
4 garlic cloves, crushed
1^1/$_2$ pounds ground beef
2 teaspoons mild chili powder
2 teaspoons ground cumin
^{1}/$_2$ teaspoon cayenne pepper
2 cans (14^1/$_2$ ounces each) diced tomatoes, undrained
2^1/$_2$ cups Beef Stock (see page 189)
2 medium potatoes, peeled and cut into 1-inch cubes
1 large carrot, peeled and cut into 1-inch pieces
2 celery ribs, diced
1 red bell pepper, seeded and diced
1 can (15 ounces) red kidney beans, drained and rinsed
1 can (15 ounces) pinto beans, drained and rinsed
Salt and freshly ground pepper
^{1}/$_2$ teaspoon chili sauce (optional)

To serve: Fried Rice (see page 155)

Method

1. Heat the oil in a dutch oven. Add the onions and cook over very low heat until almost tender, about 10 minutes. Add the garlic and ground beef and cook, stirring constantly with a fork to break up meat.

2. Stir in the chili powder, cumin, and cayenne and cook for 3 minutes.

3. Mix in the tomatoes, stock, potatoes, carrot, celery, and bell pepper and bring to a boil.

Reduce the heat, cover and simmer for 40 minutes.

4. Stir in the beans, season to taste with salt, pepper, and chili sauce and continue simmering for 15 minutes, or until all the flavors are well blended. Serve with Fried Rice.

NOTE: This recipe is best made a day in advance and then reheated. Any leftovers can be used in pies, empanadas, Pancake Stack Pie (see page 91), tamales, or tacos.

WINE SUGGESTION: Full-bodied red.

Grilled Steak with Spiced Parsley Sauce

Parsley sauce is a traditional Argentinian accompaniment to grilled or roasted meat. With 97 percent of the population claiming European descent, and a large percentage of that from Great Britain, it is no surprise to find Worcestershire sauce as an ingredient in this recipe.

Ingredients

4 (6-ounce) rump or sirloin steaks

For the marinade:
$1/4$ cup white wine
2 garlic cloves, crushed
1 tablespoon white rum
2 tablespoons Worcestershire sauce
6 peppercorns
1 teaspoon dried marjoram
1 bay leaf

For the parsley sauce:
$1/2$ cup vegetable oil
$1/4$ cup white wine vinegar
1 red onion, chopped
$1/2$ garlic clove, crushed
$1/4$ cup chopped fresh Italian flat-leaf parsley
   leaves
1 teaspoon finely chopped fresh oregano leaves
$1/2$ teaspoon cayenne pepper
Dash chili sauce
Salt and freshly ground pepper

Method

1. Trim the steaks of all excess fat.

2. Combine all the marinade ingredients in a small bowl. Put the steaks in a shallow dish, pour the marinade over them, cover and refrigerate for 2 hours, turning once.

3. Mix all the sauce ingredients together in a blender or food processor until smooth. Season to taste with salt and pepper and transfer to a small bowl. Let the sauce stand at room temperature to develop its flavor for up to 2 hours before serving.

4. Prepare the grill. Remove the meat from the marinade and pat it dry. Discard the marinade.

5. Grill the steaks over hot coals 8 to 10 minutes, turning once, or to the desired doneness. Season with salt and pepper. Transfer the meat to a hot serving plate and serve at once with the parsley sauce.

NOTE: The steaks can also be cooked on a very hot griddle or in a skillet.

WINE SUGGESTION: Full-bodied, dry red.

Beef Stew in Dried Chile Sauce

The much-loved dried ancho chile from Mexico is the chief seasoning in the sauce for this rich and aromatic casserole.

Ingredients

1^1/$_2$ pounds chuck steak, trimmed
1 tablespoon vegetable oil

For the sauce:
^{3}/$_4$ cup Beef Stock (see page 189)
3 dried ancho chiles (see page 199)
Generous pinch hot red pepper flakes or mild
  chili powder
2 cans (14^1/$_2$ ounces each) diced tomatoes,
  undrained
2 large onions, chopped
2 garlic cloves, crushed
1 tablespoon tomato paste
2 tablespoons vegetable oil
^{1}/$_2$ teaspoon ground cumin
1 tablespoon flour
1 teaspoon dried oregano
^{1}/$_2$ teaspoon sugar
Salt and freshly ground pepper

For the garnish:
2 tablespoons chopped fresh parsley leaves

To serve: Sweet Potato Purée (see page 146)

Method

1. Cut the beef into 1^1/$_2$-inch cubes, discarding any fat.

2. Heat 1 tablespoon oil in a large saucepan over medium-high heat. Add the beef, a few pieces at a time, and cook until well browned. Put the browned pieces into a bowl as they are done. If the bottom of the pan becomes very dark or too dry, deglaze it by pouring in a little stock and scraping off any browned bits stuck to the bottom; bring it to a boil and pour over the browned meat in the bowl. Heat up a little more oil and continue to brown the meat. When it is all browned, repeat the deglazing process. Rinse and dry the saucepan.

3. Heat the remaining stock until hot. Remove the stalks from the dried chiles and cut them in half. Remove and discard the seeds and any large ribs. Tear the chiles into small pieces, put them into a bowl and pour over the hot stock. Soak for 20 minutes, then drain, reserving the liquid.

4. In a blender or food processor, process the pepper flakes, soaked chiles, tomatoes, onions, garlic, and tomato paste until smooth.

5. Preheat the oven to 300°F.

6. Heat 2 tablespoons oil in the rinsed-out pan over medium heat. Add the cumin and cook for 1 minute. Add the flour and oregano and cook for a minute. Add the tomato mixture and the reserved soaking liquid from the chiles. Cook for 10 minutes over medium heat, stirring occasionally. Stir in the sugar and season with salt and pepper.

7. Combine the meat and sauce in an ovenproof dutch oven. Cover; bake for 2^1/$_2$ hours or until the meat is tender. Mix in half of the parsley; transfer to a serving dish. Sprinkle with the remaining parsley. Serve with the Sweet Potato Purée.

WINE SUGGESTION: Full-bodied, fruity red.

Ground Beef with Apples, Olives, and Almonds

This is a festive version of Picadillo (see page 92) and has an exquisite flavor from the sweetness of the raisins and apples and the heat of the chiles.

Ingredients

2 tablespoons vegetable oil
1 large onion, finely chopped
1^1/$_2$ pounds ground beef
2 red chiles, seeded and coarsely chopped (see page 194)
1 garlic clove, crushed
3 tomatoes, peeled, seeded, and chopped
2 green apples, peeled, cored, and coarsely chopped
^{1}/$_3$ cup raisins
10 green olives, pitted and halved
^{1}/$_2$ teaspoon ground cinnamon
Pinch ground cloves
Salt and freshly ground black pepper
^{2}/$_3$ cup sliced almonds

To serve: Refried Beans (see page 151)
Yellow Coconut Rice (see page 157)

Method

1. Heat the oil in a large saucepan, add the onion and cook over low heat until soft, about 10 minutes. Add the ground beef and cook, stirring constantly with a fork to break up meat.

2. Add the chiles and garlic and cook for 5 minutes.

3. Reduce the heat and add the tomatoes, apples, raisins, olives, cinnamon, and cloves and season with salt and pepper to taste. Simmer, covered, for 40 minutes, stirring occasionally.

4. Toast the almonds in a small skillet over medium heat, stirring constantly until they are light brown.

5. Stir half the almonds into the meat mixture and transfer to a warm serving dish. Sprinkle the remaining almonds on top and serve with Refried Beans and Yellow Coconut Rice.

NOTE: Like picadillo, this recipe can be used as a stuffing for tamales, pies, and turnovers.

WINE SUGGESTION: Fruity, full-bodied red.

Spicy Shredded Beef

The beef produced on the plains around the Orinoco River in Venezuela and Colombia can be quite tough, so the cooks from both countries have developed numerous recipes for tenderizing the meat without losing any of the flavor. This recipe comes from Venezuela and is mildly hot.

Ingredients

$1^1/_2$ pounds flank steak
$1^3/_4$ cups Beef Stock (see page 189)

For the sauce:
3 tablespoons vegetable oil
2 onions, finely chopped
2 garlic cloves, crushed
$1/_2$ teaspoon ground cumin
$1/_2$ teaspoon ground coriander
4 red Indian or Thai chiles, seeded and finely chopped (see page 194)
2 cans ($14^1/_2$ ounces each) diced tomatoes, undrained
1 teaspoon tomato paste
$1/_2$ teaspoon sugar
2 bay leaves
Salt and freshly ground black pepper
2 tablespoons chopped fresh cilantro leaves

For the garnish:
2 tablespoons chopped fresh parsley leaves

Method

1. Put the meat into a large, heavy saucepan and cover with the stock. Bring to a boil; reduce the heat, cover and simmer until the meat is very tender, about 2 hours. Remove the meat from the pan and allow to cool. Reserve the cooking stock.

2. Heat the oil in a large skillet over medium heat. Add the onions and cook until tender. Stir in the garlic, cumin, coriander, chiles, tomatoes, tomato paste, sugar, bay leaves, and salt and pepper and cook for 5 minutes. Add $2/_3$ cup of the reserved stock. Bring to a boil; reduce the heat and simmer, uncovered, for 35 minutes or until the sauce is slightly thickened. Discard the bay leaves and keep the sauce warm.

3. Transfer the cooled meat to a carving board and shred, using a fork. Mix the shredded meat and cilantro into the sauce and cook over medium heat for 5 minutes or until the meat is heated through.

4. Transfer to a serving plate and sprinkle with the chopped parsley.

NOTE: The meat can be finely sliced rather than shredded, if desired. It can also be cooked the day before and assembled just before serving.

WINE SUGGESTION: Full-bodied red.

Brazilian Meat and Black Bean Stew

Originally an African slave concoction, *feijoada* is now the national dish of Brazil. Where pig's ears, feet, tail, and other minor cuts were once slowly cooked together in a pot with black beans, today better cuts of smoked and salted pork, dried meat, and sausages are used, making a deliciously rich and unique dish. Traditionally, it is eaten for lunch on Saturdays and followed by a long siesta. Because it is a costly and time-consuming dish to prepare, it is reserved for special occasions and large parties. This recipe will feed up to 12 people if all the accompaniments are served with it.

Ingredients

2 pounds dried black beans, soaked overnight
1 pound smoked chorizo sausages
1 pound sirloin beef, in one piece
6 ounces smoked ham hock, in one piece
1 pound smoked pork loin, in one piece
1 fresh pig's foot (optional)
4 garlic cloves, crushed
1 bouquet garni (sachet of parsley stems, celery, thyme, leeks, and carrots)
2 bay leaves, crumbled
1 bunch scallions, white and green parts, chopped
$^1/_4$ cup chopped fresh parsley leaves
Salt and freshly ground pepper

To serve: Shredded Kale (see page 145)
Fried Rice (see page 155)
Creoja Sauce (see page 179)
6 oranges, peeled and sliced
Toasted Cassava Meal (see page 248)

Method

1. Preheat the oven to 400°F.

2. Drain and rinse the beans under running water. Put into a large saucepan and cover with water (do not add salt as this toughens the skins). Bring to a boil and continue boiling for 10 minutes. Reduce the heat to low; simmer gently for 30 to 35 minutes or until the beans are just tender. Drain the beans and discard the cooking liquid.

3. Meanwhile, put all the meat cuts and the pig's foot (if using) into a roasting pan and roast 20 minutes. Remove the sausages and hock and continue cooking the remaining cuts for 20 minutes.

4. Once all the meat is cooked, cut it into large chunks and cut the pig's foot in half. Reserve the pan drippings and reduce the oven temperature to 300°F.

5. Place all the meat, the garlic, bouquet garni sachet, bay leaves, half the scallions and parsley, the beans, salt, and pepper in an ovenproof dutch oven. Stir thoroughly and add enough water to cover the beans and meat completely. Cover and bake for 1$^1/_2$ hours, adding more water after 45 minutes if the stew looks dry. The meat and beans should be covered with liquid. Just before serving, remove the bouquet garni and mix in the remaining parsley and scallions. Season to taste with salt and pepper. The meat and beans should be very tender and the liquid syrupy.

6. Add 3 tablespoons of liquid from the beans to the *Creoja Sauce.*

7. To serve: A buffet table is the best way to serve a feijoada. Place the bean and meat stew in the center and arrange the other dishes around it. Serve with pickled chiles and beer.

WINE SUGGESTION: Spicy, oak-aged red.

Pancake Stack Pie

This is a delicious dish where all the ingredients can be prepared in advance and assembled just before cooking.

Ingredients

10 (10-inch) Crêpes (see page 219)
$^1/_2$ recipe Two-Bean Chili with Vegetables (see page 85)
1 recipe Spicy Tomato Sauce (see page 181)
$^1/_4$ cup shredded Cheddar cheese

To serve: mixed green salad

Method

1. Preheat the oven to 400°F. Lightly grease a 12-inch round baking dish.

2. Layer the crêpes in the baking dish, spreading 4 to 5 tablespoons chili and 1 tablespoon sauce between each layer. Finish with a crêpe and pour remaining sauce around the stack. Sprinkle the cheese over the top. Bake for 25 minutes or until the cheese is golden brown and the sauce is bubbly and very hot. Serve at once with a mixed green salad.

VARIATION: To make a vegetarian dish, substitute Drunken Beans (see page 152) for the chili in the filling, omitting the bacon in the recipe and increasing the cheese to $^3/_4$ cup. Sprinkle some cheese on top of the beans in each layer.

WINE SUGGESTION: Fruity red.

Picadillo

This dish, sometimes known as *picadinho*, is found throughout Latin America, where it is also called "hangover hash" because it is believed to cure the aftereffects of alcohol. There are many variations: pork, sausages, potatoes, eggs, and carrots can be added according to taste and budget. Picadillo is used in empanadas, tacos, burritos, turnovers, and pies, or eaten with beans and rice.

Ingredients

1 tablespoon vegetable oil
1 large onion, finely chopped
2 garlic cloves, crushed
1$^1/_2$ pounds ground beef
2 tablespoons tomato paste
1 green Kenyan or Fresno chile, seeded and
   finely chopped (see page 194)
1 can (14$^1/_2$ ounces) diced tomatoes, undrained
$^1/_2$ teaspoon ground cumin
1 teaspoon dried oregano
2 tablespoons chopped fresh parsley leaves
3 scallions, finely chopped
Pinch sugar
Salt and freshly ground black pepper
$^2/_3$ cup Beef Stock (see page 189)
1 large potato, peeled and cut into small cubes

Method

1. Heat the oil in a large saucepan and add the onion and garlic. Cook over very low heat until the onions are almost tender, about 10 minutes.

2. Add the ground beef and cook, stirring constantly with a fork to break up meat.

3. Stir in the tomato paste, chile, tomatoes, cumin, oregano, half the parsley and scallions, and the sugar; mix well. Season to taste with salt and pepper. Bring to a boil, reduce the heat and cook, covered, for 20 minutes.

4. Add the stock and potato and continue cooking, uncovered, for 20 minutes or until the potato is tender and most of the liquid has evaporated. Mix in the remaining parsley and scallions and season to taste with salt and pepper. Serve hot or use to fill empanadas, pies, etc.

WINE SUGGESTION: Full-bodied California red.

Veal Chops in Chile Paste

There are not many recipes for veal in Latin America. Argentina—with its Italian ancestry—is the country where it is mostly eaten.

Ingredients

4 (8-ounce) veal chops
Juice of 2 limes
2 teaspoons chili powder
2 teaspoons paprika
1 teaspoon ground cumin
5 garlic cloves, crushed
4 tablespoons olive oil
Salt
$^2/_3$ cup Chicken Stock (see page 188)
2 tablespoons chopped fresh cilantro leaves

To serve: Root Vegetable Gratin (see page 134)

Method

1. Trim the veal chops of any excess fat and place in a shallow dish. Pour $^1/_4$ cup of the lime juice over the chops, then cover and refrigerate for 1 hour.

2. Combine the chili powder, paprika, cumin, garlic, and 2 tablespoons of the oil in a small bowl. Brush over both sides of the chops and season with salt.

3. Heat the remaining 2 tablespoons oil in a large skillet over medium heat. Add the veal and cook for about 5 minutes on each side, turning only once. The meat should be tender and browned all over.

4. Remove the meat from the pan and keep warm. Add the stock to the hot pan, scraping off any browned bits stuck to the bottom. Add the remaining lime juice and the cilantro. Season with salt and pepper, then pour over the meat and serve at once with the Root Vegetable Gratin.

WINE SUGGESTION: Fruity red with good acidity.

Roast Breast of Veal Stuffed with Jalapeño Purée

This recipe combines the delicate flavor of veal with the popular jalapeño chile. It also works well with pork.

Ingredients

3 pounds boneless veal breast
2 tablespoons butter
2 tablespoons vegetable oil
1 cup orange juice

For the purée:
8 jalapeño or Fresno green chiles (see page 196)
6 tablespoons olive oil
Juice of 1 lime
2 garlic cloves, crushed
1 big bunch of fresh Italian flat-leaf parsley
  leaves
4 tablespoons fresh bread crumbs
Salt and freshly ground pepper

To serve: Sweet Potato Purée (see page 146)

Method

1. Make the purée: put the whole chiles on a baking sheet and broil, turning them until the skin is blistered and charred. Put the chiles into a plastic bag, seal the bag, and set aside until cool enough to handle.

2. Wearing rubber gloves, remove the skins and seeds from the chiles and discard. Put the chiles, olive oil, lime juice, garlic, parsley leaves, and bread crumbs in a blender or food processor and process until smooth. Season with salt and pepper.

3. Preheat the oven to 350°F.

4. Place the veal on a work surface, open it up and spread the chile purée inside. Roll up the meat and tie it for roasting.

5. Put the butter and oil in a roasting pan and place in the oven until the butter melts. Add the veal and roast for 30 minutes. Add the orange juice and continue roasting for about 50 minutes, basting frequently with the pan juices, until a meat thermometer inserted into the veal registers 155°F.

6. Remove the veal from the roasting pan, cover with foil and let it stand for 10 minutes. Season the pan juices with salt and pepper and strain into a small saucepan. Slice the meat and arrange it on a serving plate. Reheat the juices and spoon over the meat. Serve with Sweet Potato Purée and a green vegetable.

WINE SUGGESTION: Full-bodied red.

Hot Pork Roast

Pork is the favorite meat in many Latin American countries, and country cooks still tend to use lard for cooking. In this recipe, a mixture of orange juice and honey gives the pork a golden crust and sweet sauce, while the chiles impart a gentle heat.

Ingredients

3 pounds boneless pork loin roast, rolled and tied

For the marinade:
Grated zest and juice of 2 lemons
Juice of 1 orange
1 teaspoon tomato paste
2 tablespoons honey
2 green Dutch chiles, finely chopped (see page 194)
1 tablespoon ground ginger
1 teaspoon chopped fresh thyme leaves
2 garlic cloves, crushed
Salt and freshly ground pepper
$^1/_2$ cup water
2 tablespoons vegetable oil

To serve: Potato, Cheese, and Cayenne Puffs (see page 136)

Method

1. Make the marinade: in a small saucepan, combine the lemon zest and juice, orange juice, tomato paste, honey, chiles, ginger, thyme, garlic, and salt and pepper. Bring to a boil, remove from the heat and set aside to cool.

2. Put the pork into a glass bowl or dish and pour the cooled marinade over it. Cover and refrigerate for 8 to 12 hours, turning the meat occasionally.

3. Preheat the oven to 400°F.

4. Remove the meat from the marinade and pat dry with paper towels. Put the marinade and water into a roasting pan.

5. Heat the oil in a large skillet over medium-high heat. Add the meat, brown evenly on all sides, then put into the roasting pan with the marinade. Roast for $1^1/_4$ hours (see page 63), basting the meat frequently with the marinade, until a meat thermometer inserted into the roast registers 160°F. Cover the roast with foil and let it stand for 10 minutes before carving. Serve with the Potato, Cheese, and Cayenne Puffs and pass the marinade as a sauce separately.

WINE SUGGESTION: Dry white.

Spicy Pork with Root Vegetable Gratin

The use of citrus juice to tenderize and flavor meat dishes is common in many Latin American recipes. Orange and lime juice are the most commonly used citrus fruits, but in more tropical areas, pineapple and papaya juice are used as well.

Ingredients

2 (12-ounce) pork tenderloins
5 garlic cloves, crushed
2 teaspoons ground cumin
1 teaspoon ground annatto or achiote (see note and page 274)
$^1/_2$ teaspoon cayenne pepper
$1^1/_4$ cups white wine vinegar
$^2/_3$ cup orange juice
2 tablespoons vegetable oil
Salt and freshly ground pepper
2 tablespoons chopped fresh cilantro leaves

To serve: Root Vegetable Gratin (see page 134)

Method

1. Trim the tenderloins and put into a glass bowl.

2. Combine the garlic, cumin, annatto, cayenne, vinegar, and orange juice in a small bowl. Pour over the tenderloins and mix thoroughly to coat. Cover and refrigerate for 8 hours or overnight.

3. Strain and reserve the marinade. Heat the oil in a large sauté pan with a tight-fitting lid. Cook the tenderloins over medium-high heat until golden brown on all sides. Add the reserved marinade; cover and cook over very low heat until the meat is tender and registers 160°F on a meat thermometer, about 35 minutes.

4. Transfer the pork to a carving board, cover with foil and let it stand for 10 minutes before slicing. Season the pan juices with salt and pepper and mix in the cilantro. Serve the pork with the juices and Root Vegetable Gratin.

NOTE: If neither annatto nor achiote is available, ground turmeric may be substituted.

WINE SUGGESTION: Full-bodied white.

Sweet Roast Pork

The combination of milk and vinegar (or sometimes lemon juice) in this Peruvian recipe is unusual but easily explained. The acid in the vinegar curdles the milk and tenderizes the meat. The addition of raisins, cinnamon, and butter adds sweetness and richness to the exotic character of the dish.

Ingredients

2 pounds boneless pork shoulder roast, rolled, tied, and skin left on
Salt and freshly ground pepper

For the marinade:
$^3/_4$ cup dry white wine
4 whole cloves
$^1/_4$ cup packed light brown sugar
$^1/_4$ cup unsalted butter, melted
$^3/_4$ cup whole milk
$^1/_2$ teaspoon ground cinnamon
$^1/_2$ teaspoon ground nutmeg
$^2/_3$ cup raisins

Method

1. Season the meat with salt and pepper and score the skin with a sharp knife.

2. In a large, nonmetallic bowl, combine the wine, cloves, and sugar. Add the meat and turn it well to coat with the marinade. Cover and refrigerate overnight.

3. Preheat the oven 350°F.

4. Remove the meat from the marinade, pat it dry with paper towels, and put into a roasting pan.

5. Add the melted butter, milk, cinnamon, nutmeg, and raisins to the marinade; mix thoroughly and pour over the meat. Roast for $1^3/_4$ hours (see page 63), basting occasionally, until a meat thermometer inserted into the roast registers 160°F.

6. Transfer the meat to a carving board, cover with foil and let it stand for 10 minutes before slicing. Season the pan juices to taste with salt and pepper and serve with the pork.

NOTE: This recipe works equally well with a rolled veal breast.

WINE SUGGESTION: Dry white.

Pork Chops with Pineapple and Lime Salsa

Pork chops are not as common in Latin American cuisine because the loin joint, from which they are cut, is usually cooked whole. If you prefer, this dish can be made using small pork tenderloins.

Ingredients

4 (6-ounce) pork loin chops
2 tablespoons butter
1 tablespoon vegetable oil

For the marinade:
1/4 cup white wine vinegar
2 tablespoons vegetable oil
1 garlic clove, crushed
1 teaspoon chopped fresh oregano leaves
1/2 teaspoon mild chili powder
Pinch sugar

For the salsa:
5 tablespoons vegetable oil
Juice of 2 limes
3 tablespoons chopped fresh Italian flat-leaf
   parsley leaves
2 celery ribs, coarsely chopped
1 red bell pepper, seeded and coarsely chopped
1 fresh pineapple, cut into small cubes
1/2 teaspoon cayenne pepper
1 red Fresno or Kenyan chile, seeded and
   coarsely chopped (see page 194)
Salt and freshly ground pepper

Method

1. Prepare the chops by scoring the fat at regular intervals with a sharp knife.

2. Combine all the marinade ingredients in a large bowl. Add the chops and turn to coat all sides with the marinade. Cover and refrigerate for 1 hour or overnight.

3. Combine all the salsa ingredients in a large bowl and season to taste with salt and pepper. Cover and let stand at room temperature until ready to serve (see Note).

4. Remove the pork chops from the marinade, pat them dry with paper towels and discard the marinade.

5. Heat the butter and oil in a large, heavy skillet over medium-high heat until very hot. Add the pork chops and brown well on both sides. Reduce the heat and continue cooking for 5 minutes or until the meat is barely pink in the center. Season well with salt and pepper. Serve hot with the pineapple salsa.

NOTE: The salsa should not be made more than 3 hours in advance as it loses its crunch if allowed to stand.

VARIATION: Veal chops can also be used in this recipe.

WINE SUGGESTION: Full-bodied white.

Pork, Allspice, and Onion Stew with Beans

Beans and pork are two of the best-loved foods in South America; in fact, a meal without beans is considered hardly worth eating. Allspice is widely used in Central America in savory as well as sweet dishes.

Ingredients

3 tablespoons vegetable oil
1^1/$_2$ pounds pork stew meat, cut into 1^1/$_2$-inch cubes
1 large Spanish onion, thinly sliced
2 teaspoons ground allspice
1 teaspoon ground cumin
^{1}/$_2$ teaspoon paprika
^{2}/$_3$ cup white wine
^{2}/$_3$ cup Chicken Stock (see page 188)
2 (2-inch) cinnamon sticks
Salt and freshly ground pepper
1 can (15 ounces) cannellini or great Northern beans, rinsed and drained

For the garnish:
2 tablespoons chopped fresh parsley leaves

Method

1. Preheat the oven to 325°F.

2. Heat half the oil in a large skillet over medium-high heat and brown the pork pieces evenly. Transfer the meat to an ovenproof dutch oven.

3. In the same skillet, cook the onions until golden brown, adding a little more oil if necessary. Add the allspice, cumin, and paprika and continue cooking for 30 seconds. Spoon the browned onions and spices over the meat.

4. Add the wine and stock to the skillet. Bring to a boil, scrape any browned bits from the bottom of the pan, and add to the dutch oven. Add the cinnamon sticks and season with salt and pepper. Cover tightly and bake for about 1^1/$_2$ hours, or until the meat is very tender.

5. Remove the cinnamon sticks and discard. Add the beans to the meat, mix well and continue cooking, covered, for 15 minutes. Season to taste with salt and pepper. Sprinkle with the parsley and serve.

NOTE: This stew has a dry consistency.

WINE SUGGESTION: Dry, light white.

Shredded Pork

This recipe is used for stuffing tamales, tacos, and empanadas, or eaten with beans and rice.

Ingredients

1 tablespoon butter
1 tablespoon vegetable oil
3 (8-ounce) pork tenderloins
1 onion, thinly sliced
$^1/_2$ teaspoon ground cumin
1 cup chopped canned tomatoes
1 garlic clove, crushed
1 teaspoon dried oregano
2 tablespoons chopped scallions
2 tablespoons chopped fresh parsley leaves
Salt and freshly ground black pepper

Method

1. Preheat the oven to 375°F.

2. Heat the butter and oil in a large skillet over medium-high heat until hot. Add the pork and brown quickly on all sides. Transfer to a roasting pan and bake for 25 to 30 minutes, or until the tenderloins are tender.

3. Place the onion and cumin in the same skillet and cook slowly over very low heat until the onion is almost tender, about 10 minutes. Add the tomatoes, garlic, oregano, scallions, parsley, and season with salt and pepper. Bring the sauce to a boil, reduce the heat and cook, uncovered, for 20 minutes.

4. Remove the pork from the oven and set aside to cool. When cold, shred the meat or slice it thinly. Add to the sauce and reheat thoroughly before serving.

WINE SUGGESTION: Dry white.

Lamb Stew with Red Peppers

In many Ecuadorean recipes mashed bananas are added at the last minute to thicken sauces. They give a rich, sweet texture and flavor to any dish.

Ingredients

1 1/2 pounds lean boneless lamb, cut into
 1 1/2-inch cubes
3 large garlic cloves, crushed
Salt and freshly ground black pepper
4 tablespoons vegetable oil
4 large red bell peppers, seeded and cut into
 1-inch strips
2 red jalapeño or Fresno chiles, seeded and
 finely chopped (see page 194)
1 teaspoon ground cumin
1 1/4 cups dry white wine
2/3 cup Chicken Stock (see page 188)
2 limes, washed and cut into quarters
3 tablespoons coarsely chopped fresh cilantro
 leaves
2 large ripe bananas, mashed

To serve: Green Rice (see page 156)

Method

1. Season the lamb with the garlic, salt, pepper, and 1 tablespoon of the oil. Set aside at room temperature to marinate for 30 minutes.

2. In a large skillet, heat the remaining 3 tablespoons oil over medium-high heat and cook the lamb, in batches, until brown. Remove to a large saucepan.

3. Add the bell peppers, chiles, and cumin to the skillet and cook for 3 minutes. Add to the lamb.

4. Add the wine and stock to the skillet, bring to a boil and scrape the browned bits from the bottom of the pan; pour the liquid over the lamb. Add the limes to the saucepan and simmer, covered, for about 1 hour, or until the lamb is very tender.

5. Just before serving, remove and discard the lime quarters, add the cilantro and mashed bananas and mix well. Cook for 5 minutes, stirring constantly. Season to taste with salt and pepper and serve with the Green Rice.

NOTE: If you prefer, the stew can be baked in an ovenproof dutch oven at 325°F. for 1 1/2 hours.

WINE SUGGESTION: Full-bodied red.

Lamb Roast with Mint and Fried Pinto Beans

Lamb is eaten most frequently in Chile, Uruguay, and Argentina, where a large number of European immigrants settled in the 19th and early 20th centuries. Uruguay produces very good quality lamb and beef. The use of mint comes from Spain, to which it was introduced from the Middle East.

Ingredients

1 (4-pound) leg of lamb, boned
6 tablespoons butter, softened
8 garlic cloves, crushed
Salt and freshly ground pepper
1/4 cup finely chopped fresh mint leaves
1 1/4 cups white wine

For the beans:
2 tablespoons vegetable oil
1 small onion, finely chopped
1 garlic clove, crushed
1 cup dried pinto beans, cooked
Dash chili sauce
Salt and freshly ground pepper
2 tablespoons finely chopped fresh parsley
   leaves
3 scallions, white and green parts, chopped

To serve: Raisin and Walnut Rice (see page 155)

Method

1. Preheat the oven to 325°F.

2. Trim the lamb well. Combine the butter, 8 garlic cloves, salt and pepper, and mint. Cut the leg to open flat and spread the seasoned butter on the inside. Roll up the leg and tie at 2-inch intervals with string.

3. Put the meat into a roasting pan, add the wine and roast for 1 hour (15 minutes per pound) for rare lamb, until a meat thermometer inserted into the lamb registers 125°F. Baste every 20 minutes with the pan juices.

4. To prepare the beans: heat the oil in a large skillet over very low heat, add the onion and cook until almost tender, about 15 minutes. Add the garlic, cooked beans, chili sauce and season to taste with salt and pepper. Cook over medium heat until the beans begin to stick to the bottom of the pan. Add the parsley and scallions, and keep warm until the lamb is cooked.

5. When the lamb is done, transfer to a carving board, cover with foil and let it stand for 15 minutes before slicing. Strain the pan juices into the skillet with the beans and mix thoroughly. Serve the meat with the beans and Raisin and Walnut Rice.

WINE SUGGESTION: Full-bodied red.

Braised Shoulder of Lamb in Dried Chili Sauce

Chipotle chiles are smoked red jalapeños, which impart a delicious tannic and earthy flavor to this sauce. They can be quite hot, so start with two chiles and if the result is not hot enough, add some more.

Ingredients

1 (4 pound) boneless lamb shoulder roast
2 garlic cloves, crushed
2 tablespoons butter, softened
2 tablespoons chopped fresh parsley leaves
1 teaspoon dried oregano
Salt and freshly ground pepper
2 tablespoons vegetable oil

For the sauce:
2 dried chipotle chiles (see page 198)
$1/4$ cup Chicken Stock (see page 188)
2 tablespoons vegetable oil
3 onions, chopped
1 tablespoon ground cumin
2 teaspoons tomato paste
2 cans ($14^1/2$ ounces each) diced tomatoes
1 teaspoon cornstarch
3 tablespoons chopped fresh parsley leaves

Method

1. Trim the lamb of any excess fat, leaving a thin layer on the outside. Mix the garlic, butter, parsley, and oregano to a paste. Open out the lamb, season the inside with salt and pepper, and spread the garlic paste on one half. Using thin string, tie up the lamb, being careful not to pull the string too tight. Set aside while making the sauce.

2. Break the chiles into pieces, discarding the stems and seeds. Place in a small saucepan with the stock and bring to a boil. Reduce the heat, cover and simmer for about 15 minutes or until the chiles are soft. In a blender or a food processor, process the chiles with the liquid.

3. Heat 2 tablespoons of the oil in a large, heavy skillet over medium-high heat and brown the lamb on all sides. Remove the lamb from the pan, pour in a few tablespoons each of chicken stock and chile liquid to deglaze and scrape up any browned bits. Reserve the liquid.

4. Make the sauce: in a dutch oven, heat the 2 tablespoons oil over medium-high heat and add the onions. Cook quickly until the onions are lightly browned. Add the cumin, tomato paste, reserved chile liquid, the deglazing liquid, tomatoes, and salt and pepper.

5. Bring to a boil, then add the lamb, basting it well with the sauce. Reduce the heat to low, cover and cook for 1 to $1^1/2$ hours or until the lamb is very tender, turning it once or twice during cooking.

6. Remove the lamb from the sauce and carefully remove the string. Transfer the lamb to a warm serving dish.

7. Blend the cornstarch with 2 tablespoons of the sauce. Pour it back into the pan, add the parsley and stir until the mixture boils and thickens slightly. Season to taste with salt and pepper and serve with the lamb.

WINE SUGGESTION: Full-bodied red.

Lamb Brochettes with Mango and Avocado Salsa

Brochettes are very popular in many Latin American countries and sometimes involve unusual ingredients—spicy ox hearts in Peru and chicken hearts in Brazil. Fish, shrimp, beef, chicken, and pork brochettes are found in markets and on street corners throughout the continent and they are delicious.

Ingredients

2 pounds boneless lamb, trimmed and cut into
   1^1/$_2$-inch cubes
4 (12-inch) wooden skewers, soaked in water for
   at least 20 minutes
1 teaspoon paprika

For the marinade:
Juice of 4 limes
^{1}/$_2$ cup olive oil
^{1}/$_2$ teaspoon coarse sea salt
1 teaspoon chopped fresh marjoram leaves
Salt and freshly ground pepper

To serve: Mango and Avocado Salsa (see
   page 176)

Method

1. Mix the marinade ingredients in a large bowl. Add the lamb cubes and stir to coat well. Cover and marinate in the refrigerator for 3 hours, turning occasionally.

2. Prepare the grill. Remove the lamb from the marinade; reserve the marinade.

3. Thread the lamb onto the 4 soaked skewers. Baste with the marinade and sprinkle with the paprika. Grill over medium-hot coals for 10 minutes for medium lamb or 15 minutes for well done. Turn the skewers and baste the meat once or twice during grilling. Serve at once with the Mango and Avocado Salsa.

WINE SUGGESTION: Light, fruity red.

Rabbit Stew in Coconut Milk

This recipe comes from Venezuela, where coconut is used extensively in cooking savory dishes. Venezuela enjoys a rich variety of produce because of its geographical position: it has the Andes on its border with Colombia, the rain forest on its border with Brazil, and the Caribbean Sea along its coastline.

Ingredients

1 (2- to 2^1/$_2$-pound) rabbit, cut into 8 pieces
Salt and freshly ground pepper
2 tablespoons olive oil

For the sauce:
2 tablespoons butter
2 garlic cloves, crushed
1 large onion, finely chopped
1 red Kenyan or jalapeño chile, seeded and
    diced (see page 194)
2 cans (14^1/$_2$ ounces each) diced tomatoes,
    undrained
^{1}/$_2$ teaspoon paprika
1^1/$_4$ cups Chicken Stock (see page 188)
^{1}/$_2$ cup unsweetened cream of coconut
2 tablespoons finely chopped fresh parsley
    leaves

To serve: Fried Rice (see page 155)

Method

1. Season the rabbit pieces with salt and pepper.

2. Heat the oil in a large skillet over medium-high heat and brown the rabbit pieces on both sides. Set aside while making the sauce.

3. In a large saucepan, melt the butter; add the garlic and onion and cook over low heat until the onion is almost tender, about 10 minutes.

4. Add the chile, tomatoes, paprika, and stock and bring slowly to a boil. Season with salt and pepper, then add the rabbit pieces. Cook, covered, over medium-low heat until the rabbit is tender, about 1 hour.

5. Transfer the rabbit pieces to a warm serving dish. Add the cream of coconut, and parsley to the sauce and cook for 5 minutes. (If the sauce is very thin, reduce it by boiling rapidly until shiny and rich in appearance.) Season to taste with salt and pepper and pour over the rabbit pieces. Serve with Fried Rice.

WINE SUGGESTION: Rioja.

Rabbit with Peanut Sauce

This recipe comes from Chile and has been adapted from *Latin American Cooking*, by Elisabeth Lambert Ortiz.

Ingredients

1 (2- to 2^1/$_2$-pound) rabbit, cut into 8 pieces
Salt and freshly ground pepper
3 tablespoons vegetable oil
1^3/$_4$ cups Chicken Stock (see page 188)
2 large onions, finely chopped
1 garlic clove, crushed
2 teaspoons paprika
1 green Fresno or jalapeño chile, seeded and
   finely chopped (see page 194)
^{1}/$_2$ cup natural crunchy peanut butter
^{1}/$_2$ teaspoon ground cumin
1 tablespoon white wine vinegar
1^1/$_4$ cups dry white wine

To serve: Yellow Coconut Rice (see page 157)

Method

1. Season the rabbit pieces with salt and pepper. Heat 1^1/$_2$ tablespoons of the oil in a large, heavy skillet over medium-high heat and brown the rabbit pieces on both sides. Transfer the pieces to a bowl and set aside. Add ^{3}/$_4$ cup stock to the skillet and scrape up any browned bits. Pour the liquid over the rabbit pieces.

2. Add the remaining 1^1/$_2$ tablespoons of oil to the same skillet and heat over low heat. Add the onions and cook until almost tender, about 10 minutes. Add the garlic, paprika, and chile and mix well. Add the peanut butter, cumin, vinegar, the remaining 1 cup stock, and wine to the onions. Bring to a boil and season to taste with salt and pepper.

3. Return the rabbit to the pan, pressing it down into the sauce. Reduce the heat, cover and simmer until the rabbit is tender, about 1^1/$_2$ hours. Serve with Yellow Coconut Rice.

WINE SUGGESTION: Full-bodied white.

Seafood

SEAFOOD

With thousands of miles of coastline on the Atlantic and Pacific oceans, and the Caribbean Sea, the seafood in Latin America is varied, exciting, and abundant. Apart from Paraguay and Bolivia, which are inland, all the other countries are rich in fish and shellfish. Paraguay makes up for its lack of seafood with very good fresh water fish, like the much-praised dorado fish from the Paraguay River.

The countries richest in seafood are Chile, Peru, and Ecuador. The Humboldt or Peru current from the Antarctic washes the coasts of these countries, providing a variety of fish and shellfish unequalled elsewhere in Latin America. Chile alone has 2,600 miles of coastline and is the country with the largest variety of seafood. In fact, seafood constitutes the main source of protein in the Chilean diet. Many varieties of fish and shellfish are found only in Latin America, while others are common to the tropical or subtropical waters of the world. Chile boasts the famous *pibre*, a type of large sea urchin, and the *congrio*, a conger eel-type of fish; from Peru comes a pink and white scallop called *conchita*, and *corvina*, a relative of sea bass. Also found in Ecuador, corvina is widely used for making ceviches.

With the exception of the Caribbean and Bahia in Brazil, fish cookery throughout Latin America is kept simple. The slaves brought from West Africa to work on sugar plantations in the Caribbean and Brazil transformed their local cuisines into something unique from the rest of Latin America. They brought with them spices, vegetables, and flavorings. The similar climactic conditions made it possible for them to produce their native foodstuffs, such as okra, dried shrimp, yams, coconuts, plaintains, and dendê or palm oil, in their new homeland.

While white male slaves worked in planting and processing sugar cane, the women did housework and cooked. The African cook, with an almost inbred capacity for making something tasty from very little, was, and still is, a major influence in the cooking of Brazil and the Caribbean. Tropical fish like grouper, dolphin fish or mahi mahi, scad, surgeon or doctor fish, and snapper or vara vara are now found in good seafood speciality shops. More commonly known fishes such as tuna, sardines, and salt cod are widely used in Latin American cuisine and available in most supermarkets. Of all the shellfish, shrimp are the most popular, being a main ingredient in many classic dishes. Crab and lobsters are also very popular, and usually cooked in a very simple way.

Flavorings vary from country to country, annatto oil being used extensively in Caribbean and Ecuadorean cuisines. Dendê or palm oil is the main flavoring for seafood in Brazil and, when used in combination with coconut milk, chilies, and peanuts, makes fish cookery an exciting experience. Citrus juices and salt are also standard flavoring ingredients.

All the olive oil consumed in Latin American countries is imported, mostly from Spain and Portugal, and is therefore rather expensive. Consequently, it tends to be used only when the budget allows and in special recipes.

Cod with Spicy Nut Sauce

This rich, smooth, and delicious sauce from Mexico's exquisite cuisine can be served with any firm, white-fleshed fish.

Ingredients

4 (6-ounce) cod fillets, skinned and boned
Juice of 1 lemon
Salt and freshly ground white pepper
2 tablespoons chopped fresh cilantro leaves

For the sauce:
8 slices white bread
1 3/4 cups hot milk
4 tablespoons vegetable oil
2 medium onions, finely chopped
1 garlic clove, crushed
1 tablespoon red chili paste (see page 180) or
   1/2 teaspoon cayenne pepper
1 cup ground walnuts
Salt and freshly ground pepper
1/2 teaspoon ground annatto or achiote
   (see note and page 274)

For the garnish:
1 teaspoon paprika
2 tablespoons finely chopped fresh parsley

Method

1. Preheat the oven to 400°F.

2. Season the fish with the lemon juice, salt, white pepper, and cilantro. Place in a single layer in a shallow baking pan. Bake 25 minutes or until the fish flakes easily when tested with a fork.

3. Meanwhile, make the sauce. Trim the crusts from the bread and discard. Cut each bread slice into quarters; place in a large bowl. Add half of the hot milk and let stand for

5 minutes. Transfer the bread mixture to a blender or food processor and process until smooth. Or, press the bread mixture through a sieve.

4. Heat the oil in a large skillet over medium-high heat. Add the onions and garlic; cook until the onions are tender, about 10 minutes. Add the chili paste, walnuts, and salt and pepper. Reduce the heat to low and cook, stirring frequently, for about 5 minutes.

5. Stir in the ground annatto and bread purée. Gradually add the rest of the milk. Cook, stirring constantly, until the sauce thickens. (The sauce should be the consistency of heavy cream; if too thick, add more milk or water.)

6. Transfer the cooked fish to a serving plate and sprinkle with the paprika. Pour the hot sauce around the fish and sprinkle with the parsley. Serve at once.

NOTE: If neither annatto nor achiote is available, it can be substituted by adding 1/2 teaspoon each paprika and ground turmeric to the sautéed onions.

WINE SUGGESTION: Full-bodied white.

Salmon Tacos

Tacos are tortillas which have been stuffed and rolled up like cigars. These 'soft tacos' are eaten in the hand. They can also be stuffed and fried, and make an exciting meal since each person 'composes' his or her own taco. A variety of dips, salsas, beans, or salads accompanies a traditional taco (see page 165). This recipe, using salmon, is for a more sophisticated taco.

Ingredients

4 (6-ounce) salmon fillets, skinned
1 can (14 ounces) black beans, drained and
  rinsed
2 tablespoons chopped fresh cilantro leaves
2 tablespoons vegetable oil
Juice of 1 lime

For the marinade:
$^3/_4$ cup honey
2 tablespoons coarse-grained brown mustard
Juice of 1 lemon
2 teaspoons ground cumin
1 teaspoon ground cilantro
1 teaspoon chili powder
Salt and freshly ground black pepper

To serve: 8 (8-inch) whole-wheat flour tortillas
  (see page 166)
1 medium head iceberg lettuce, shredded
Lime wedges
Salsa Cruda (see page 176)
Guacamole (optional, see page 185)

Method

1. In a large shallow dish, combine all the marinade ingredients; mix well. Add the salmon; turn to coat. Cover and refrigerate up to 1 hour.

2. Heat the grill on high. Place the salmon on a baking sheet and grill without turning until fish flakes easily when tested with a fork. Remove from the grill; cover to keep warm.

3. Preheat the oven to 350°F. Wrap the tortillas in aluminum foil, place in the oven, and heat until warmed, about 10 minutes.

4. In a medium bowl, mix together the black beans, cilantro, oil, and lime juice. Season with salt and pepper to taste.

5. Arrange the grilled salmon, lettuce, bean mixture, and lime wedges on a large platter. Serve with the warmed tortillas, Salsa Cruda, and Guacamole. Allow the guests to assemble their own tacos.

WINE SUGGESTION: Full-bodied, dry white.

Fish and Shrimp in Ginger-Flavored Peanut Sauce

Featured here is another classic dish from Brazil, where the African and native cuisines meet so interestingly. Rich and exciting, *vatapa*, as this dish is called locally, can be seasoned to suit your particular tastes—really hot or very mild.

Ingredients

1 pound sea bass, halibut, or swordfish fillet, skinned and cut into large pieces
2 tablespoons vegetable oil
1 large onion, finely chopped
1 can (40 ounces) chopped tomatoes, undrained
1 dried red chili, seeded and crumbled
1 cup flaked coconut
2 tablespoons crunchy, unsweetened peanut butter
3 tablespoons dried shrimps (see page 277)
1 (1-inch) piece ginger root, peeled and grated
$1/2$ teaspoon ground ginger
$2^{1}/_{3}$ cups coconut milk
Salt and freshly ground pepper
1 tablespoon rice flour
5 teaspoons dendê or palm oil (see page 277)
3 tablespoons coarsely chopped fresh cilantro leaves
8 ounces shelled raw, medium shrimp, peeled and deveined (see page 277)

For the garnish:
$1/4$ cup peanuts, toasted
2 tablespoons coarsely chopped fresh cilantro leaves

To serve: Steamed long-grain white rice or boiled potatoes

Method

1. Cut the fish into 2-inch pieces.

2. Heat the oil in a Dutch oven over medium-high heat. Add the onion; cook and stir until tender, about 10 minutes.

3. Add the tomatoes, chili, coconut, peanut butter, dried shrimps, grated and ground ginger, and the coconut milk. Season with the salt and pepper. Bring to a boil. Reduce the heat to low, cover, and simmer 25 minutes.

4. Remove the sauce from the heat. Pour it into a blender or food processor and purée until smooth. Or, pour it through a sieve back into the rinsed-out pan.

5. In a small bowl, mix the rice flour with $1/3$ cup of the sauce. Add to the sauce and cook over medium heat, stirring constantly, until it is thick enough to coat the back of a wooden spoon. Taste and adjust seasoning.

6. Add the dendê oil, the 3 tablespoons cilantro, and the fish and shrimp and simmer for 5–8 minutes or until the fish flakes easily when tested with a fork.

7. To serve, transfer the fish and sauce to a warmed, deep plate, scatter the toasted peanuts on top, and sprinkle with 2 tablespoons cilantro. Serve with rice or potatoes.

WINE SUGGESTION: Medium-dry white.

Salt Cod Cakes with Three Pepper Salsa

Salt cod travels a long way before it reaches Latin America, where it is extremely popular. Most of it comes from Norway, where the fresh cod is soaked in brine and exported mainly to Portugal, Spain and other Mediterranean countries. Brazil inherited its love of salt cod from the Portuguese, and most of its salt cod dishes are direct copies of traditional Portuguese recipes. Among them is *bolinho de bacalhau*, a cocktail version of this fish cake recipe. Whether served as an appetizer or as a main dish, this recipe is really worth the effort of making.

Ingredients

1 pound salt cod
1 tablespoon butter
1 tablespoon all-purpose flour
Pinch cayenne pepper
$1/2$ teaspoon chili powder
$2/3$ cup milk
2 cups mashed potatoes
3 tablespoons finely chopped flat-leaf Italian
   parsley
Freshly ground pepper
All-purpose flour
2 eggs, beaten
Dry white bread crumbs
Oil for frying

To serve: Three-Pepper Salsa (see page 177)
   and/or lime wedges

Method

1. Soak the salt cod in water for a minimum of 16 hours, changing the water 4 or 5 times.

2. Place the fish, skin side up, in a large skillet. Add enough water to cover. Cook over low heat for about 20 minutes or until the skin peels off easily. Drain and discard the cooking liquid. Skin and coarsely flake the fish; set aside.

3. In a small saucepan, melt the butter over medium heat. Add the flour, cayenne, and chili powder and cook for 1 minute. Stir in the milk and bring to a boil, stirring continuously. Simmer for about 1 minute.

4. In a large bowl, mix the flaked fish with the mashed potatoes, white sauce, and parsley. Season to taste with pepper.

5. With floured hands, shape the potato mixture into 8 patties, each about 2 inches in diameter. Dip each patty into the beaten egg and then the bread crumbs. Cover and refrigerate for 1 hour.

6. Pour about 1 inch of oil into large skillet and heat over medium-high heat. Add the fish cakes and cook, turning only once, until golden brown. Drain on paper towels. Serve immediately with the Three-Pepper Salsa.

NOTE: These cakes are delicious when served as appetizers. Shape them into 2-inch balls and cook until golden brown. Serve with the lime wedges.

WINE SUGGESTION: Medium-dry white.

Shrimp with Okra and Peanuts

A typical dish from Bahia in Brazil, *caruru*, as it is known locally, includes African ingredients such as dried shrimp, okra, dendê or palm oil, and peanuts (see page 280). It makes a rich, thick sort of stew with an unusually delicious mixture of flavors. If desired, it can be made without the shrimp and served as a vegetable dish. This dish was a great favorite with the teachers at Leith's during its testing.

Ingredients

2 pounds raw large shrimp in their shells, weighed without the heads
2 tablespoons butter
1 teaspoon paprika
1 small onion, finely chopped
$^1/_2$ green bell pepper, finely diced
1 can (14$^1/_2$ ounces) chopped tomatoes, undrained
8 ounces fresh okra, washed and trimmed
1 tablespoon dried shrimps, finely chopped or pounded in a mortar (see page 277)
1$^3/_4$ cups coconut milk
2 tablespoons crunchy, unsweetened peanut butter
5 tablespoons coarsely chopped fresh cilantro leaves
Salt and freshly ground pepper

To serve: Fried Rice (see page 155)
Jalapeño and Lime Salsa (see page 177)

Method

1. Shell and devein the shrimp (see page 277), leaving 3 shrimp unshelled for garnish.

2. Melt the butter in a large, heavy skillet over medium-high heat. Add the paprika and shrimp and cook for 3 minutes or until the shrimp are firm and turn pink. Transfer to a plate, cover, and place in the refrigerator while making the sauce.

3. Add the onion and green pepper to the same skillet and cook over medium heat until tender but not browned, about 10 minutes.

4. Add the tomatoes with their juice, the okra, and dried shrimps. Stir in the coconut milk. Cover, reduce the heat to low, and simmer for 25 minutes or until the okra is very tender.

5. Add the cooked shrimp, peanut butter, cilantro, and salt and pepper to taste. Cook, stirring frequently, for about 5 minutes or until the shrimp are heated through. Serve with Fried Rice and the Jalapeño and Lime Salsa.

VARIATION: Although not traditional, the okra can be cooked separately (sauté with 1 tablespoon of oil and the juice of $^1/_2$ lemon for 8 minutes) and added at the last minute. This will help the okra keep its bright green color and crisp texture.

WINE SUGGESTION: Dry white with good acidity.

Fresh Tuna Steamed with Fruit Juice

Fresh tuna is now relatively easy to find. In this recipe, the firm pink flesh marinates in a combination of citrus juice and spices, and when the cooked parcels are unwrapped, a delicious sweet aroma is released. Although not essential to the flavor of the finished dish, the annatto imparts an attractive bright yellow color to the sauce.

Ingredients

4 (6-ounce) fresh tuna fillets or steaks
4 (10-inch) circles of aluminum foil
Salt and freshly ground black pepper

For the marinade:
$^2/_3$ cup fresh orange juice
Juice of 1 lime
1$^1/_2$ teaspoons ground annatto (see page 274)
1 garlic clove, crushed
1 teaspoon finely chopped fresh oregano leaves
$^1/_2$ teaspoon ground cumin
$^1/_4$ teaspoon ground cloves
$^1/_2$ teaspoon ground cinnamon

To serve: 8 (8-inch) whole-wheat flour tortillas
(see page 166)

Method

1. Skin the fish if using fillets, or bone and skin if using steaks; cut into 1$^1/_2$-inch cubes.

2. Combine all the marinade ingredients in a large bowl. Add the tuna chunks and stir to coat thoroughly. Cover and marinate in the refrigerator for at least 6 hours, or overnight.

3. Preheat the oven to 375°F.

4. Brush the foil circles lightly with oil. Spoon the tuna chunks and marinade evenly onto the foil circles. Season with salt and pepper to taste. Bring the edges of the foil together and give a firm twist to the top, sealing the parcel well. Place the parcels on a baking sheet and bake for 15 minutes.

5. To warm the tortillas, wrap them in additional foil and place in the oven along with the fish. (They will be ready at the same time.)

6. To serve, put one parcel on each plate and serve with the warmed tortillas.

VARIATION: Chicken can be used in this recipe with very good results. Chop 4 skinned and boned chicken breasts into 1$^1/_2$-inch cubes and follow the recipe as directed.

WINE SUGGESTION: Fruity red.

Salt Cod Bahian Style

Salt cod is a legacy from the Portuguese in Brazil. Although it is imported from Norway and therefore quite costly, Brazilians always manage to find a way to eat it. This recipe is authentically Brazilian, using ingredients such as coconut milk and chilies.

Ingredients

1 1/4 pounds salt cod
3 tablespoons vegetable oil
2 medium onions, thinly sliced
1 pound tomatoes, peeled, seeded, and chopped
2 green bell peppers, seeded and thinly sliced
5 scallions, coarsely chopped
5 tablespoons coarsely chopped fresh cilantro leaves
1 cup flaked coconut
1 can (14 ounces) thick coconut milk
Juice of 1 lime
2 green chilies, Kenyan or serrano, seeded and finely chopped (see page 194)
Freshly ground pepper
1 pound potatoes, peeled and sliced 1/2 inch thick

To serve: Green Rice (see page 156)

Method

1. Soak the salt cod in water for a minimum of 16 hours, changing the water 4 or 5 times.

2. Preheat the oven to 375°F.

3. Place the fish, skin side up, in a large skillet. Add enough water to cover. Cook over low heat for about 20 minutes or until the skin peels off easily. Drain and discard the cooking liquid. Skin and flake the fish into fairly large pieces and set aside.

4. Heat the oil in a large saucepan over medium-high heat. Add the onions; cook and stir until tender, about 10 minutes. Add the tomatoes, peppers, scallions, cilantro, flaked coconut, coconut milk, lime juice, and chilies. Reduce the heat to low and cook for about 10 minutes, stirring occasionally. Season to taste with pepper. (The cod is quite salty, so it might not need any more salt.)

5. In a large ovenproof serving dish, place layers of potatoes, fish, and a few tablespoons of the sauce. Finish with a layer of the sauce.

6. Bake 30–35 minutes or until the potatoes are tender and the mixture is hot and bubbly. Serve hot with the Green Rice.

WINE SUGGESTION: Medium-dry white.

Shrimp in Pimiento, Pumpkin Seed, and Cilantro Sauce

Apart from their beautiful red color, pimientos have a delicate and deliciously sweet flavor. Here they are blended with dried chilies and pumpkin seeds to create a rich and unique sauce.

Ingredients

2 pounds raw large shrimp in their shells, weighed with the heads on
2 dried cayenne or tabasco chilies, crumbled (see page 194)
1/4 cup vegetable oil
1/2 cup roasted, salted pumpkin seeds
1 medium onion, chopped
1 can (14 ounces) whole red pimientos, drained and coarsely chopped
1 1/2 teaspoons ground coriander
1 garlic clove, crushed
1/2 teaspoon sugar
5 tablespoons coarsely chopped fresh cilantro leaves
Salt and freshly ground black pepper
Juice of 1 lime

To serve: Yellow Coconut Rice (see page 157)

Method

1. Shell and devein the shrimp (see page 277). Place the shells with the dried chilies in a medium saucepan and add enough cold water to cover. Bring to a boil over high heat, reduce the heat to low, and simmer, uncovered, for about 15 minutes or until the stock is reduced by one third.

2. Place the shrimp shells with the chilies and their liquid in a food processor or blender and process for a few seconds. Strain the liquid through a sieve, pressing the shells well to extract all of the liquid. Discard the pulp.

3. Heat half of the oil in a large skillet over medium-high heat. Add the pumpkin seeds, onion, pimientos, ground coriander, garlic, sugar, and half of the fresh cilantro. Season with the salt and pepper. Cook, stirring occasionally, for 5 minutes. Add the shell stock and cook for an additional 15 minutes. Transfer the pumpkin seed mixture to a blender or food processor and process to a smooth consistency.

4. In a large skillet, heat the remaining oil over medium-high heat. Add the shrimp and cook for 3 minutes or until they are firm and opaque. Add the sauce to the shrimp and stir lightly to coat.

5. Stir in the remaining cilantro and cook 2 minutes. Season with salt to taste and stir in the lime juice. Serve at once with the Yellow Coconut Rice.

WINE SUGGESTION: Still or sparkling rosé.

Grilled Snapper with Mango Chili Sauce

Try this simple and delicious way to serve snapper. The sauce can be made up to a day in advance and reheated just before serving.

Ingredients

4 (6-ounce) snapper fillets, skins on

For the marinade:
Juice of 2 lemons
3 tablespoons peanut oil
2 tablespoons chopped fresh cilantro leaves
Salt and freshly ground pepper

For the garnish:
Few sprigs fresh cilantro

To serve: Thick Mango and Chili Sauce
(see page 181)

Method

1. Wash and thoroughly dry the snapper fillets.

2. In a large shallow dish, mix the marinade ingredients together. Season with salt and pepper. Add the fish fillets, turn to coat, and set aside to marinate for at least 30 minutes.

3. Heat the grill to high. Remove the fish from the marinade and discard the marinade. Oil a baking sheet and arrange the fillets on it, skin sides down. Grill until the flesh is firm to the touch and completely opaque, 5–8 minutes. Gently transfer the fish to a warmed serving plate and top each fillet with a generous spoonful of mango sauce. Garnish with the sprigs of cilantro and serve immediately.

NOTE: The fish can also be cooked on an hot oiled griddle or in a large skillet.

WINE SUGGESTION: Full-bodied white.

Baked Stuffed Trout

This simple recipe reveals its Spanish influences in the use of olives, pimientos, and olive oil.

Ingredients

4 (12-ounce) whole trouts, cleaned, heads and
  tails on
$^3/_4$ cup green olives, pitted and halved
1 medium onion, finely chopped
3 canned red pimientos, drained and diced
$^1/_2$ cup sliced almonds
$^1/_2$ teaspoon cayenne pepper
$^1/_2$ cup button mushrooms, sliced
Salt and freshly ground black pepper
$^1/_4$ cup olive oil
Juice of 1 lemon

To serve: Lemon and lime wedges

Method

1. Preheat the oven to 400°F.

2. Wash the trout well and pat dry with paper
    towels.

3. In a large bowl, mix the olives, onions,
    pimientos, almonds, cayenne, and
    mushrooms. Season to taste with salt
    and pepper.

4. Grease an ovenproof dish. Spoon the
    stuffing evenly into the fish and secure with
    wooden toothpicks. Arrange the fish in the
    prepared dish and make two cuts in the skin
    of each fish. Pour the olive oil and lemon
    juice evenly over them. Season with salt
    and pepper.

5. Bake for 25 minutes or until the flesh feels
    firm and the skin is lightly browned. Remove
    the toothpicks. Serve hot or cold with lemon
    and lime wedges.

WINE SUGGESTION: Chilled fino sherry.

Baked Haddock with Lime and Tomato Sauce

Apart from the countries with a strong African heritage, fish recipes in Latin America tend to be simple, making the most of the wonderful and plentiful variety of fish and shellfish.

Ingredients

4 (6-ounce) haddock fillets, skinned and boned

For the sauce:
3 tablespoons vegetable oil
2 medium red onions, finely chopped
$^1/_2$ tablespoon ground coriander
$^1/_2$ teaspoon cayenne pepper
1 red bell pepper, seeded and diced
1 green bell pepper, seeded and diced
4 tomatoes, peeled, seeded, and diced
Juice of 3 limes
Salt and freshly ground black pepper
2 tablespoons chopped fresh cilantro leaves

To serve: Mexican Rice (see page 158)

Method

1. Preheat the oven to 375°F.

2. Rinse the fish fillets well under cold water. Pat dry and set aside.

3. In a large saucepan, heat the oil over medium-high heat. Add the onions; cook and stir until tender, about 10 minutes. Stir in the coriander and cayenne and cook for 2 minutes.

4. Add the diced peppers and tomatoes. Reduce the heat to low and cook, uncovered, for 10 minutes. Remove the saucepan from the heat. Stir in the lime juice and season with salt and pepper.

5. Arrange the fish fillets in a buttered, shallow ovenproof dish. Cover with the sauce. Bake, uncovered, for 20–25 minutes or until the fish flakes easily when tested with a fork.

6. Sprinkle with the cilantro and serve with the Mexican Rice.

VARIATION: A whole emperor bream or 2 whole snappers can be used in this recipe. Clean the fish, leaving the heads and tails on, and follow the recipe as directed.

WINE SUGGESTION: Dry, acidic white.

Snapper with Anaheim Chili Sauce

Anaheim, or New Mexican, chilies are large mild green or red chilies. They develop an intense flavor once they are grilled or roasted, and can be used to enhance the flavor of sweet red and green bell peppers.

Ingredients

4 (11-ounce) whole snappers, cleaned, heads and tails on
Salt and freshly ground pepper
Juice of 2 lemons

For the sauce:
3 red Anaheim chilies, halved and seeded (see page 194)
3 red bell peppers, halved and seeded
3 garlic cloves, crushed
$1/4$ cup vegetable oil
2 tablespoons white wine vinegar
2 tablespoons fresh white bread crumbs
2 tablespoons chopped fresh cilantro leaves
Salt and freshly ground pepper

Method

1. Preheat the oven to 400°F. Heat the grill to high.

2. Season the fish, both insides and out, with salt and freshly ground pepper. Place the fish in a single layer in an ovenproof dish and make two shallow cuts on the top side of each fish. Drizzle with the lemon juice and set aside.

3. Place the chilies and bell peppers, skin sides up, on the grill and cook until they are blistered and blackened all over, about 15 minutes, turning occasionally. Place the hot chilies and peppers inside a plastic bag, close tightly, and let stand at room temperature until they are cool enough to handle. Remove and discard the skins and coarsely chop the chilies and peppers.

4. Transfer the chilies and peppers to a blender or food processor. Add the garlic, oil, vinegar, bread crumbs, and cilantro and process until the mixture forms a thick paste. Season to taste with salt and pepper.

5. Spread the paste over the fish. Bake, uncovered, for about 20 minutes or until the fish flakes easily when tested with a fork.

WINE SUGGESTION: Dry, acidic white.

Fish Stew with Coconut and Shrimp Sauce

Moqueca, as this is known in Brazil, is a simple and popular fish stew. It traditionally uses thick white fish steaks, with some extra shrimps added to the sauce for flavor. It is equally delicious when made without the coconut milk.

Ingredients

4 (6-ounce) white fish steaks, such as cod or halibut
Juice of 2 limes
Salt and freshly ground pepper
3 tablespoons vegetable oil
2 medium onions, thinly sliced
1 teaspoon ground cumin
2 green bell peppers, seeded and thinly sliced
2 Fresno or jalapeño chilies, seeded and chopped (see page 194)
4 scallions, chopped
5 tablespoons coarsely chopped fresh cilantro leaves
3 tablespoons chopped flat-leaf Italian parsley
1 can (29 ounces) chopped tomatoes, undrained
$3/4$ cup flaked coconut, chopped
$1/2$ cup thick coconut milk
4 ounces shrimp, shelled and cooked

To serve: Boiled rice
Red Chili Paste (see page 180)

Method

1. Place the fish steaks in a large shallow glass dish, add half of the lime juice, and season with salt and pepper. Toss the steaks with the lime juice to coat and set aside while preparing the sauce.

2. In a large, heavy-bottomed saucepan or Dutch oven, heat the oil over medium-high heat. Add the onions; cook and stir until tender, about 10 minutes. Add the cumin, bell peppers, and chilies and cook, stirring constantly, 1 minute.

3. In another large saucepan, combine the scallions, half each of the cilantro and parsley, the tomatoes with their juice, the flaked coconut, and coconut milk. Bring to a boil over high heat. Reduce the heat to low and simmer for 20 minutes.

4. Add the fish steaks and marinade to the sauce. Cover and cook for 10–12 minutes. Transfer the fish to a serving dish and keep warm.

5. Bring the sauce to a boil. Add the shrimp, the remaining cilantro, parsley, and lime juice. Cook 3 minutes. Season to taste with salt and pepper. Pour the sauce over the fish. Serve at once with boiled rice and the Red Chili Paste.

NOTE I: *For an authentic Bahian flavor, add $1/4$ cup of dendê oil (see page 277) to the sauce at the beginning of step 5.*

NOTE II: *An authentic accompaniment is made by adding enough sauce to toasted cassava meal (see page 247) to give it a very thick, doughlike consistency.*

WINE SUGGESTION: Off-dry white with good acidity.

Vegetable Dishes

VEGETABLE DISHES

When visiting a local farmer's market, it is interesting to see how many vegetables believed to be of local origin actually come from Latin America. Tomatoes, peppers, chiles, green beans, corn, avocados, all types of potatoes, to name just a few, are all "imports" but now form an integral part of many different cuisines.

Vegetables are also an important part of the Latin American diet, and in poor areas are the only foodstuff affordable. Root vegetables, such as potatoes and cassava, are favorites and have given rise to many recipes. Cassava or manioc is restricted to Brazil since it is one of the few Brazilian Indian foods incorporated into the Portuguese and African cooking that emerged after the colonizing.

The potato is important because of its social and culinary impact. Originally from Peru, potatoes were cultivated in the high Andes for hundreds of years before the Conquest. The Incas discovered a way of freeze-drying in order to preserve them, and the same method is still used today by Andean people. With more than 100 varieties, and colors ranging from black to bright orange, potatoes are a very important staple food in high-altitude regions, where rice and corn cannot grow.

In the late 19th century and early 20th century many South American countries received large numbers of immigrants from Japan, China, Germany, Italy, and elsewhere. With them came a variety of different vegetables and fruits, which all found a place to flourish in the huge continent's many types of climate and soil. Today, food markets in São Paulo are full of vegetable stalls run by descendants of the Japanese immigrants. Further south, and in countries like Argentina, Chile and Uruguay, the European influence is most dominant. Germans and Italians settled in these areas because of the cooler climate and worked the land, just as they did in their homelands. Within a few decades their own food culture was established and they even started producing beer and wine. As with most Europeans, the staple diet is based on meat; vegetables play a smaller role in their eating habits.

The vegetable recipes that follow reflect the way in which local cooking has combined with imported cuisines. Main courses are followed by side dishes.

Herb Potato and Eggplant Roulade with Spicy Tomato Sauce

This roulade is very easy to make and best served hot.

Ingredients

For the roulade:
1 cup cold mashed potatoes
$1/2$ cup shredded Cheddar cheese
$1/4$ cup butter, melted
4 eggs, separated
1 tablespoon finely chopped fresh parsley leaves
Salt and freshly ground black pepper

For the filling:
2 tablespoons vegetable oil
1 large onion, finely chopped
1 garlic clove, crushed
2 medium eggplants, cut into $1/2$-inch cubes
3 tomatoes, peeled, seeded, and chopped
Salt and freshly ground pepper
2 tablespoons finely chopped fresh parsley
  leaves
$1/2$ teaspoon hot red pepper flakes

For the garnish:
Small bunch of watercress

To serve: Spicy Tomato Sauce (see page 181)

Method

1. Preheat the oven to 375°F. Line a
   13 x 9-inch pan with parchment paper.

2. Make the roulade: in a large bowl, mix the
   potato, $1/4$ cup of the cheese, the melted
   butter, egg yolks, and 1 tablespoon parsley
   and season to taste with salt and pepper.

3. Whisk the egg whites until stiff but not dry
   and gently fold into the potato mixture.
   Spread the mixture evenly into the prepared

pan. Bake for 10 minutes, or until cooked,
but not colored. Invert on to a clean dish
towel.

4. Make the filling: heat the oil in a large skillet
   over low heat. Add the onion and cook for
   5 minutes or until beginning to soften. Add
   the garlic, eggplants, and tomatoes and
   season with salt and pepper. Cook,
   uncovered, for about 20 minutes or until
   the eggplants are reduced to a pulp. Add
   the 2 tablespoons parsley and pepper flakes
   and season to taste with salt and pepper.
   Spread the mixture over the potato roulade,
   then roll it up, beginning at a short side,
   jelly-roll style. Place the roulade, seam side
   down, on a greased baking sheet. Sprinkle
   the remaining $1/4$ cup cheese on top.

5. Just before serving, bake the roulade at
   375°F. until the cheese is melted and slightly
   browned, about 15 minutes. Cut crosswise
   into slices and serve hot with the Spicy
   Tomato Sauce; garnish with the watercress.

*NOTE: The roulade can also be placed in an
ovenproof serving dish and the tomato sauce
poured around it. Bake until golden brown and the
sauce is hot.*

VARIATION: Beef Picadillo (see page 92) makes a
wonderful nonvegetarian filling for this roulade.

WINE SUGGESTION: Fruity red.

Root Vegetable Gratin

Any root vegetable can be used for this gratin, which makes a perfect accompaniment for roast meat and poultry.

Ingredients

$3/4$ pound sweet potatoes, peeled and shredded
$3/4$ pound celery root, peeled and shredded
$3/4$ pound turnips, peeled and shredded
$1^{1}/4$ cups heavy cream
$1/2$ teaspoon cayenne pepper
Salt and freshly ground pepper
2 tablespoons shredded Cheddar cheese
1 tablespoon dry white bread crumbs

Method

1. Preheat the oven to 400°F.

2. In a large bowl, combine the shredded vegetables, cream, and cayenne. Season with salt and pepper. Spoon into a greased shallow gratin dish. Cover tightly foil and bake for about 30 minutes or until the vegetables are cooked. Remove the gratin from the oven.

3. Heat the broiler.

4. Combine the cheese and bread crumbs; sprinkle evenly over the gratin. Broil, uncovered, until the cheese is brown and bubbly. Serve at once.

WINE SUGGESTION: Dry rose.

Vegetable Stew with Almonds and Dried Chiles

This dish is made with what Mexicans call a *pipian*. Pipians are pesto-type sauces made with dried or fresh chiles, and thickened with seeds. Traditionally, they should not be salted until the moment of serving or they will separate.

Ingredients

3 tablespoons vegetable oil
1 large eggplant, cut into large cubes
2 zucchini, cut into 1-inch slices
2 red bell peppers, seeded and cut into 1-inch strips
$1/4$ pound green beans, ends trimmed
$3/4$ pound small new potatoes, scrubbed
$1/4$ pound okra, ends trimmed

For the sauce:
2 ancho chiles (see page 199)
1 tablespoon vegetable oil
$3/4$ cup whole blanched almonds
1 teaspoon sugar
$1/2$ teaspoon dried oregano
$1/2$ teaspoon ground cinnamon
$1/2$ teaspoon ground cumin
Pinch ground cloves
$2^{1}/3$ cups Vegetable Stock (see page 188)
Salt
$1/4$ cup chopped fresh cilantro leaves

To serve: Spicy Corn Muffins (see page 240)

Method

1. Heat the 3 tablespoons oil in a dutch oven over medium-high heat. Add the eggplant, zucchini, and peppers in batches and cook until browned. Return them all to the pan, add the beans and potatoes and remove from the heat while making the sauce.

2. Make the sauce: shake the seeds out of the chiles and discard. Rinse the pods, tear them up and put into a small bowl. Cover with hot water; soak for 20 minutes.

3. Heat the oil in a small skillet over medium heat. Add the almonds; cook until lightly browned. Add the sugar, oregano, and spices and cook for 30 seconds.

4. Drain the chiles and discard the soaking liquid. In a blender or food processor, process the chiles, almonds, spices, and 1 cup of the stock to form a smooth purée.

5. Pour the purée over the vegetables, add the remaining $1^{1}/3$ cups stock, then cover and cook over medium-low heat for 20 minutes or until the vegetables are tender.

6. Just before serving, gently mix the okra into the other vegetables and cook over medium heat for 8 to 10 minutes or until the okra are tender.

7. Season with salt and stir in the cilantro. Serve hot with Spicy Corn Muffins.

NOTE: This dish is also delicious served at room temperature with baked sweet potatoes or tortillas.

VARIATION: To make chicken pipian, omit the vegetables and make the sauce as described above. Cut 3 whole chicken breasts, boned and skinned, into large cubes. Heat 2 tablespoons vegetable oil and brown the chicken pieces in two batches. Add the browned chicken to the sauce and bring to a boil. Reduce the heat and simmer for 15 to 20 minutes, or until the chicken is no longer pink in the center. Season with salt and serve with tortillas.

WINE SUGGESTION: Medium-bodied red.

Potato, Cheese and Cayenne Puffs

Potatoes, corn, and rice are the principal starchy foods in the Latin American diet—it is actually difficult to find a meal served without one of them. These simple puffs are good served with roast meat, poultry, or fish.

Ingredients

2 cups cold mashed potatoes
Salt and freshly ground pepper
1 tablespoon chopped fresh parsley leaves
1 tablespoon chopped fresh cilantro leaves
1 tablespoon snipped fresh chives
2 tablespoons grated Parmesan cheese
1 teaspoon baking powder
3 tablespoons milk
2 tablespoons butter
1 teaspoon cayenne pepper
3 eggs, separated

Method

1. Preheat the oven to 425°F. Grease twelve (2¹/₂-inch) muffin pan cups.

2. Season the mashed potatoes with salt and pepper. Mix in the herbs, cheese, and baking powder.

3. Heat the milk, butter, and cayenne in a small saucepan until warm and add to the mashed potatoes. Mix in the egg yolks and beat thoroughly.

4. Whisk the whites to soft peaks and gently fold into the potato mixture.

5. Spoon the mixture into the muffin cups and bake for about 20 minutes, or until the puffs have risen and are golden brown. Serve at once.

VARIATION: Substitute sweet potatoes for the white potatoes and follow the recipe as above.

NOTE: This recipe can also be baked in a greased gratin dish until golden brown.

WINE SUGGESTION: Fruity, dry white.

Layered Polenta and Vegetable Pie

Dishes derived from corn are widely eaten, with slight variations, throughout Latin America. Polenta takes many forms and has many uses. It is eaten soft with stews and spicy casseroles, or cooled and cut into wedges with roasted meats and barbecues, or simply layered with a meat or vegetable stuffing, as in this recipe.

Ingredients

For the stuffing:
2 tablespoons olive oil
2 red onions, thinly sliced
2 garlic cloves, crushed
$1/2$ teaspoon ground coriander
1 teaspoon chopped fresh oregano leaves
$1/2$ teaspoon hot red pepper flakes
2 red bell peppers, roasted, peeled, and thinly sliced (see page 141)
2 green bell peppers, roasted, peeled, and thinly sliced (see page 141)
2 green Anaheim chiles, roasted, peeled, and thinly sliced (see page 194)
2 tomatoes, peeled, seeded, and diced
12 green olives, pitted and halved
Salt and freshly ground pepper

For the polenta:
1 quart water or Vegetable Stock (see page 188)
1 teaspoon salt
$2/3$ cup coarse instant polenta
2 tablespoons olive oil

For the garnish:
2 tablespoons chopped fresh parsley leaves

To serve: Spicy Tomato Sauce (see page 181)

Method

1. Make the stuffing: heat the oil in a large skillet over very low heat. Add the onion and cook until almost tender, about 10 minutes. Stir in the garlic, coriander, oregano, and pepper flakes and cook, stirring, for 2 minutes.

2. Add the peppers, chile, and tomatoes and mix thoroughly. Cook over low heat, uncovered, until the tomatoes become a pulp and almost all of the liquid has evaporated. Remove from the heat, add the olives and season to taste with salt and pepper. Set aside to cool.

3. Make the polenta: bring $3^{1}/2$ cups of the water to a boil in a large saucepan. In a large, heatproof bowl, stir the remaining $1/2$ cup water into the polenta until smooth. Gradually stir the boiling water into the polenta. Return polenta to the pan; stir until thickened. Reduce the heat to low; cook for 5 to 10 minutes or until thick. Season to taste.

4. Lightly grease a 2-quart round glass bowl; spread one fourth of the polenta in the bottom. Top with one third of the stuffing, leaving a $1/2$-inch border at the edge. Continue layering, finishing with the polenta; cool.

5. When ready to serve, heat the broiler. Invert the pie onto a cutting board and cut into 6 wedges. Lightly brush a baking sheet with olive oil and place the wedges on it, cut sides down. Brush the wedges with olive oil and broil until golden brown and hot.

6. Arrange the wedges on a serving plate and spoon the Spicy Tomato Sauce around them. Sprinkle with chopped parsley and serve.

VARIATION: This recipe can be made using Beef Picadillo (see page 92) for the stuffing.

WINE SUGGESTION: Medium-bodied red.

Mexican Crêpe Gratin

Mexicans have very inventive recipes using tortillas, and this is one of them. Here, the Latin American staple of corn tortillas have been substituted by cornmeal crêpes.

Ingredients

For the batter:
$1/2$ cup fine cornmeal
3 tablespoons all-purpose flour
2 eggs
1 tablespoon vegetable oil
$1^1/4$ cups milk
2 tablespoons water

For the filling:
2 tablespoons vegetable oil
2 medium onions, finely chopped
1 garlic clove, crushed
1 red bell pepper, seeded and diced
$1/2$ teaspoon dried oregano
$1^1/2$ pounds tomatoes, peeled, seeded, and
    chopped
Dash chili sauce
Salt and freshly ground pepper
4 hard-cooked eggs, peeled and sliced
$1^1/2$ cups shredded Cheddar cheese

Method

1. Mix the batter ingredients in a blender or a food processor until smooth. Refrigerate for 30 minutes. (This allows the starch cells to swell, and gives a lighter result.)

2. Meanwhile, make the filling. Heat the oil in a large skillet over very low heat. Add the onions and cook until almost tender but not browned, about 10 minutes. Add the garlic, bell pepper, oregano, and tomatoes. Cook, uncovered, over medium heat for 20 minutes or until slightly thickened. Remove from the heat, add a dash of chili sauce and season to taste with salt and pepper.

3. Heat a crêpe pan or small skillet over medium-high heat and lightly grease with oil. When hot, pour in about 1 tablespoon of the batter, swirling the pan to evenly spread it over the bottom. Cook for 1 minute, then, using a small metal spatula and fingers, carefully turn the pancake over. Continue cooking 30 seconds or until the underside is lightly browned.

4. Stack 3 or 4 cooked crêpes together, roll up like a cigar and cut them crosswise into $1/2$-inch strips.

5. Preheat the oven to 425°F.

6. Grease a gratin dish. Layer half the tomato sauce, egg slices, crêpe strips, and cheese. Repeat the layers, finishing with a layer of cheese. Cover with foil and bake for 10 minutes.

7. Remove the foil and continue cooking for 10 minutes or until the cheese is bubbly and brown. Serve at once.

WINE SUGGESTION: Medium-bodied red.

Stuffed Peppers with Tomato Sauce

This is a classic Mexican way of serving stuffed peppers. They can also be filled, dipped in batter, and then fried. In this version the peppers are filled with beans and baked with a spicy tomato sauce.

Ingredients

4 large green bell peppers
1 recipe Refried Beans (see page 151)
1 recipe Spicy Tomato Sauce (see page 181)

To serve: sour cream and Green Rice (see page 156)

Method

1. Heat the broiler.

2. Wash and pat dry the whole peppers, including the stems. Brush the skin slightly with vegetable oil and place them on a baking sheet. Broil the peppers, turning them, until they are black on all sides.

3. Preheat the oven to 400°F.

4. Put the hot peppers into a plastic bag, seal the bag and let them stand until cool enough to handle. Peel off and discard the skin from the peppers. Make a cut in the flesh on one side and gently remove the seeds and veins, still leaving the stems intact. Fill each pepper with the Refried Beans and secure with a wooden toothpick.

5. Pour half the Spicy Tomato Sauce into a medium baking dish, arrange the peppers in it upright and pour the remaining sauce on top. Bake for about 25 minutes or until the sauce and peppers are hot. Remove the toothpicks. Serve with Green Rice and pass the sour cream separately.

VARIATION: For meat-stuffed peppers, stuff the peppers with Picadillo (see page 92) instead of Refried Beans.

WINE SUGGESTION: Full-bodied, dry red.

Ricotta and Vegetable Empanada Pie

Cornmeal is used extensively in many Latin American countries to make cakes, breads, pastries, porridge-type dishes, and even drinks. This cornmeal pastry can also be used to make sweet pies filled with apples, pears, or quinces.

Ingredients

For the pastry:
1 cup plus 2 tablespoons cornmeal
1$^{1}/_{4}$ cups self-rising flour
1 teaspoon salt
$^{1}/_{2}$ cup butter
2 tablespoons shortening or lard
1 egg yolk
$^{1}/_{4}$ cup cold water
1 beaten egg, for glazing

For the filling:
1 tablespoon vegetable oil
1 onion, thinly sliced
1 garlic clove, crushed
1 red bell pepper, seeded and finely sliced
1 green bell pepper, seeded and finely sliced
1 red Fresno or Kenyan chile, seeded, and sliced
  (see page 194)
$^{1}/_{2}$ teaspoon mild chili powder
$^{1}/_{2}$ teaspoon ground allspice
1 teaspoon dried oregano
3 tomatoes, peeled, seeded and chopped
3 tablespoons chopped fresh parsley leaves
Salt and freshly ground pepper
1 cup ricotta cheese

Method

1. Preheat the oven to 400°F.

2. Make the pastry: sift the cornmeal, flour, and salt together into a large bowl. Cut in the butter and shortening until the mixture resembles coarse crumbs. Combine the egg yolk and water, then add to the cornmeal mixture. Stir to form a firm dough, first with a fork, then with one hand. It may be necessary to add more water, but the pastry should not be too moist. Knead the dough briefly on a lightly floured surface until smooth.

3. Divide the dough in half. On a floured surface, roll out half of the pastry to a 10$^{1}/_{2}$-inch circle. Place in a 9$^{1}/_{2}$-inch tart pan with a removable bottom. Wrap the other half of the dough in plastic wrap and chill.

4. Meanwhile, make the filling. Heat the oil in a large skillet. Add the onion and cook over medium heat for 5 minutes. Add the garlic, peppers, chile, chili powder, allspice, oregano, tomatoes, and parsley. Mix thoroughly, season to taste, and cook, uncovered, over medium heat for 25 minutes or until the mixture is almost dry. Transfer to a bowl and cool slightly.

5. In a small bowl, break up the ricotta with a fork and season with salt and pepper.

6. Spread the ricotta into the chilled pastry shell. Spoon the pepper mixture over the cheese. Roll out the remaining pastry and gently lay it on top; press the edges together to seal.

7. Cut a few slits in the top of the pie and brush with the beaten egg.

8. Bake in the middle of the oven for about 35 minutes or until slightly browned.

WINE SUGGESTION: Full-bodied red.

Cured Onions

Cured onions, also known as pink onions, are used as a garnish in many dishes from Ecuador, and can be added to salads, cold dishes and sandwiches. The acidity in the onions reacts with metal, so it is important to use a plastic sieve or colander to drain them or they will have a metallic taste.

Ingredients

2 red onions, very thinly sliced
3 teaspoons salt
2 tablespoons lemon juice
1 teaspoon sugar

Method

1. Put the onions in a plastic colander or sieve; sprinkle them with salt and toss to coat evenly. Place the sieve over a bowl and let the onions drain for 20 minutes.

2. Rinse the onions with plenty of cold water and pat them dry with paper towels.

3. Transfer the onions to a glass bowl and mix in the lemon juice and sugar. Cover and set aside at room temperature until they turn pink, about 2 hours. This dish can be made up to 24 hours in advance, in which case the onions will get very pink.

Shredded Kale

This is a traditional dish to serve with Brazilian Meat and Black Bean Stew or *feijoada* (see page 90). Kale is a very popular vegetable in Brazil.

Ingredients

2 pounds kale or collard greens
3 tablespoons vegetable oil
1 garlic clove, crushed
Salt and freshly ground pepper
Juice of ¹/₂ lime

Method

1. Wash the kale thoroughly. Cut the leaves from their tough stems. Stack several leaves at a time on top of each other, roll up like a cigar and cut crosswise into thin slices to shred finely.

2. Heat the oil in a large sauté pan over low heat. Add the garlic and cook for 1 minute. Increase the heat to medium, add the shredded kale and stir for 1 minute. Cover and cook for 5 to 8 minutes or until wilted. Remove the lid, turn the heat to high and boil for 2 minutes, or until all the liquid has evaporated. Season to taste with salt and pepper and add the lime juice. Serve hot or cold.

Sweet Potato Purée

A favorite ingredient in Latin American cuisine, the sweet potato is used widely for savory and sweet dishes. A delicious canned purée, looking and tasting very much like pumpkin purée, is sold in many countries.

Ingredients

1$^1/_2$ pounds sweet potatoes
Milk
Heavy cream
Butter
$^1/_2$ teaspoon ground cumin
$^1/_2$ teaspoon ground coriander
$^1/_2$ teaspoon hot red pepper flakes
Salt and freshly ground pepper

Method

1. Peel the sweet potatoes and cut into 2-inch chunks.

2. Put the potatoes into a saucepan, cover with cold salted water, and bring to a boil. Cook over medium heat until they are tender, about 15 minutes.

3. Drain the potatoes well, return to the saucepan and stir over medium heat for a few minutes to dry. Press the potatoes through a sieve or food mill with a fine plate.

4. In a small saucepan, heat about $^1/_3$ cup milk with a few tablespoons of cream, then add a few tablespoons butter and the spices. Beat this mixture into the potato.

5. Continue with more warm milk, cream or butter until the desired consistency is reached. Season to taste with salt and pepper and serve hot.

VARIATION: This recipe is equally delicious without the milk and cream. Melt 2 tablespoons butter in a large skillet over low heat. Add 1 finely chopped onion and cook until tender but not browned. Add the spices and stir in the mashed sweet potatoes. Season well with salt and pepper and serve hot.

Fried Plantains

This very popular dish is usually served as a side dish, but is also delicious sprinkled with cinnamon-sugar and eaten as a dessert. It goes particularly well with bean dishes, is easy to make and tastes best when eaten hot.

Ingredients

4 large plantains (see page 280)
Vegetable oil for frying
Salt and freshly ground black pepper

Method

1. Peel the plantains and cut them in half lengthwise.

2. Heat about 1-inch of oil in a large skillet until a crumb sizzles in it. Carefully put the plantain halves into the oil and fry until golden brown, about 2 minutes.

3. Remove the plantains with a slotted spoon and drain on paper towels. Season with salt and pepper and serve hot.

VARIATION: To make sweet fried plantains, mix 1 tablespoon sugar with 1 teaspoon ground cinnamon and sprinkle on the plantains as soon as they are fried. Serve warm with vanilla ice cream or yogurt.

NOTE: Plantains are used in this recipe because, unlike bananas, they keep their shape when cooked or fried.

Beans and Rice

BEANS AND RICE

Beans are a staple food in almost any Latin American country, and they are served, in one form or another, at most meals. Together with maize and potatoes, beans played an important part in the diet of the Mayas and Aztecs in Mexico and Central America, and the Incas in Peru.

Black, red kidney, pink, pinto, haricot, lima beans, and peas are among the pulses native to Mexico or Peru, and were taken by the *conquistadores* back to Europe, where they were readily incorporated into the cuisines of Spain and Portugal before spreading throughout the Continent. In Latin America, it is a common habit to cook large quantities of beans and store them in the refrigerator ready to be used day by day. Cooks take pride in the way they prepare and serve their beans, so canned beans are not commonly used, although I have used them for convenience in many of the recipes in this book.

Rice was introduced to the New World in the 16th century and was immediately integrated into the local diet. Together with beans, it makes a "complete protein" and is the dietary basic in much of Latin America where long-grain white rice is the variety used most frequently. Rice recipes vary from country to country, but the final result has one common characteristic: tender, fluffy and separate grains.

Refried Beans

The Spanish name for this dish, *frijoles refritos*, implies that the beans are fried twice, which is not true—they are first boiled and then fried. Variations of this basic recipe are numerous and there are no written rules; some people prefer their beans with a little liquid, while others prefer none at all. The same applies to texture and seasoning.

Ingredients

9 ounces (about 1 1/4 cups) dried pinto beans
1/2 cup water
2 tablespoons vegetable oil
1 medium onion, finely chopped
2 tomatoes, peeled, seeded, and chopped
2 garlic cloves, crushed
2 teaspoons ground cumin
2 red Fresno or Kenyan chilies, seeded and finely diced (see page 194)
Salt and freshly ground black pepper
2 tablespoons freshly chopped fresh cilantro leaves

Method

1. Place the beans in a large saucepan or bowl. Add enough water to cover and soak the beans overnight, then cook according to the instructions on the package. Drain the beans and discard the cooking water.

2. In a blender or food processor, purée the beans and 1/2 cup water until smooth.

3. In a large skillet, heat the oil over medium-high heat. Add the onion, cook and stir until tender, about 10 minutes. Add the tomatoes, garlic, cumin, and chilies and cook, stirring frequently, 3 minutes.

4. Stir in the bean purée and season with salt and pepper. Reduce the heat to medium and cook, stirring occasionally, 20 minutes.

5. Stir in the cilantro and serve hot or cold.

VARIATIONS:
- Red kidney, borlotti, black, or brown beans can be used with very good results. For a bean purée with texture, process only half of the beans and leave the other half whole.
- If no blender or food processor is at hand, just mash the beans with a fork or potato masher as they cook with the onions.

NOTE: For a quicker version of this recipe 2 (14-ounce) cans of rinsed and drained pinto beans can be used instead of the dried beans.

Drunken Beans

In this recipe, the beans are left whole and cooked in a mixture of spices and beer until there is almost no liquid left. They can replace refried beans (see page 151) in tacos, burritos, and tostadas.

Ingredients

9 ounces (about 1^1/$_4$ cups) dried pinto beans
  or 2 (14-ounces each) cans pinto beans,
  rinsed and drained
1 tablespoon vegetable oil
3 bacon slices, chopped
1 large onion, finely chopped
2 garlic cloves, crushed
1 teaspoon ground cumin
1 teaspoon chili powder or 1 teaspoon red
  pepper flakes
1 teaspoon chopped fresh oregano
1 can (14 ounces) chopped tomatoes, drained
^{3}/$_4$ cup light beer
^{3}/$_4$ cup water
Salt and freshly ground black pepper

Method

1. Place the beans in a large saucepan or bowl. Add enough water to cover and soak the beans overnight, then cook according to the instructions on the package. Drain the beans and discard the cooking water.

2. In a large saucepan, heat the oil over medium-high heat. Add the bacon and cook for 3 minutes. Add the onion, garlic, cumin, chili powder, and oregano and cook, stirring occasionally, until the onion is tender, about 10 minutes.

3. Add the beans, tomatoes, beer, and water and mix well. Season with salt and pepper to taste and bring to a boil over high heat. Reduce the heat to low, cover, and simmer for 30 minutes.

4. Remove the lid, stir well, and simmer an additional 20 minutes or until there is very little liquid left. Season to taste with salt and pepper and serve hot.

Milky Coconut Beans

This unusual bean recipe, which comes from Bahia in Brazil, is delicious when served with a spicy fish dish.

Ingredients

8 ounces dried black beans
1 can (14 ounces) thick coconut milk
$1/2$ teaspoon cayenne pepper
$1/2$ tablespoon granulated sugar
1 teaspoon salt

Method

1. Place the beans in a large saucepan or bowl. Add enough water to cover and soak the beans overnight, then cook according to the instructions on the package.

2. Drain the beans and discard the cooking water. Process the beans with the coconut milk in a blender or food processor, leaving a little texture in the beans.

3. Place the mixture in a large saucepan, add the cayenne pepper, sugar, and salt and bring to a boil. If the mixture is too thick, add a few tablespoons of water; if not thick enough, boil the mixture until it has the consistency of creamy mashed potatoes. Serve hot or warm.

Fried Rice

Latin Americans from Mexico to Argentina immediately incorporated rice into their diets as soon as it was brought to the continent by the Spanish. As a staple food, rice forms the basis of numerous recipes, with two main types being used—long-grain white for most recipes, and pudding rice for soups and desserts.

Ingredients

1 cup plus 2 tablespoons uncooked long-grain white rice
3 tablespoons vegetable oil
1 garlic clove, crushed
Salt and freshly ground pepper
2 cups hot water

Method

1. Rinse the rice thoroughly and let it drain well in a colander or sieve, about 30 minutes.

2. Heat the oil in a large saucepan or skillet over medium-high heat. Add the rice and cook, stirring constantly, until the rice is hot, about 5 minutes. Add the garlic and season with salt and pepper. Add the water and bring to a boil. Reduce the heat to low, cover, and simmer until the rice is tender and all the liquid absorbed, about 20 minutes.

3. If the rice is not cooked after 20 minutes, add a few tablespoons of hot water and cook, covered, for an additional 5 minutes. The water should be completely absorbed and the rice tender with each grain separate.

VARIATIONS: This basic rice recipe can be changed in many ways.
- The water can be substituted by chicken or vegetable stock.
- Yellow rice: add $1/2$ teaspoon of turmeric to the rice when frying.
- Vegetable rice: blanched diced carrots, zucchini, bell peppers, and peas can be stirred in at the end.
- Raisin and walnut rice: $1/2$ cup each raisins and coarsely chopped walnuts can be stirred in halfway through the cooking time.

Green Rice

Originally from Mexico, this is a deliciously different way to serve rice. For an authentic appearance, press the rice mixture into a lightly oiled ring mold and serve unmolded, garnished with watercress or fresh cilantro leaves.

Ingredients

1 cup plus 2 tablespoons uncooked long-grain white rice
3 tablespoons vegetable oil
4 garlic cloves, crushed
2 medium onions, chopped
3 green Fresno or jalapeño chilies, halved, seeded, and chopped (see page 194)
2$^1/_4$ cups hot Chicken Stock (see page 188)
3 tablespoons chopped fresh parsley
3 tablespoons chopped fresh cilantro leaves
Salt and freshly ground black pepper

Method

1. Rinse the rice thoroughly and let it drain well in a colander or sieve, about 30 minutes.

2. Heat 1 tablespoon of the oil in a large skillet over medium-high heat. Add the garlic, onions, and chilies; cook and stir until the onions are tender, about 10 minutes. Add half the stock to the pan and stir to scrape any browned bits from the bottom of the pan.

3. Transfer the onion mixture to a blender or food processor. Add the parsley and cilantro and blend until smooth. Set aside.

4. In a large saucepan, heat the remaining 2 tablespoons oil over medium-high heat. Add the rice and cook, stirring constantly, until the rice is lightly browned, about 5 minutes.

5. Stir in the onion mixture, the remaining stock, and the salt and black pepper. Bring to a boil. Reduce the heat to low, cover, and simmer for about 20 minutes or until the rice is tender and fluffy.

6. Remove the saucepan from the heat but keep the pan covered for another 5 minutes before serving.

Yellow Coconut Rice

This rice makes a wonderful accompaniment to spicy dishes—the coconut milk soothes a burning palate and cleanses it between mouthfuls.

Ingredients

1 cup plus 2 tablespoons uncooked long-grain white rice
1 cup flaked coconut
$2^2/_3$ cups hot Chicken Stock (see page 188)
$^1/_4$ cup vegetable oil
2 medium onions, finely chopped
$^1/_2$ teaspoon ground annatto or achiote (see page 274)
$^1/_2$ teaspoon mild chili powder
6 whole cloves
$^1/_2$ teaspoon ground cinnamon
Salt

Method

1. Rinse the rice thoroughly and let it drain well in a colander or sieve, about 30 minutes.

2. In a medium bowl, combine the coconut and hot chicken stock; mix well. Set aside.

3. Heat the oil in a large, heavy saucepan over medium-high heat. Add the onions; cook and stir until tender, about 10 minutes. Add the annatto and the chili powder and cook 1 minute.

4. Add the rice to the onions and cook, stirring frequently, until the rice is lightly browned, about 5 minutes.

5. Add the coconut mixture, cloves, cinnamon, and salt. Bring to a boil and simmer 5 minutes. Reduce the heat to low, cover, and simmer until the rice is tender and all the liquid is absorbed, about 20 minutes.

NOTE: If neither annato nor achiote is available, use turmeric instead.

Mexican Rice

Grilled tomatoes, onions, and garlic mixed with stock give a wonderful flavor to this recipe. When served with beans and guacamole, this is a delicious vegetarian meal.

Ingredients

1 cup plus 2 tablespoons uncooked long-grain white rice
3 medium tomatoes, halved
1 medium onion, halved
2 garlic cloves, crushed
4 tablespoons vegetable oil
Salt and freshly ground black pepper
1 3/4 cups hot Chicken Stock (see page 188)
2 carrots, peeled and finely diced
3/4 cup frozen peas, thawed
1 green chili, seeded and finely diced (see page 194)
1/2 red bell pepper, seeded and finely diced

For the garnish:
1 tablespoon chopped fresh parsley

Method

1. Heat the grill to high.

2. Wash the rice in several changes of water and let it soak for 15 minutes. Drain thoroughly.

3. Place the tomatoes, onion, and garlic on a baking sheet. Drizzle with 2 tablespoons of the oil and season with salt and pepper. Grill, stirring occasionally, until the tomatoes and onions are lightly browned, about 10 minutes.

4. Transfer the grilled vegetable mixture to a blender or food processor and blend until smooth. If too thick, add a few tablespoons chicken stock. Transfer to a colander or sieve to drain.

5. Heat the remaining 2 tablespoons oil in a large, heavy saucepan over medium-high heat. Add the rice and cook, stirring constantly, until the rice is lightly golden but not burned, about 5 minutes. Add the drained vegetable mixture and cook 5 minutes.

6. Stir in the carrots, peas, chili, red pepper, and chicken stock. Season with salt and pepper. Bring to a boil. Reduce the heat to low, cover, and simmer until the rice is tender and the liquid absorbed, about 20 minutes.

7. Transfer the rice mixture to a serving dish and sprinkle with the parsley. Serve at once.

VARIATIONS:
- Sweet corn, zucchini, mushrooms, finely chopped green beans, celery, and even diced ham and bacon can be added to this rice.
- For a delicious variation, sprinkle the rice with shredded Cheddar cheese 5 minutes before the end of the cooking time and cover tightly with a lid. When ready to serve, bring the pan to the table and remove the lid. The cheese will be completely melted and the rice moist.

Baked Red Rice

Very popular in Brazil, this rice recipe is easy to make. Since it can be prepared well in advance and baked just before serving, it is ideal for parties or other large gatherings.

Ingredients

1 cup plus 2 tablespoons uncooked long-grain white rice
2 tablespoons vegetable oil
1 small onion, finely chopped
1 garlic clove, crushed
1 tablespoon tomato purée
1 teaspoon chopped fresh oregano
3 tomatoes, peeled, seeded, and chopped
$1/2$ teaspoon cayenne pepper
Salt and freshly ground black pepper
$1/2$ cup shredded Cheddar cheese

Method

1. Preheat the oven to 375°F. Lightly grease a medium shallow ovenproof dish.

2. Rinse the rice thoroughly under cold water; drain well. Bring about 2 cups lightly salted water to a boil over high heat. Reduce the heat to low and simmer 5 minutes. Place the rice in a colander and rinse with the cooking water to remove the excess starch. Set aside while preparing the sauce.

3. Heat the oil in a large skillet over medium-high heat. Add the onion; cook and stir until the onion is tender, about 10 minutes. Add the garlic, tomato purée, and oregano and cook 2 minutes. Add the tomatoes and cayenne and season to taste with salt and black pepper.

4. Add the rice and mix well. Spoon the rice mixture into the prepared baking dish and sprinkle with the cheese. Bake 20 minutes or until the rice is tender and the cheese is melted. Serve at once.

NOTE: Alternatively, the rice can be baked in the oven for 15 minutes, then placed under the broiler for about 2 minutes to lightly brown the cheese.

Tortilla Dishes

TORTILLA DISHES

Tortillas are flat breads made from corn or wheat flour. Before the Spaniards introduced wheat to the Americas in the late 15th century, maize or corn was the main grain used to make breads. Corn has very little gluten, so it is difficult to make it into a leavened bread. As a result, the people of Mexico and Central America shaped corn dough into thin, unleavened cakes and cooked or toasted them briefly on a hot pottery griddle.

The Spaniards called the Mexican bread *tortilla*, the same name used for a popular round potato omelette found in Spain. With the integration of ingredients brought by the *conquistadores* into the local cuisine, wheat tortillas appeared, especially in the northern part of Mexico. The new leavened bread never replaced the tortilla in the Mexican diet, and many of the dishes tasted by the *conquistadores* are still very popular today.

Tortillas are the basis of numerous Mexican dishes, as well as being served as bread. The fillings used with them vary little; it is how the dish is assembled or cooked that makes for the variety.

Types of tortilla

Chalupa are oblong tortillas, a speciality of the Puebla region in Mexico.

Gorda, literally meaning 'fat', is a thicker tortilla than the usual variety.

Sope is a tortilla that is thicker at the edges.

Totopos are pieces of *tortilla gorda* fried in butter and served with refried beans.

Tortilla dishes

Burritos, thought to be a North American invention, are large, wheat-flour tortillas used as a wrapper for any filling, rather like soft tacos.

Chilaquiles are usually made with stale tortillas that have been shredded, fried, and layered in a casserole with cheese or vegetables. A chile-based sauce or stock is then poured over them. They are served with radishes and slices of onions.

Chimichangas are uncooked wheat tortillas that are filled, then fried.

Enchiladas are corn tortillas that are dipped in a thin savory sauce and then in hot oil. They are then filled, rolled up like tacos, arranged in a serving dish, and covered with the remaining sauce. The dish is then baked and garnished with cheese and onions.

Quesadillas are like turnovers made with uncooked corn tortillas. They usually have a savory filling and are deep-fried or baked in the oven until crisp.

Tacos are corn tortillas wrapped around a savory filling, which can consist of such things as meat, beans, guacamole, salsa, or shredded poultry. There are two types of tacos, soft and hard. A soft taco is spread with the filling, then rolled up and eaten like a sandwich; a hard taco is filled and then fried in hot oil.

Tostadas are tortillas deep-fried or baked until crisp. They are flat or shaped into baskets and used as containers for savory toppings and garnishes. They can also be made sweet for puddings.

Tostaditas, or tortilla chips, are wedges or strips of tortilla fried until crisp. They can be made of different types of corn, hence the dark tortilla chips, which are made of blue corn.

Classic fillings and garnishes

The most popular meat fillings are:

- shredded chicken (poached or leftover roast chicken)
- Shredded Pork (see page 103)
- Picadillo (see page 92)

Accompaniments

After selecting one type of meat, the following accompaniments are used:

- Salsa Cruda (see page 176) or Tomatillo and Apple Salsa (see page 183)
- shredded iceberg lettuce
- shredded cheese (Cheddar or Gouda)
- Refried Beans (see page 151)
- Guacamole (see page 185)
- sour cream
- sliced onions and radishes
- pickled chilies or hot chili sauce

Corn Tortillas

Masa harina, the flour used to make tortillas, is made by boiling corn kernels with lime. The kernels are then dried and ground into flour. Masa harina is available in speciality shops and large supermarkets.

Ingredients

1 1/4 cups instant masa harina mix
1 teaspoon salt
about 1 1/4 cups warm water

Method

1. Combine the masa harina and salt in a medium bowl. Pour in two thirds of the water and mix with a knife to a doughy consistency. Add enough of the remaining water to make a soft but not sticky dough. Knead until well combined and smooth. Cover and rest for 15 minutes.

2. Divide the dough into 12 equal balls. Place each ball between sheets of waxed paper or plastic wrap and use a rolling pin to flatten them into discs about 6 inches in diameter. Peel off the paper or plastic wrap.

3. Heat an ungreased griddle or heavy sauté pan and cook the tortillas one at a time for about 1 minute on each side until flecked with brown.

4. Keep the cooked tortillas warm by stacking them in a clean napkin and serving them wrapped.

NOTE: The tortilla dough can also be flattened in a tortilla press—a quick, efficient gadget developed by the Spanish and found in speciality shops.

Taco Fiesta

Tacos are tortillas wrapped around a variety of savory fillings. Traditionally, corn tortillas are served, but filled wheat-flour tortillas (called burritos) are just as delicious. All the different fillings and garnishes are put on the table and each person assembles his or her taco according to taste and eats it with their hands. Many of the garnishes can be prepared in advance and are served at room temperature. The meat and bean fillings are best served warm. Allow 2 or 3 fresh warm tortillas per person and plenty of salsa cruda and hot chile paste on the side.

Ingredients

12 (6-inch) Corn or Wheat-Flour Tortillas (see page 164 or 166)
2 recipes Guacamole (see page 185)
1 recipe Refried Beans (see page 151)
1 recipe Picadillo (see page 92)
2 chicken breast halves, poached and shredded
$1/2$ head iceberg lettuce, finely shredded
$1^1/4$ cups shredded Cheddar cheese
1 recipe Cured Onions (see page 144)
2 recipes Salsa Cruda (see page 176)
$1/2$ pint sour cream or crème fraîche
1 recipe Fresh Chile Paste (see page 180)

To serve: mixed green salad

Method

1. Preheat the oven to 325°F. To reheat the tortillas, wrap them loosely in foil as they are made. Heat in the oven for 10 minutes before serving, then pile them on to a plate and cover with a large napkin.

2. Each person takes a tortilla and spoons on some guacamole, beans, meat or chicken, some lettuce, cheese and onions, then a small quantity of salsa cruda and sour cream on top. Roll up like a cigar—not too tightly or the filling will squeeze out of the ends when being eaten. Brave individuals can add a few drops of red chile paste before rolling up the taco, or place a little on the plate and dip the taco into it now and again. Serve with a mixed green salad.

NOTE: Hard taco shells are not as good as freshly made tortillas, but they are good as a shortcut for a taco fiesta; allow 2 or 3 per person.

WINE SUGGESTION: Light-bodied red.

Flour Tortillas

Wheat was introduced to Mexico after the Conquest in 1519. Although flour tortillas are common in northern parts of Mexico, they don't rival the popularity of corn tortillas.

Ingredients

1¼ cups all-purpose flour
1 teaspoon salt
¼ cup lard or shortening
about ¾ warm water
1 teaspoon vegetable oil

Method

1. Sift the flour and salt into a medium bowl. Rub in the lard. Stir in enough water to form a soft but not sticky dough.

2. Knead the dough well on a floured surface for about 10 minutes or until smooth and elastic. Put the dough into the cleaned bowl, cover, and set aside to rest for 1 hour.

3. Divide the dough into 12 equal pieces. Roll each piece on a lightly floured surface until about 8 inches wide.

4. Cook the tortillas one at a time in a heated comal or heavy-based skillet until the underside is flecked with brown and bubbles appear on the surface. Turn the tortilla and cook the other side, pressing down the bubbles with a rolled-up dish towel. Grease the pan very lightly with the oil only if the tortilla is sticking.

5. Keep the tortillas warm by wrapping them in a clean cloth when they are cooked.

Crab Tostadas

This is a very good dinner party dish since all the preparation can be done in advance and the tostadas just heated up before serving. It is important not to fill them in advance or they will get soggy. The tostadas can be baked flat, but they look much nicer when cooked in a basket shape.

Ingredients

1/2 recipe Flour Tortilla dough (see page 166)
Vegetable oil for brushing

For the filling:
1 pound cooked crabmeat
2 tablespoons vegetable oil
1 small onion, finely chopped
2 scallions, finely chopped
3 tablespoons chopped fresh cilantro leaves
2 tomatoes, peeled, seeded, and finely chopped
3 tablespoons lime juice
Salt and freshly ground pepper

To serve: 1/2 head iceberg lettuce, finely
   shredded
1 recipe Refried Beans (see page 151)
1 recipe Guacamole (see page 185)
Sour cream
1 recipe Salsa Cruda (see page 176)

Method

1. Preheat the oven to 250°F.

2. Divide the dough into 4 equal pieces and shape each into an 8-inch circle. Brush the tortillas on both sides with a little oil. Using inverted small ovenproof mixing bowls or cereal bowls, put the tortillas on top and bake for 30 minutes, or until they are crisp. Remove to a wire rack to cool. (They can be made up to a day in advance and reheated slightly just before serving.)

3. Pick over the crabmeat. In a sauté pan, heat the oil over medium heat and cook the onion for 10 minutes. Add the scallions, half

the cilantro, the tomatoes, lime juice, and crabmeat. Season with salt and pepper and cook for 5 minutes over low heat. Just before serving mix in the remaining cilantro.

4. To serve, arrange the tortillas on a plate and put a handful of shredded lettuce at the bottom of each. Layer the beans, crab mixture, and guacamole on top, finishing with 1 tablespoon of sour cream. Pass the salsa cruda separately.

VARIATION: To make sweet tostadas, melt 2 tablespoons butter and brush each tostada. Mix 2 tablespoons of sugar with 1 teaspoon ground cinnamon and sprinkle over the buttered surface. Bake as above and fill with Tropical Fruit Salad (see page 212). Serve with plain yogurt, Rich Vanilla Ice Cream (see page 229) or Cinnamon and Vanilla Ice Cream (see page 227).

NOTE I: This dish is a complete meal in itself, so it is not necessary to serve anything else with it.

NOTE II: The tostadas can be made finger-food size and filled with different meats or salsas.

NOTE III: Picadillo (see page 92) or shredded chicken breasts can be used instead of crabmeat; for a vegetarian tostada, substitute the meat with shredded Cheddar cheese.

WINE SUGGESTION: Full-bodied white.

Chorizo Sausage Quesadillas

These are delicious turnovers made with uncooked tortilla dough and filled with a savory or sweet stuffing.

Ingredients

3 Spanish chorizo sausages, skinned and finely chopped
$1/4$ cup grated Parmesan cheese
2 tomatoes, peeled, seeded, and chopped
2 scallions, finely chopped
1 recipe Flour Tortilla dough (see page 166)
Vegetable oil for brushing

To serve: Marinated Vegetable Salad (see page 57)

Method

1. Preheat the oven to 400°F.

2. Put the chopped sausage into a sauté pan and cook over medium heat for about 10 minutes, stirring until most of the fat has come out. Using a slotted spoon, transfer the sausage pieces to a bowl and add the tomatoes and scallions. Set aside to cool.

3. Divide the tortilla dough into 16 equal parts. Roll them on a lightly floured surface into 6-inch circles and place a portion of the filling on one half of each circle. Fold the other half over and pinch the edges together to seal. Transfer to an oiled baking sheet and brush the quesadillas with a little oil.

4. Bake in the middle of the oven for about 15 to 20 minutes or until they are crisp and golden. Serve warm with the Marinated Vegetable Salad.

VARIATIONS:
*   The quesadillas can also be deep-fried in hot oil until crisp.
*   Shredded chicken, Picadillo (see page 92), shrimp and crabmeat can be used as alternative fillings.

WINE SUGGESTION: Full-bodied red.

Tamales

Tamales are corn husks filled with masa harina dough, then steamed. They appear in many varieties throughout Latin America: in some countries they are made with fresh corn and called *humitas* or *pamoulas*. Although they can be left unfilled, they are usually stuffed with meat, vegetables, or cheese. They can be very spicy and are a good way of using up leftovers, such as picadillo or shredded beef. They also make a delicious dessert when filled with tropical fruit and nuts and served with coffee or hot chocolate.

Ingredients

$1/3$ cup lard or shortening
1 cup instant masa harina (see page 279)
$1^1/2$ teaspoons baking powder
$1^1/2$ teaspoons salt
$2/3$ cup lukewarm water
12 corn husks (see Note I, page 171), or 12
  sheets of waxed paper measuring 9 x 4 inches

For the filling:
Picadillo (see page 92)
Poached and shredded chicken breasts
9 ounces mozzarella cheese, cut into rounds

Method

1. In a medium bowl, cream the lard with a wooden spoon.

2. Sift together the masa harina, baking powder, and salt. Add 3 spoonfuls of the masa harina mixture at a time to the creamed lard, and beat with a wooden spoon until all the masa harina is thoroughly combined with the lard.

3. Slowly pour in the lukewarm water and bring the dough together with one hand. Knead lightly for 1 minute or until the dough is soft and smooth.

4. To assemble the tamales: put about 1 tablespoon of dough in the center of a corn husk or sheet of paper and spread with your fingers into a rectangle, leaving a 1-inch border. Put 1 tablespoon of your chosen filling, or a piece of the cheese, in the center

of the dough. Fold one side of the wrapper a little more than halfway across the filling and bring the opposite side over the first fold. Turn the ends up to cover the seam, overlapping them across the top. Tie with a piece of string. If using corn husks, use a thin strip of husk to tie the tamales.

5. Lay the tamales in a large colander in as many layers as necessary and place the colander over a deep pan filled with hot water. Cover, reduce the heat and steam the tamales for 1 hour, adding more water to the pan if necessary. When the tamales are done, remove them from the colander with tongs, arrange on a plate and serve at once. They may be prepared in advance and reheated by steaming them again for 30 minutes.

VARIATIONS:
*   Sweet tamales: Add $1/2$ cup sugar, 1 tablespoon ground almonds and 1 cup flaked coconut to the masa harina when making the dough. Fill with $1/3$ cup chopped walnuts mixed with $1/4$ cup apricot jam. Shape them half the size of the above tamales and steam for 35 minutes. Serve warm or cold.
*   Using leftover plain or cheese tamales, remove the tamale from the wrapping and cut in half. Heat a little oil in a shallow skillet and fry the tamales until golden brown. Serve at once with coffee as a snack or as part of a meal.

NOTE I: If using dried corn husks, soak in warm water for 15 minutes, then drain and pat dry before using. Waxed paper is a perfect substitute for the corn husks, although the appearance is not as authentic.

NOTE II: The water used for the dough can be substituted by stock, according to the filling used, or by coconut milk if making a sweet tamale.

WINE SUGGESTION: Full-bodied dry red for savory tamales, Moscatel for sweet tamales.

Making Tamales

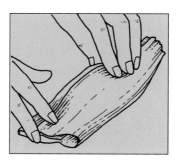

1.

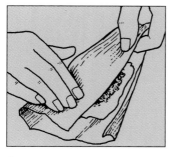

2.

3.

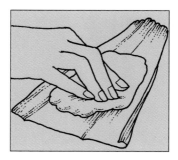

4.

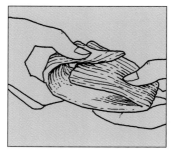

5.

6.

Salsas,
Sauces and Stocks

SALSAS AND SAUCES

Literally meaning 'sauce', the term *salsa* is applied to any kind of sauce in Latin America. Elsewhere, it is used to describe a sauce or relish made with freshly chopped, uncooked ingredients. A basic salsa consists of tomatoes; onions; an herb such as cilantro; lime juice, lemon juice, or vinegar; and fresh chilies.

To keep its freshness, a salsa should be made no more than two hours before eating and all the ingredients used should be very fresh. It is essential to use good-quality vinegar, oils, and spices. The other ingredients are chopped finely, but not so fine that they cannot be identified. A spoonful of salsa should contain a bit of everything.

Salsas are a healthy and delicious substitute for rich butter and cream sauces and offer a nice change from traditional gravies. They serve as a tasty complement to roast, grilled, barbecued, or pan-fried meats, and have the added advantage of being fresh, low in sugar and fat, and easy to make.

A good salsa has no more than three or four basic ingredients (apart from the herbs and liquid), so it keeps a clean, fresh flavor. It is best to use ingredients which are in season because they are cheaper and taste better. Although most salsas have chilies added to them, they are not essential. Different types of chilies go well with different types of foods (see Chili Chart, pages 195–9), so it is worth experimenting to discover your preferred combination.

A salsa is a simple, quick sauce, so the tomatoes, peppers, and chilies that go into it are usually not skinned. However, grilled peppers and large chilies, which have a nice, full flavor, are skinned. While they lose some of their crispness in the process of grilling, the robust flavor of the grilled vegetables adds special interest to the salsa.

Ideally, a salsa should be made about one hour before serving and left at room temperature. Take care if using raw onions in a salsa as they can be quite strong. If you like, you can degorge the onions first (see page 277), or substitute scallions, which have a milder flavor.

Fruit salsas are exciting and delicious when served with barbecued foods. Start with the proven combinations, like Pineapple and Chili Salsa with barbecued pork chops, and then move on to the more unusual salsas. Note that fruit salsas do not keep as long as vegetable salsas.

Normally, the salsa is placed in a serving bowl and left on the table so that people can help themselves. For a more refined presentation, small ramekins can be filled and placed on individual plates.

Salsa Cruda

This is also called "table salsa" because it is the basic tomato and chili salsa served with every meal in Mexico and other Latin American countries. It goes well with meat, vegetables, rice, and potatoes, and is even used as a salad dressing!

Ingredients

6 medium tomatoes, seeded and finely diced
1 medium red onion, finely chopped
2 scallions, white and green parts, coarsely chopped
2 tablespoons finely chopped fresh cilantro leaves
1 green Dutch or Westland chili, seeded and finely chopped (see page 194)
$^1/_2$ teaspoon finely chopped fresh oregano
Pinch of sugar
Juice of 1 lime or 2 lemons
3 tablespoons vegetable oil
Salt and freshly ground black pepper

Method

1. Combine all ingredients except the salt and black pepper in a medium bowl; mix well. Season to taste with the salt and pepper. Serve at room temperature.

NOTE: The fresh green chili can be substituted by a few drops of hot pepper sauce or $^1/_2$ teaspoon chili powder.

Mango and Avocado Salsa

This salsa goes particularly well with grilled and barbecued chicken, fish, and lamb.

Ingredients

1 large mango, peeled and finely diced
$^1/_2$ medium red onion, finely chopped
$^1/_2$ medium green bell pepper, diced
$^1/_2$ medium red bell pepper, diced
3 tablespoons white wine vinegar
2 tablespoons lime juice
2 tablespoons coarsely chopped fresh cilantro leaves
5 tablespoons vegetable oil
1 tablespoon coarsely chopped fresh chives
Salt and freshly ground black pepper
1 small avocado, peeled, pitted, and diced

Method

1. Mix together all the ingredients, except the salt, black pepper, and avocado in a medium bowl. Season to taste with salt and black pepper, then gently stir in the avocado. Serve at room temperature.

Three-Pepper Salsa

Here the grilling of the peppers and Anaheim chili gives this salsa a unique flavor, which complements roasted or barbecued meat, and fried fish recipes. Unlike other fresh salsas, this recipe will keep for several hours in the refrigerator.

Ingredients

1 red bell pepper, grilled, peeled, and finely diced
1 yellow bell pepper, grilled, peeled, and finely diced
1 green pepper, grilled, peeled, and finely diced
2 green Anaheim chilies, grilled, peeled, and finely diced (see page 194)
$1/3$ cup vegetable oil
$1/4$ cup white wine vinegar
1 garlic clove, cut in half
Pinch of sugar
2 tablespoons finely chopped flat-leaf Italian parsley
2 tablespoons finely chopped fresh cilantro leaves
1 teaspoon chopped fresh oregano
Dash Tabasco sauce
Juice of 1 lime
Salt and freshly ground black pepper

Method

1. Mix all the ingredients except the salt and black pepper together in a bowl. Season to taste with the salt and pepper and set aside for 1 hour to allow the flavors to develop.

2. Just before serving, remove the garlic.

Jalapeño and Lime Salsa

This salsa, with its clean, vegetable flavor, goes well with any type of roasted meat. The combination of lime and lemon juices gives it a nice amount of tartness.

Ingredients

1 large onion, finely chopped
1 teaspoon salt
Juice of 2 limes
Juice of 1 lemon
$1/2$ garlic clove, crushed
2 green jalapeño or Fresno chilies, seeded and finely chopped (see page 194)
2 tablespoons chopped flat-leaf Italian parsley
1 teaspoon freshly chopped fresh marjoram or oregano
Salt

Method

1. Place the onion in a plastic colander or sieve and sprinkle with the salt. Let stand 5 minutes. Rinse the onion under cold running water and drain well.

2. In a non-metallic bowl, mix together the onions, lime and lemon juices, garlic, chilies, parsley, and marjoram. Season to taste with salt and let stand at room temperature for 1 hour. Serve with grilled or barbecued fish, chicken, or pork.

Pineapple and Chili Salsa

This salsa is delicious when served with grilled sausage or roast pork.

Ingredients

1 small red onion, finely chopped
1 teaspoon salt
Boiling water
3 medium tomatoes, seeded and finely diced
1 dried ancho chili, seeded and finely chopped
(see page 194)
1 tablespoon coarsely chopped fresh cilantro
leaves
1 red bell pepper, skinned, seeded, and finely
diced
Juice of 3 limes
$1/2$ fresh ripe pineapple, peeled, cored, and finely
diced
Salt

Method

1. Place the onion in a plastic sieve or
    colander and sprinkle with the salt. Let
    stand 10 minutes and rinse well with the
    boiling water.

2. In a large bowl, combine the onion with all
    the remaining ingredients except the salt.
    Season with the salt. Cover and refrigerate
    for at least 30 minutes before using.

NOTE: For a more intense flavor, lightly heat the
ancho chili under the broiler.

VARIATION: To make melon and chili salsa, use
half a honeydew melon, diced, instead of the
pineapple.

Scotch Bonnet and Papaya Salsa

Scotch bonnet, Jamaican hot, and habañero chilies are all from the same family; in fact, they look and taste very similar. They are the hottest chilies in the world, so should be handled with care and eaten with caution.

Ingredients

1 large onion, finely chopped
1 green Scotch bonnet or habañero chili, seeded and finely chopped (see page 194)
1 ripe papaya, peeled, seeded, and diced
1 small garlic clove, crushed
Juice of 2 limes
3 tablespoons white wine vinegar
2 tablespoons chopped flat-leaf Italian parsley
Salt

Method

1. Place the onion in a sieve, rinse with hot water, and drain.

2. Mix the onion with all the remaining ingredients except the salt in a bowl and let stand at room temperature 1 hour. Season with salt and serve with cooked seafood or fish.

Creoja Sauce

This is more of a dressing than a salsa, and delicious as a substitute for gravy with roast pork or veal. It can also be used to marinate and baste barbecued meats.

Ingredients

Juice of 2 limes
$1/4$ cup olive oil
1 tablespoon coarsely chopped fresh cilantro
1 tablespoon coarsely chopped flat-leaf parsley
1 teaspoon chopped fresh thyme
$1/2$ garlic clove, crushed
$1/2$ teaspoon fresh Chili Paste (see page 180)
Salt and freshly ground black pepper

Method

1. Thoroughly combine all of the ingredients except the salt and black pepper in a medium bowl. Season to taste with salt and black pepper.

NOTE I: The hot chili paste can be substituted by $1/2$ teaspoon hot red pepper flakes or hot pepper sauce.

NOTE II: When using this salsa as a baste for barbecued meats, tie 3 or 4 large sprigs of fresh rosemary and/or thyme together to use as a brush. It will impart a delicate flavor to the meat.

Spicy Avocado Salsa

In Venezuela, a finely chopped hard-boiled egg is added to this salsa—the result is called *guasacaca*. It is especially delicious served as a dip with tortilla chips or with Spicy Chicken Wings (see page 71).

Ingredients

5 tablespoons peanut oil
3 tablespoons white wine vinegar
Juice of 1 lime
$1/2$ teaspoon hot chili powder
2 small tomatoes, seeded and diced
2 avocados, peeled, pitted, and cut into 1-inch
  cubes
$1/2$ yellow bell pepper, seeded and finely diced
$1/2$ red bell pepper, seeded and finely diced
2 tablespoons finely chopped fresh parsley
1 tablespoon chopped scallions, white and
  green parts
Salt and freshly ground black pepper
Hot pepper sauce (optional)

Method

1. Combine the oil, vinegar, lime juice, and chili powder in a large bowl and mix well. Add the tomatoes, avocados, yellow and red peppers, parsley, and scallions; mix thoroughly. Season to taste with salt, black pepper, and a few drops of hot pepper sauce.

Fresh Chili Paste

A good thick sauce for chili growers or lovers, this is also an invaluable seasoning companion for the daring cook.

Ingredients

7 ounces fresh red chilies (Fresno or jalapeño),
  seeded and halved (see page 194)
Boiling water
2 teaspoons tomato purée
1 garlic clove, crushed
4 tablespoons peanut oil
1 teaspoon ground cumin
1 tablespoon chopped fresh oregano
$1/2$ cup Chicken Stock (see page 188)

Method

1. Rinse the chilies and drain. Place them in a small bowl and add enough boiling water to cover. Let stand 1 hour, then drain.

2. Place the chilies along with the remaining ingredients in a blender or food processor and blend until smooth.

3. Transfer the chili purée to a small saucepan and simmer, uncovered, over low heat about 10 minutes or until the mixture is thickened. Season to taste with salt if desired. Remove from the heat and cool completely. Store in a glass jar.

NOTE: This paste is also called salsa roja *and can be made using small, fiercely hot red chilies, like tabasco or Thai chilies. Keep covered in the refrigerator for up to 2 weeks and use to flavor dips, stews, and soups.*

Thick Mango and Chili Sauce

This sauce is very good with lean and not too strongly flavored meat or fish. The sweetness of the mango and the heat from the chilies make a perfect match.

Ingredients

2 ripe mangoes
2 tablespoons vegetable oil
1 large onion, chopped
1 teaspoon ground cumin
1 tablespoon finely chopped fresh oregano
2 red Thai or Indian chilies, seeded and chopped (see page 194)
3 tablespoons white rum
3 tablespoons white wine vinegar
2 tablespoons light brown sugar
Salt

Method

1. Peel the mangoes and cut the flesh into chunks.

2. Heat the oil in a large saucepan over medium-high heat. Add the onion; cook and stir until tender, about 10 minutes.

3. Add the cumin, oregano, chilies, and mangoes. Reduce the heat to medium and simmer about 10 minutes.

4. Add the rum, vinegar, and sugar and bring to a boil. Reduce the heat to low and simmer for 15 minutes or until the mangoes are completely softened. Remove the saucepan from the heat and season to taste with salt.

5. Transfer the mango mixture to a blender or food processor and blend until smooth. The sauce should have the consistency of a soft purée. If is too thick, add a little water. Serve warm or cold.

Spicy Tomato Sauce

This sauce, which tastes and smells delicious, can be used in many different ways. If desired, it can be made up to two days in advance, refrigerated, and reheated when ready to use.

Ingredients

1 can (29 ounces) chopped tomatoes, undrained
3 tablespoons vegetable oil
2 Kenyan or Fresno red chilies, seeded and finely chopped (see page 194)
2 garlic cloves, crushed
$1/2$ teaspoon ground cinnamon
$1/2$ teaspoon ground cumin
$1/2$ teaspoon ground coriander
$1/8$ teaspoon cayenne pepper
$1/8$ teaspoon paprika
1 tablespoon tomato purée
3 tablespoons chopped fresh parsley
4 scallions, white and green parts, chopped
$1/2$ teaspoon sugar
Salt and freshly ground black pepper

Method

1. Mix all of the ingredients except the salt and black pepper together in a large, heavy saucepan and bring to a boil over medium-high heat. Season with salt and pepper, reduce the heat to low, and simmer, uncovered, for 30 minutes.

2. Taste and adjust the seasoning if necessary. Serve hot or cold.

NOTE: For a smooth sauce, purée the cooked mixture in a blender or food processor.

Yellow Chili Paste

The many varieties of pale yellow chilies vary greatly in their intensity of heat . The most common ones are the Hungarian wax or the Cera, but any of the other varieties can be used. Just make sure to taste for heat.

Ingredients

6 cups water
24 wax chilies (see page 196)
2 tablespoons vegetable oil
2 tablespoons distilled white vinegar
2 tablespoons salt

Method

1. Bring the water to a boil in a large saucepan. Add the whole chilies and boil, uncovered, for 5 minutes. Drain and rinse under cold running water.

2. Split the chilies in half, remove the seeds, and discard (see page 194).

3. In a blender or food processor, place the chilies along with the oil, vinegar, and salt and process to a smooth purée. Transfer to a bowl, cover, and use as a substitute for fresh mild chilies.

Red Dried Chili Paste

This is a basic recipe for a good chili paste that will keep in the refrigerator for up to one month. It's easy to make and ideal as a table salsa for the more adventurous.

Ingredients

2 ounces dried tabasco or hot red chilies (see page 199)
$2/3$ cup boiling Chicken Stock (see page 188)
5 tablespoons olive oil
1 garlic clove, crushed
Salt

Method

1. Break the chilies in half, brush out the seeds, and discard. Place the chilies in a bowl and add the boiling stock. Let stand 2 hours.

2. Place the chili mixture in a blender or food processor. Add the oil and garlic; season to taste with the salt. Process until the mixture forms a smooth purée. Transfer to a bowl, cover, and refrigerate until ready to serve.

NOTE: This chili paste can be used as a flavoring for dressings, mayonnaise, dips, and sauces.

Chipotle Chili Salsa

Chipotles are smoked, dried jalapeño chilies. They have a wonderful nutty flavor that goes well with stews, soups, and salsas.

Ingredients

3 chipotle chilies (see page 198)
$^2/_3$ cup cider vinegar
6 medium tomatoes, seeded and finely diced
1 red bell pepper, seeded and finely diced
Pinch of sugar
2 tablespoons chopped fresh parsley
$^1/_2$ teaspoon chopped fresh oregano
Salt

Method

1. Halve the chilies, brush out the seeds, and discard. Finely chop the flesh.

2. In a small saucepan, bring the vinegar to a boil and remove from the heat. Add the chilies and let stand for 30 minutes.

3. Transfer the chile mixture to a medium bowl and add all the remaining ingredients except the salt. Mix thoroughly and season to taste with the salt.

Tomatillo and Apple Salsa

Tomatillos, also known as husk tomatoes, are small, green Mexican tomatoes with a distinctive tart flavor. Very popular in Mexico, they are sold fresh or in cans at speciality shops and can be substituted by green gooseberries.

Ingredients

5 fresh tomatillos, coarsely chopped, or 12 gooseberries
1 yellow bell pepper, seeded and diced
1 small green apple, unpeeled, cored, and finely diced
1 small onion, finely chopped
3 tablespoons chopped fresh cilantro leaves
2 tablespoons olive oil
2 tablespoons lime juice
2 green chilies, Fresno or jalapeño, seeded and finely chopped (see page 194)
$^1/_2$ teaspoon salt

Method

1. Mix all of the ingredients together in a bowl. Let stand at room temperature at least 1 hour before serving.

Escabeche Sauce

Escabeche is a vinegar-based sauce and is also the name given to recipes where food is marinated or pickled in vinegar. It is a commonly used sauce for fried fish, but is also delicious with cooked vegetables. If desired, chilies and peppers can be added to this easy-to-make recipe.

Ingredients

^{1}/$_4$ cup olive oil
3 medium onions, thinly sliced
3 tomatoes, peeled, seeded and cut into strips
1 green bell pepper, seeded and cut into strips
1 green jalapeño or Fresno chili, seeded and
  thinly sliced (optional, see page 194)
^{1}/$_2$ teaspoon ground cumin
^{1}/$_4$ cup white wine vinegar
^{1}/$_4$ cup warm water
Salt and freshly ground black pepper
12 green olives, pitted

Method

1. In a large saucepan, heat the oil over medium-high heat. Add the onions; cook and stir until tender, about 10 minutes.

2. Add the tomatoes, green bell pepper, chili, and cumin and cook 5 minutes, stirring once or twice and taking care not to crush the tomatoes.

3. Add the vinegar and water and season with the salt and pepper to taste. Bring to a boil, remove from the heat, and add the olives. Transfer to a serving dish and serve hot or cold.

NOTE: For a classic serving, fried fillets of white fish are placed on a bed of lettuce. The escabeche sauce is then poured over the fish and garnished with chopped fresh cilantro leaves.

Guacamole

Guacamole is a dip so well known outside Latin America that it scarcely needs an introduction. In Mexico, the cooks put the avocado pit on top of the guacamole as it is believed to prevent the avocado from discoloring. Try it and see!

Ingredients

2 very ripe avocados
Juice of 1 lime
1 small onion, finely chopped
1 teaspoon salt
Boiling water
2 medium tomatoes, seeded and chopped
2 red jalapeño or Fresno chilies, seeded and
   finely chopped (see page 194)
Dash Tabasco sauce
2 tablespoons chopped fresh cilantro leaves
Salt and freshly ground pepper

Method

1. Halve the avocados, remove the pits, and mash the flesh slightly in the skins using a fork. Transfer the mashed avocado to a medium bowl. Add the lime juice and mix thoroughly.

2. Place the onion into a non-metallic sieve or colander, sprinkle with the salt, and let stand 10 minutes. Pour boiling water over the onions and drain well. Pat dry with paper towels.

3. Add the onions, tomatoes, chilies, Tabasco sauce, and fresh cilantro to the avocado mixture and mix well. Season to taste with the salt and pepper. Add a little more Tabasco if not hot enough.

4. Keep covered at room temperature until ready to use.

Peanut, Chili, and Ricotta Cheese Dip

A versatile recipe, this can be used as a sandwich filling or dip.

Ingredients

1 cup creamy peanut butter
$^1/_4$ cup heavy cream
$^1/_4$ cup milk
$^1/_4$ cup ricotta or cottage cheese
$^1/_4$ cup vegetable oil
3 tablespoons chopped fresh cilantro leaves
Salt and freshly ground pepper
1 teaspoon mild chili powder

Method

1. Place all of the ingredients except the seasonings together in a blender or food processor and process until smooth.

2. Taste and season with the salt, pepper, and chili powder.

Mayonnaise

This basic mayonnaise recipe can be flavored with chili purées for a Latin twist and used in salads, sandwiches, and dips.

Ingredients

2 egg yolks
Salt and freshly ground white pepper
1 teaspoon mustard
1¹/₄ cups olive oil or ²/₃ cup *each* olive oil and
  vegetable oil
Squeeze of lemon juice
1 tablespoon white wine vinegar

Method

1. Place the yolks in a medium bowl. Add a pinch of salt and the mustard and beat well with a wooden spoon.

2. Add the oil literally drop by drop, beating constantly. The mixture should be very thick by the time half of the oil is added.

3. Beat in lemon juice to taste.

4. Continue pouring in the remaining oil, going rather more confidently now, but alternating the dribbles of oil with small quantities of vinegar, beating constantly.

5. Add salt and white pepper to taste.

VARIATION: To make spicy red pepper mayonnaise, grill 2 red bell peppers and 1 red Kenyan or jalapeño chili, skin sides up, until blistered and blackened, about 15 minutes. Peel, then process or chop finely to a pulp. Prepare the mayonnaise as directed above, seasoning with 1 teaspoon mild chili powder instead of the mustard, and mixing in the pepper purée once the mayonnaise is made.

NOTE: If the mixture curdles, another egg yolk should be beaten in a separate bowl, and the curdled mixture beaten into it drop by drop.

Stocks

Most cooking in Latin America is done on top of the stove. In fact, it is not unusual, especially in Mexican recipes, for meat or poultry to be poached before being added to a sauce for further cooking, leaving behind valuable stock to be used in other dishes. As in most countries, however, stock cubes are frequently used – sometimes added to the water for boiling pasta, rice, and beans. Most cooks would not dream of making fresh stock for a specific dish, mainly because many sauces are tomato or pepper based.

The secret of making good stocks is slow, gentle simmering. If the liquid is the slightest bit greasy, vigorous boiling will produce a murky, fatty stock. Skimming, especially of meat stocks, is vital. As fat and scum rise to the surface, they should be lifted off with a slotted spoon, perhaps every 10 or 15 minutes.

Vegetables, particularly onions, carrots, and celery, add flavor and color to stocks; leeks, tomato skins and seeds, and mushroom stalks can also be used if you like. The total weight of vegetables should be equal to or less than the weight of the bones.

A good way of storing a large batch of stock is to boil it down to double strength and then dilute it with water when using it. Alternatively, it can be boiled down to a thick syrupy glaze, which can be used like stock cubes. Many cooks freeze the glaze in ice-cube trays, then transfer the frozen cubes to a plastic bag in the freezer. If fat-free, they will keep for at least a year.

Chicken Stock

MAKES ABOUT 3 CUPS

Ingredients

1 onion, sliced
1 celery stalk, sliced
1 carrot, sliced
Bones of 1 chicken
1 bunch parsley
$^1/_2$ bunch thyme
2 bay leaves
6 peppercorns

Method

1. Place all of the ingredients in a large saucepan. Add enough water to cover and bring to a boil over high heat, occasionally skimming off any fat and/or scum.

2. Reduce the heat to low and simmer for 2–3 hours, skimming frequently and adding additional water if necessary. The liquid should reduce to half the original quantity.

3. Strain the stock and let cool. Remove and discard all the fat.

Brown Stock (Beef)

Ingredients

2 pounds beef bones
1 tablespoon vegetable oil
1 medium onion, peeled and chopped (remove the skins)
2 medium carrots, cut into quarters
1 bunch parsley
2 bay leaves
6 black peppercorns

Method

1. Preheat the oven to 425°F.

2. Place the beef bones in a roasting pan and bake in the oven until well browned. This may take up to 1 hour.

3. Heat the oil in a large stock pot over medium-high heat. Add the onion and carrots and cook, stirring occasionally, until browned, about 15 minutes. It is essential that the vegetables do not burn.

4. When the bones are browned, add them to the vegetables along with the onion skins, parsley stalks, bay leaves, and black peppercorns. Add enough cold water to cover and bring to a boil, skimming off any scum as it rises to the surface.

5. When the stock is clear of scum reduce the heat to low, and simmer for 3–4 hours, or even longer, skimming off the fat as necessary and adding additional water if necessary. The longer the stock simmers and the more the liquid is reduced, and the stronger the stock will be.

6. Strain the stock and let cool. Remove and discard any remaining fat.

NOTE: To make glace de viande (concentrated beef stock), boil the fat-free stock in a heavy saucepan over a medium-high heat until thick, clear, and syrupy. Pour into small containers and let cool completely. Cover with polythene or jam covers and secure. This stock will keep in the refrigerator for several weeks, or can be frozen in an ice-cube tray up to 6 months.

Fish Stock

Ingredients

1 onion, sliced
1 carrot, sliced
1 celery stalk, sliced
1–1½ pounds fish bones, skins, fins, heads, tails
1 pound crustacean shells, e.g. shrimp or mussel
1 bunch parsley
1 bay leaf
Pinch chopped thyme
3 black peppercorns

Method

1. Place all of the ingredients in a large saucepan. Add enough cold water to cover and bring to a boil over high heat. Reduce the heat to low and skim off any scum.

2. Simmer 20 minutes if the fish bones are small and 30 minutes if large. Strain.

NOTE: Avoid cooking the bones for too long. Once strained, however, the stock may be strengthened by reducing it further.

Chiles

CHILES

Archaeological evidence in Mexico shows the presence of chiles as far back as 6,000 years ago. All chiles belong to the *Solanaceae* family, as do tomatoes, potatoes, and eggplants. The genus *Capsicum* (from the Latin *capsa*, meaning "case") includes all peppers, from the sweet bell pepper to the hottest of chiles. There are 20 to 30 separate species of *Capsicum*: the *Annuum* includes almost all the most common chiles like ancho, ball, cayenne, jalapeños, pasilla, serrano. Most of the chiles found in South America, like the aji, belong to the *Baccatum* species, while the Habañero and New Mexican or Anaheim chiles belong to the *Chinense* species. Given the widespread use of chiles in modern times, it is hard to believe that until the end of the 15th century, the people of Central and South America were the only ones using them in their cuisine. The Spanish and Portuguese took chiles to their colonies in Africa, Asia, and India, where they were immediately incorporated into the local cuisines. By the end of the 16th century, chiles were known around the world and had become a major source of flavoring for millions of people.

There are hundreds of chile varieties throughout the world, and one variety can have several different names, which is a source of confusion for the occasional chile buyer. In North America, chiles tend to keep their Spanish, Mexican, or South American names. In Europe, chiles come via Africa or the Far East, where they are named differently. To confuse things even further, supermarkets tend to name the chiles by their country of origin, hence Thai, Indian, and Kenyan.

Outside places like Mexico, India, South America, and Spain, where they are part of a gastronomic heritage, chiles are often considered only as a source of heat. The variety of subtle flavors and the uses of fresh and dried chiles are just beginning to be discovered and appreciated. The 'heat' comes from capsaicin, a bitter alkaloid concentrated mostly in the seeds and internal ribs or veins, which is measured in units called Scovilles. A mild chile, such as Anaheim, rates 300–600 Scoville units, while the hottest of all the chiles, the habañero, rates 200,000–350,000 Scoville units. As a general rule, the smaller the chile, the hotter it will be. Small chiles also tend to have lots more seeds and veins. As a rough guideline, expect the same heat from fresh and dried chiles, but as with dried fruit, dried chiles have a more intense and richer flavor, especially the mild large ones.

Fresh chiles are a very good source of vitamin C, while powdered chile is rich in vitamin A. Chiles have been used in folk medicine for centuries and are believed to cure numerous illnesses, including bronchitis. They are also believed to help digestion and relieve congested noses. One of the reasons for their success in the hot areas of the world is that their spiciness makes people perspire, which lowers the body temperature.

While it cannot be said that chile-eating is addictive, the palate does get used to the burning sensation they produce, so regular consumption means that hotter and hotter food is needed to give any impact.

Cooking with chiles

It is important to remember the following points when cooking with chiles.

1. The longer the chile is cooked in a dish, the hotter the result. Capsaicin is not destroyed by heat or freezing, so start with very little chile and adjust at the end of cooking.

2. Chile pods of the same variety from the same tree vary in hotness, so taste a little piece before adding to a dish.

3. Chiles vary enormously in flavor, as well as in heat, so if possible, find out which variety you are using (see chile chart, pages 195–9). There is no way of decreasing the heat once the dish is cooked, although adding sugar is believed to help. But since one can add just so much sugar to a savory dish, it is best to taste the chile beforehand.

4. Commercially made chili sauces tend to contain too much vinegar and too many spices; they make up with heat what they lack in flavor. Homemade chile paste and sauces are very easy to make and keep for a long time in the refrigerator. They can be used in a variety of dishes, such as dips, dressings, pasta, potatoes, rice, soups, stews, and sandwiches, to name just a few.

5. Sensitivity to hot food varies enormously; what is unbearably hot for some is quite mild for others. To sooth the burning sensation of chiles, dairy products are useful. Try a little yogurt, milk, or sour cream to take away the heat. Alternatively, a mouthful of bland food, such as tortillas, rice, beans, or potatoes, will also help "wash off" the heat from chiles.

    Capsaicin, the chemical responsible for the hotness of chiles, dissolves in milk fat or alcohol, so contrary to popular belief, high-alcohol drinks, such as tequila or vodka, are more cooling than beer. (Alcohol also acts as a painkiller.) Very cold drinks (and that is where the beer comes in) are also thought to be a good antidote, simply because they numb the taste buds and make the "burning" less obvious. The only drink that makes the burning worse is water, so avoid it!

6. To reduce the heat of chiles before cooking, remove the seeds and veins, which contain around 80 percent of their heat. Soak the flesh in 3 parts vinegar to 1 part salt for 1 hour, rinse and follow the recipe.

Buying, storing, and drying chiles

How to prepare chiles

WARNING Capsaicin, the substance in chiles responsible for their heat, can cause a very painful burning sensation if it comes into contact with the eyes, mouth, or sensitive skin. Be sure to follow the instructions below.

FRESH CHILES

Buy firm, smooth-skinned chiles with a bright color. If the skin is wrinkled, the chiles have lost their moisture and will quickly start to decay where soft spots appear. Fresh chiles lose their flavor and moisture quickly, so avoid buying large quantities. Store wrapped in a cool, dry place, preferably the vegetable drawer in the refrigerator.

DRIED CHILES

Look for clear, plastic packaging so that the chiles can be checked. Large dried chiles should be supple and fragrant, a sign that their natural oils have not been lost during the drying process. Once opened, small or large dried chiles should be put into an airtight container and kept in a cool place. Alternatively, they can be frozen and defrosted just before being used. If they are dusty, just wipe them with a dry cloth.

DRYING CHILES

If you have a large amount of chiles on hand, they can be dried at home very easily. Most chile varieties are suitable for drying, but only fully matured and preferably red chiles should be used. Using a large needle with heavy cotton thread, string the pods through their flesh close to their stems and hang in a warm, dry place inside, or a sunny, breezy place outside for a week, or until they are completely dry. They can then be crushed, powdered, frozen, or kept in an airtight container.

PREPARING FRESH CHILES

Wearing rubber gloves, cut the chile in half and wash under running water, discarding the seeds. To improve the flavor, and because the skin can be tough and bitter, chiles can be peeled. Grill or roast them until their skin is black, or, if using a small quantity, char them over an open gas flame using tongs or a fork. Once the skin is black, put the chiles in a plastic bag until they are cool enough to handle. Still using rubber gloves, remove the skins and discard. Any surfaces that came into contact with chiles should be washed very carefully.

PREPARING DRIED CHILES

Large dried chiles are safe enough to handle until they have been soaked, after which they should be handled as fresh chiles. To prepare a dried chile, snap off the stalk and cut the pod in half lengthwise. Brush out and discard the seeds, removing the internal ribs or veins. Tear the chile into small pieces or snip with a scissors, place in a bowl, and cover with hot water or stock. Set aside to soak for at least 20 minutes. The smaller varieties of dried chile should be handled with care and gloves should be worn. They do not need soaking and can be added directly to soups, stews, and sauces.

Dried chiles develop a depth of flavor and increase their pungency if roasted or grilled for 5 minutes in a medium-hot oven or 3 minutes under a hot broiler. They can also be dry-roasted in a nonstick skillet until they begin to soften, about 2 minutes on each side. Overdoing it will make the chiles taste bitter.

FRESH CHILES

Fresh Chiles

1. **Anaheim**

2. **Red Fresno**

3. **Jalapeños**

4. **Habañeros**

5. **Dutch or Westland**

6. **Wax**

7. **Thai or Indian**

Fresh Chiles

NAME/CHARACTERISTICS	COLORS	USES	SUBSTITUTES	HEAT SCALE
AJI or orange Thai chile (*Capsicum baccatum*) Aji is a generic name for any chile in South America. It measures 3–5 inches long and ½ inch wide with thin flesh. It has a fruity flavor and is quite hot. When dried it is called canagueño.	Yellow to orange.	In all Peruvian dishes, particularly ceviches. It is also good pickled in any Thai or Malayan dishes.	Brazilian malagueta (smaller and hotter) or 2 Indian chiles to 1 Aji.	🌶🌶🌶🌶
ANAHEIM or New Mexican (*Capsicum chinense*) 4–6 inches long, 1 inch wide and flattish. Smooth medium-thick flesh and a mild, sweet, vegetable flavor. The red Anaheim is sweeter than the green and also known as chile Colorado.	Green and red.	Very versatile chile. Flavor is improved by roasting, a delicious addition to roasted sweet pepper salads, sandwich fillings & green chile sauces.	New Mexico green or red are a little bit hotter, but a good substitute.	🌶🌶
CAYENNE (*Capsicum annuum*) 3–5 inches long. Long, thin, sharply pointed. The many varieties include Hot Portugal or Ring of Fire, grown for their heat.	Green, red, yellow.	Primarily used for grinding into cayenne pepper or in bottled sauces.	Thai or Indian	🌶🌶🌶🌶
DUTCH or holland red chile, or Red or Green Westland chile 4 inches long with a curved, tapering point; it has a thick flesh with a strong, fresh flavor.	Bright red or green.	Salsas, pickles, stews, soups, and pipians (see Glossary, page 280).	Red Thai or frescos.	🌶🌶🌶
FRESNO or Kenyan (*Capsicum chinense*) 2 inches long, 1 inch wide on the shoulders, tapering to a round end. Sometimes mistaken for a red jalapeño, fresno has a medium-thick flesh with a sweet flavor.	Light green, red.	Good in everything, raw, cooked or grilled. Used in salsas, ceviches, soups, and stir-fries.	Jalapeño, red or green, although less hot, make a perfect substitute.	🌶🌶🌶
HABAÑERO, or Jamaican hot, Scotch bonnet, rocoto, rocotillo (*Capsicum chinense*) These chiles are all of the same family and have a very similar shape and taste. They are 2 inches long and roundish with an irregular shape which resembles a bonnet. The habañero and its cousins are the hottest chiles in the world with an intense, fruity flavor.	Deep green to orange and light red.	Its fierce heat goes really well with seafood and shellfish. Good for flavoring oils, vinegars, salsas, and pickles.	Any *Capsicum chinense* will be a perfect substitute, although the heat varies slightly.	
JALAPEÑO (*Capsicum chinense*) About 2–3 inches long, 1 inch wide and tapered to a round end. Juicy, thick-fleshed and rather stringy, with a clean, fresh vegetable flavor.	Grass green to dark green or red.	A very popular and versatile chile that can be stuffed or grilled and used in anything from salsas to pickles, marinades to curries.	Fresno, even though slightly hotter, is a good substitute when roasted for salsas.	🌶🌶🌶

CHILES ~ KEY: 🌶🌶🌶🌶 = VERY HOT   🌶 = FIERCELY HOT

NAME/CHARACTERISTICS	COLORS	USES	SUBSTITUTES	HEAT SCALE
PIMIENTO (*Capsicum annuum*) 4 inches long, 3 inches wide, with almost a heart shape. It is a mild chile, with thick flesh and found mostly canned or pickled. Once powdered it becomes paprika, a well-known spice.	Scarlet.	As a substitute for red bell peppers, pimentos can be stuffed, used in sauces and marinades, or grilled and cut into strips for sandwich fillings, salads, or pasta dishes.	Hungarian sweet chile has a paler color but similar flavors and uses.	🌶
POBLANO (*Capsicum annuum*) 5.5 inches long, 3 inches wide on the shoulders, looking like a triangle with a tapered point. The poblano has a thick flesh with a mild but rich flavor. It is the most popular of the fresh chiles in Mexico.	The green-fleshed poblano has a purplish skin color that becomes deep red-brown when ripe.	The green variety is not eaten raw, but is always roasted and skinned and used mainly for stuffing. Poblanos also make good *mole* sauces and pipians (see Glossary, page 280).	Although hotter, New Mexico red can be used.	🌶
SERRANO or Mountain Chile (*Capsicum annuum*) Small, bullet-shaped chiles with a rounded end. Measuring 1–2 inches long, serranos have a thick, smooth flesh with a hard appearance. They are high in acidity with a pungent flavor.	Bright green and scarlet red	Used in salsas, pickles, and relishes; thinly sliced to flavor stews, curries, and other slow-cooking dishes, and also as a decoration chile.	Thai chiles or ajis. (1 Thai to 3 Serranos)	🌶🌶🌶
TABASCO (*Capsicum frutescers*) 1 inch long, these small tapered chiles have a smooth skin and thin flesh. With a very hot and sharp flavor they constitute the main ingredient of the world-famous McIlhenny Tabasco pepper sauce.	Bright yellow, orange or red.	Soups, stews, and flavoring oils.	Brazilian malagueta or Thai chiles	🌶🌶🌶🌶
THAI or Indian chile (*Capsicum annuum*) 1–2 inches long, slender with a pointed end. These are thin-fleshed with lots of seeds.	Bright red and dark green.	Used extensively in Asian cuisines, the Thai chile is very good for flavoring oils and as a decorative element in soups, stews, stir-fries, and noodle dishes.	Serranos or Brazilian malagueta (a bit hotter than the Thai).	🌶🌶🌶🌶
WAX chiles (*Capsicum annuum*) Includes chiles with very different characteristics, such as Hungarian wax, banana, caribe, Santa Fe, Cera, Gierro. Sizes vary from 3–4 inches long and the heat varies from medium to hot. They usually have a sweetish, waxy taste.	Pale yellow green to pale yellow.	Good for salsas (grilled, skinned and cut into strips) and for chile purées.	Use any light yellow chile with thick flesh, but make sure to taste a small piece before using any of them, as hotness can vary.	🌶🌶

DRIED CHILES

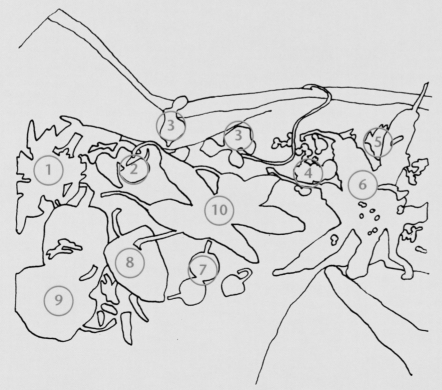

Dried Chiles

1. Cayenne

2. Chipotle

3. Habañero

4. Tepin

5. Bird's Eye

6. Pasilla

7. Cascabel

8. Ancho

9. Mulato

10. Guagillo

Dried Chiles

NAME/CHARACTERISTICS	USES	HEAT SCALE
ANCHO or dried poblano Dark mahogany in color, 4–5 inches long and 3 inches on the shoulders. It is the sweetest dried chile, with a mild flavor of prunes.	Stuffed rajas (strips), *moles*, salsas, soups, stews, chile paste.	
BIRD'S EYE, Pequin, Chile Pequeño or Piquin $\frac{1}{2}$ inch long, small, bright orange to bright red, usually oval or arrowhead-shaped. Thin-fleshed with a smoky, sweet flavor.	Ideal for flavoring oils and vinegars, or in stews and soups.	
CASCABEL, Little Rattle or Chile Bola Round in shape, about $1\frac{1}{2}$ inches long. Dark reddish-brown in color, thick-fleshed and smooth-skinned with lots of seeds. Nutty, woody flavor, slightly acidic and tannic.	Soups, salsas, chile paste with nuts.	
CAYENNE, Ginnie Pepper 2–4 inches long, tapering to a point. Bright red, thin-fleshed. Cayenne chiles have an acidic, tart flavor.	Most used in powdered form and in bottled sauces. Good for flavoring oils and vinegars.	
CHIPOTLE, Chile Ahumado or Meco Chipotle is a smoked, dried red jalapeño. 1 inch long, $\frac{1}{2}$ inch wide, dark brick to coffee color with cream veins and ridges. A distinctive smoky and hot flavor.	Chipotle is good with everything; its smoky flavor gives an interest to all dishes, especially soups, salsas, and stews.	
GUAJILLO 4–6 inches long, 1 inch wide, slightly curved and tapered at the end. Shiny dark cherry in color with thin skin and slightly tannic taste.	Guajillo is widely used in Mexico, mainly in sauces, soups, and stews.	
HABAÑERO 1 inch round, golden orange in color. Thin-fleshed with intense heat, aroma, and flavor. Dried or fresh, the habañero is the hottest chile available. Its rich fruity flavor can be tasted even through all its heat.	It goes particularly well with fish soups and in stews, salsas and in chile pastes. A little goes a long way.	
MULATO 4–5 inches long, 2–3 inches wide. Dark brown in color, the mulato is similar to the ancho, but larger and flatter. It has a medium-thick flesh and a smoky, pungent flavor with hints of tobacco and licorice.	Very good stuffed, in salsas and mixed with pasilla for mole sauces.	
PASILLA or Chile Negro 5–6 inches long, 1 inch wide. Shiny graphite color, with twisted, tapered body. Licorice and earthy flavor. It can be used instead of ancho, but it has a more pungent flavor.	Ideal chile for any seafood. Pasilla is also used in powdered form and can be used in any salsa.	

Chile-Flavored Oil

This oil can be used to make salad dressings, drizzled over potatoes or rice, used as a cooking oil or in marinades. You will need a 2¹/₂ cup (20-ounce) heatproof glass bottle.

Ingredients

1³/₄ cups peanut oil
10 dried tabasco or bird's eye chiles (see page 199)
1 teaspoon coriander seeds
1 teaspoon cayenne pepper
1 marjoram sprig or 1 teaspoon dried marjoram

Method

1. Place the glass bottle in a pan filled with water; make sure the bottle fills with water and bring to the boil. Boil for at least 10 minutes, remove from the water, drain, and leave to dry completely.

2. Warm the oil in a large saucepan. Add the chiles, coriander seeds, cayenne, and marjoram; mix carefully and simmer for 5 minutes.

3. Strain the oil through a funnel into the sterilized bottle. Add some of the chiles to the bottle for a decorative effect, but discard the remaining flavorings.

4. Cover and keep in a cool place. Alternatively, the chiles and herbs can be left in the oil and the bottle topped up with fresh oil as you use the original contents. This however, will gradually dilute the flavor.

Desserts
and Ice-creams

DESSERTS AND ICE-CREAMS

Although fresh fruit is the dessert most commonly served on a daily basis in Latin America, there are numerous dessert recipes for those special and festive occasions. Of these, crème caramel and milk pudding are the undisputed favorites. The former, probably the first dessert a young cook will learn to make, is intensely sweet and may be flavored with vanilla, chocolate, sweet corn, cheese, nuts, or coffee. Milk pudding is, if anything, even sweeter and, traditionally, a labor of love. Sugar and milk are boiled together for hours and must be stirred constantly. It is no exaggeration to say that the biggest gastronomic advance in Latin America has been the introduction of sweetened condensed milk in cans. Now milk pudding can be produced by boiling an unopened can of condensed milk for a mere $1\frac{1}{2}$ hours. Of course, purists deride this method . . .

The flavorings used in sweet dishes are many and various. Chocolate, a product native to Mexico, is used in desserts, cakes, and drinks, but chocolate bars, as eaten in the northern hemisphere, take second place to the wide range of sweets made with coconut, sweet potatoes, nuts, caramel, and candied fruit. Milk fudges, with nuts or coconut and amazingly bright food colorings, are sold in the streets and markets, usually by children, and are a feast for the eyes as well as the stomach.

Cream is very rarely used as an ingredient for making desserts, and seldom served with them; the only exception is ice cream, which generally contains more fruit than cream anyway.

Sugar is used very heavily, mainly because of its keeping properties in hot climates, but also because Latin American countries are large producers of cane sugar, which makes it cheap and readily available.

The following recipes are a mixture of updated classics and new creations inspired by the variety of fruits, nuts, seeds, and flavorings found in Latin America. Many, such as charlottes, mousses, and ice creams, resemble their European ancestors but with an added tropical twist.

Flambé Bananas with Vanilla Ice-cream

Flambé bananas is a very popular dessert in South America and is usually served in good restaurants with a lot of panache.

Ingredients

6 large bananas
Grated zest and juice of 1 lime or lemon
$^1/_2$ teaspoon ground cinnamon
Pinch of ground cloves
$^1/_2$ teaspoon ground allspice
$^1/_4$ cup butter
3 tablespoons brown sugar
Grated zest and juice of 1 orange
3 tablespoons Grand Marnier or Curaçao

To serve: Vanilla Ice Cream (see page 229)

Method

1. Peel the bananas and slice them lengthwise in half. Toss them in the lime or lemon juice to prevent them discoloring.

2. Place the spices in a large skillet and cook over medium heat, stirring constantly, for 1 minute. Add the butter and heat until melted. Add the bananas with the lime juice. Using two wooden spoons, turn the bananas gently, taking care not to crush them. Add the sugar, the orange juice and zest, and the lime zest, and gently toss the bananas in the liquid.

3. Increase the heat to high and continue to cook, shaking the pan occasionally, to allow the bananas to get some color.

4. Place the Grand Marnier in a ladle, heat it over a flame, then pour over the bananas. Light a match, stand back, and light the alcohol. Shake the pan gently until the flames subside.

5. To serve, place 2 banana halves on a plate, add a generous serving of vanilla ice cream, and spoon the remaining sauce over the bananas. Serve at once.

Nut and Coffee Tart with Coffee Cream

Latin American desserts tend to be very sweet but not particularly rich. In this recipe, however, sugar and nuts meet with a vengeance, to make a deliciously rich and sweet confection with just a hint of coffee.

Ingredients

1 recipe Sweet Rich Shortcrust Pastry (see page 251)

For the filling:
2 tablespoons instant coffee granules
$^1/_4$ cup hot water
3 large eggs
$^1/_2$ cup packed dark brown sugar
$^1/_4$ cup corn syrup
Juice of 1 lime
$^1/_2$ cup unsalted butter, melted and cooled
Pinch of salt
$^3/_4$ cup walnuts, coarsely chopped
$^3/_4$ cup Brazil nuts, coarsely chopped
$^1/_2$ cup pine nuts

To serve: $^2/_3$ cup heavy cream
1 teaspoon confectioners' sugar

Method

1. Preheat the oven to 400°F.

2. On a lightly floured surface, roll out the pastry and place in a 9-inch loose-bottomed flan pan. Chill in the refrigerator for 20 minutes.

3. Bake the pastry 'blind' (see page 274), then reduce the oven temperature to 350°F.

4. Place the instant coffee in a large bowl, add the hot water, and stir until the coffee granules are dissolved. Reserve 1 teaspoon of the dissolved coffee for flavoring the cream. Whisk in the eggs, brown sugar, corn syrup, lime juice, butter, and salt. Scatter the nuts onto the bottom of the pastry and gently pour the egg mixture over the nuts.

5. Bake on the middle rack of the oven until set, about 30 minutes. Remove from the oven and transfer to a wire rack to cool.

6. Lightly whip the cream, add the reserved dissolved coffee and sugar, and mix well. Serve with the tart.

Pineapple Charlotte

This is a very popular dessert in Brazil, where it is made using pineapples, peaches, or prunes and layered in a shallow dish instead of in the traditional deep charlotte mold.

Ingredients

$2^{1}/_{2}$ cups water
$1^{1}/_{4}$ cups granulated sugar
$^{1}/_{2}$ of a medium pineapple, peeled, cored, and cut into 1-inch cubes
$^{1}/_{4}$ cup water
2 scant tablespoons unflavored gelatin
$2^{1}/_{2}$ cups milk
4 egg yolks
$^{1}/_{2}$ cup granulated sugar
$^{3}/_{4}$ cup all-purpose flour
5 tablespoons white rum
24 ladyfingers
$^{1}/_{2}$ cup flaked coconut

Method

1. Combine the $2^{1}/_{2}$ cups water with the $1^{1}/_{4}$ cups sugar in a large saucepan. Cook over low heat, stirring occasionally, until the sugar is dissolved, then add the pineapple chunks. Cook 20 minutes or until the pineapple is soft. Drain and reserve the syrup.

2. Place the $^{1}/_{4}$ cup water in a small, heavy saucepan. Sprinkle with the gelatin and let stand for 10 minutes.

3. In a separate saucepan, heat the milk over medium heat until it just comes to a boil. Remove from the heat. In a medium bowl, lightly beat the yolks with the $^{1}/_{2}$ cup sugar. Add the flour and mix thoroughly to form a paste. Pour the hot milk over the flour mixture, mix well, and pour it back into the pan. Cook over low heat for 2 minutes or until it thickens slightly to form a custard.

4. Heat the gelatin over low heat until it is dissolved, about 5 minutes. Stir in half of the rum. Add to the custard and mix well.

5. Add the remaining rum to the reserved pineapple syrup.

6. Line a charlotte mold or soufflé dish ($6^{1}/_{2}$ inches wide x 3 inches deep) with plastic wrap. Dip one ladyfinger at a time into the syrup and place, rounded side out, around the sides of the mold. Place half of the pineapple chunks on the bottom of the mold and pour in half of the custard. Sprinkle with half of the coconut and top with the remaining diced pineapple. Cover with the remaining custard and top with a layer of the remaining ladyfingers.

7. Cover with a piece of lightly oiled plastic wrap, then place a plate and a $^{1}/_{2}$-pound weight on top. Refrigerate at least 6 hours. Unmold and garnish with the remaining coconut.

VARIATIONS: Prune Charlotte: Poach 4 ounces dried prunes in syrup until soft, then follow the recipe.
- Peach Charlotte: Substitute 1 (14 ounce) can sliced peaches, chopped, for the pineapple.
- Add 1 cup toasted and ground peanuts to the custard and dip the ladyfingers in $1^{1}/_{4}$ cups coffee mixed with the rum. Sprinkle the top with toasted ground peanuts.

NOTE: To prepare this recipe in a shallow dish, layer the syrup-dipped ladyfingers alternately with the custard, finishing with a layer of custard. Sprinkle with the coconut, then cover, and chill.

Lime and Lemon Mousse with Pistachio Praline

Lemons are not easily found in South America, so the more commonly grown limes are extensively used. Since limes have a more sour taste than lemons, they help balance the sweetness in this recipe in a very delicious way.

Ingredients

1 can (14 ounces) sweetened condensed
  skimmed milk
Grated zest and juice of 3 limes
Grated zest and juice of 2 lemons
3 egg whites
Pinch of salt
1 tablespoon granulated sugar
$^2/_3$ cup heavy cream

For the praline:
$^1/_4$ cup pistachio nuts, unsalted and shelled
$^1/_4$ cup granulated sugar

Method

1. In a large bowl, whisk the condensed milk with the juice and zest of the limes and lemons until thickened, about 1 minute.

2. In another large bowl, whisk the egg whites with a pinch of salt until stiff but not dry. Add the sugar and whisk until shiny, about 1 minute.

3. Beat the cream until it forms soft peaks.

4. Fold the whipped cream and then the whisked egg whites into the lime and lemon mixture. Taste and add more lemon juice if not tart enough. Pile the mousse into individual glasses or into a large glass serving dish and chill for at least 4 hours.

5. Meanwhile, make the praline: grease a baking sheet. Place the pistachio nuts and sugar in a heavy saucepan and place over low heat. As the sugar begins to melt, stir carefully with a metal spoon to coat the nuts. Continue cooking until the mixture is thoroughly caramelized (browned). Quickly pour the nut mixture into the oiled baking sheet and let stand to cool completely. Break into pieces or pound to a coarse powder in a mortar or blender. This praline mixture can be stored up to a week in an airtight container.

6. Just before serving, cover the mousse completely with a very fine layer of the praline and serve at once.

NOTE: This mousse should have a very tart lime/lemon taste to balance the sweetness of the pistachio praline.

Crunchy Banana Dessert

Bananas are so delicious in the tropics that they are usually eaten fresh. They are sometimes cooked to prevent discoloration, but even then they tend to become quite brown. For optimum flavor, use very ripe bananas in this dessert recipe.

Ingredients

6 ripe bananas
$^1/_2$ cup packed brown sugar
Juice of 1 lime
3 tablespoons water
$^1/_2$ cup *plus* 2 tablespoons plain unflavored
   yogurt
$^3/_4$ cup heavy cream

For the crunchy topping:
$^1/_4$ cup butter
5 tablespoons fresh bread crumbs
$^1/_4$ cup packed brown sugar
$1^1/_2$ teaspoons ground cinnamon

For the garnish:
1 tablespoon confectioners' sugar

Method

1. Peel the bananas and mash with a fork. In a large skillet, combine the mashed bananas with the sugar, lime juice, and water and cook over medium heat about 5 minutes. Transfer to a large bowl, add the yogurt, and mix well.

2. Whip the cream until it forms soft peaks, then gently fold it into the banana mixture. Taste and a few teaspoons lemon juice if it is too sweet. Pour into a glass bowl or individual glasses and refrigerate.

3. To make the crunchy topping: melt the butter in a medium skillet over medium-low heat. Add the bread crumbs and cook, stirring frequently, until the crumbs have absorbed most of the butter and are crisp and golden brown. Add the brown sugar and cinnamon and stir until the crumbs are coated with the caramelized sugar. Transfer to a plate to cool.

4. Just before serving, sprinkle the banana cream with the bread crumb mixture and the confectioners' sugar. Serve at room temperature.

Mexican Bread Pudding

This is a richer and sweeter version of bread and butter pudding. It is delicious served warm or cold. When making it for children, replace the rum with apple juice.

Ingredients

1$^1/_4$ cups raisins
$^3/_4$ cup dried prunes, roughly chopped
$^1/_4$ cup light rum
14 stale white bread slices (about 11 ounces),
    cut into 1-inch cubes
1$^1/_4$ cups walnuts, coarsely chopped
1$^1/_3$ cups light cream
1$^1/_3$ cups milk
1$^1/_3$ cups Applesauce (see page 222)
$^2/_3$ cup granulated sugar
6 tablespoons unsalted butter, melted
3 large eggs, beaten
1 teaspoon ground cinnamon
$^1/_2$ teaspoon ground nutmeg
2 tablespoons plus 2 teaspoons packed brown
    sugar

Method

1. Combine the raisins, prunes, and rum in a bowl and set aside to marinate for 1 hour. Drain and discard the liquid.

2. Preheat the oven to 350°F.

3. Generously butter an 11 x 7$^1/_2$-inch baking dish and scatter the drained raisins and prunes onto the bottom. Cover with the bread pieces and walnuts.

4. Place the cream, milk, applesauce, granulated sugar, melted butter, eggs, cinnamon, and nutmeg in a large bowl and mix well.

5. Strain the egg mixture over the bread and cover the dish with foil. Bake until the center of the pudding is set, about 1 hour.

6. When ready to serve, sprinkle the brown sugar evenly over the pudding and broil until the sugar is slightly caramelized, about 3 minutes. Serve warm or cold.

Tropical Fruit Salad with Cinnamon Crème Chantilly

Fruit salads are very popular everywhere in South America, and the leftovers are usually puréed in a blender with some orange juice to make a fresh fruit shake. Throughout Brazil, fruit bars specialize in making fresh fruit drinks in almost any combination of flavors to suit the customer's taste.

Ingredients

1 ripe mango
2 small ripe papayas
2 bananas
$^1/_2$ fresh pineapple
1 honeydew melon
2 oranges
1 pink grapefruit
4 passion fruit, halved
1 (1-inch) piece gingerroot, peeled and grated
$^2/_3$ cup Coconut Milk (see page 276)
1 tablespoon light rum (optional)

For the crème Chantilly:
2 cup heavy cream
Few drops vanilla essence or $^1/_2$ teaspoon vanilla
  extract
1 tablespoon confectioners' sugar
$^1/_8$ teaspoon ground cinnamon

To serve: Ginger Tuiles (see page 250)

Method

1. Peel the mango, papayas, bananas, pineapple and half of the melon, and cut $1^1/_2$-inch cubes.

2. Peel and segment the oranges and grapefruit and mix with the cubed fruit in a large bowl.

3. Peel the remaining melon half and place the fruit in a blender or food processor. Add the passion-fruit pulp, ginger, coconut milk, and rum and process until smooth. Press the fruit mixture through a sieve and add it to the fruit in the bowl. Mix thoroughly, cover, and refrigerate.

4. Meanwhile make the crème Chantilly. Beat together the cream, vanilla, confectioners' sugar, and cinnamon in a small bowl until the mixture forms soft peaks.

5. To serve: spoon a generous amount of the crème Chantilly over individual servings of fruit salad. Serve with the Ginger Tuiles.

Peruvian Coffee Chocolate Cups

The combination of chocolate and coffee appears in many recipes for desserts, baked goods, and drinks. This is a deliciously rich and creamy dessert which develops a better flavor if made a day in advance.

Ingredients

1 cup whole milk
1 cup light cream
1 vanilla bean, split in half lengthwise
2 tablespoons instant coffee granules
$^{1}/_{4}$ cup granulated sugar
6 tablespoons plus 2 teaspoons water
3 ounces dark chocolate, finely chopped
3 egg yolks
$^{1}/_{4}$ cup granulated sugar

For the garnish:
Chocolate shavings

Method

1. Preheat the oven to 300°F.

2. In a small saucepan, bring the milk, cream, and vanilla bean to a boil. Add the instant coffee granules, stir well until dissolved, and set aside.

3. Place the $^{1}/_{4}$ cup granulated sugar in a heavy saucepan. Add half the water and cook over high heat, stirring occasionally, until the sugar is dissolved. Continue to boil the sugar mixture until it has turned to caramel. Immediately add the remaining water (it will spatter dangerously, so stand back). Stir, then remove the saucepan from the heat. Add the chocolate and stir until melted. Strain the coffee mixture into the caramel/chocolate mixture and mix well.

4. In a medium bowl, beat together the egg yolks and remaining $^{1}/_{4}$ cup granulated sugar with a wooden spoon until pale. Add the milk mixture and mix thoroughly.

5. Strain the mixture into 6 individual ramekins or 1 large soufflé dish and cover with foil. Place the pots in a shallow baking pan and add enough hot water to reach one third of the way up the sides of the ramekins. Bake for 25 minutes (35 minutes if using one large dish) or until just set. Remove from the oven, uncover, and let cool. Refrigerate overnight or for at least 4 hours before serving.

6. Garnish with chocolate shavings.

Grilled Pineapple Skewers with Coconut Ice-cream

Pineapple is a very popular fruit in tropical America, used mainly in sweets, puddings, ice creams, and drinks. Large slices of freshly cut pineapple are sold on market stalls as a fruit snack.

Ingredients

1 large fresh pineapple
1 tablespoon cornstarch
2 tablespoons butter

For the marinade:
Grated zest and juice of 2 limes
2 tablespoons brown sugar
1 teaspoon ground cinnamon
$^{1}/_{2}$ teaspoon ground allspice
2 tablespoons honey
2 tablespoons rum
Grated zest and juice of $^{1}/_{2}$ orange

For the garnish:
Mint leaves

To serve: Coconut Ice Cream (see page 226)

Method

1. Remove the peel from the pineapple and cut into 4 lengthwise pieces. Remove and discard the core, then cut the flesh into 2-inch cubes.

2. Mix all the marinade ingredients together in a large bowl, add the pineapple chunks, and toss well. Cover and let marinate at room temperature for 1 hour.

3. Heat the grill to high. Brush a baking sheet with oil.

4. Thread the pineapple cubes onto 4 large or 8 small skewers and baste with some of the marinade. Put the skewers on the oiled baking sheet. Grill for 5 minutes on each side or until the pineapple is lightly browned.

5. Meanwhile, mix the cornstarch with 2 tablespoons of the marinade. Pour the remaining marinade into a small pan and bring to a boil. Add the cornstarch mixture and cook, stirring constantly, until slightly thickened, about 5 minutes.

6. Whisk in the butter with a fork or small whisk until the sauce is shiny and the butter completely melted.

7. To serve: spoon some of the sauce onto a dessert plate, add 2 small scoops of coconut ice cream on one side, and arrange the pineapple skewer on the other side. Garnish with a sprig of mint and serve with any remaining sauce.

Pineapple and Star Anise Compote

This easy-to-make recipe is sometimes cooked until the compote almost sets; it can then be rolled into small balls, dusted with sugar, and served as petits fours or used as a stuffing for stoned prunes. In any form it is simply delicious.

Ingredients

1 large ripe pineapple
Granulated sugar (see step 1)
2 whole star anise
Grated zest and juice of 1 lemon
$1/2$ teaspoon ground cloves
Pinch of ground cinnamon

To serve: Coconut Ice Cream (see page 226)
Light Peanut Oil Cake (see page 237)

Method

1. Peel, core, and cut the pineapple into chunks. Weigh the fruit, then measure out the same weight of granulated sugar.

2. In a blender, process half of the sugar with the whole star anise until the sugar is powdery and the star anise is finely ground.

3. In a large saucepan, mix both sugars, the pineapple chunks, lemon zest and juice, ground cloves, and cinnamon and let stand for 30 minutes.

4. Bring the mixture to a boil over medium heat and cook, stirring constantly, until the pineapple breaks up into shreds and almost no liquid is left, about 25 minutes.

5. Serve warm with Coconut Ice Cream or use to sandwich the Light Peanut Oil Cake. This is also delicious served well chilled with plain yogurt.

VARIATION: For a Caribbean flavor, add $3/4$ cup freshly grated coconut in step 3.

'Burnt' Coconut Crème Caramel

Crème caramel, known as *flan* in Spanish, is a favorite dessert throughout Latin America, where it is made in a variety of flavors, including cheese, walnut, chocolate, sweet corn, and coffee. It is usually made using sweetened condensed milk and is much sweeter than its European counterpart.

Ingredients

$^3/_4$ cup flaked coconut
$^1/_2$ cup granulated sugar
$^1/_4$ cup water
4 eggs
2 tablespoons granulated sugar
$2^1/_3$ cups milk

Method

1. Preheat the oven to 350°F.

2. Place the coconut on a baking sheet and bake for 20 minutes or until lightly toasted, stirring occasionally.

3. Reduce the oven temperature to 300°F. Place a 6-cup ring mold or gratin dish in the oven for 10 minutes.

4. Place the $^1/_2$ cup granulated sugar in a heavy saucepan with $^1/_4$ cup water and allow it to melt slowly over low heat. When the sugar has melted completely, bring it to a boil over high heat and cook until it becomes a rich brown caramel. Stir in half of the toasted coconut, then pour the coconut mixture into the warmed mold, tilting it carefully to coat the inside. Cool completely.

5. In a bowl, beat the eggs and remaining 2 tablespoons sugar with a wooden spoon until pale.

6. Bring the milk just to a boil and stir into the egg mixture along with the remaining toasted coconut. Mix thoroughly and strain it into the caramel-coated mold.

7. Fill a deep baking dish with hot water and place the filled mold in the middle. Bake for about 1 hour or until the custard is set. Remove from the oven and cool in the mold. Refrigerate overnight or for at least 4 hours before unmolding to serve.

VARIATIONS:
- Walnut: Add 1 cup ground walnuts along with the toasted coconut in step 6, then follow the recipe as above. Unmold the pudding and decorate with walnut halves.
- Chocolate: Add 1 cup cocoa powder along with the toasted coconut in step 6, then follow the recipe. After unmolding the pudding, decorate with chocolate shavings.

NOTE: Heating the mold slightly helps the caramel coating to stick more easily and evenly.

Quince Purée

Quinces belong to the apple and pear family; in fact, they look very much like apples but are not eaten raw. Quinces can be used with apples, or as a substitute for them, in tarts, pies, and pork dishes. When cooked, the firm, pale yellow, dry flesh becomes pale pink. Quinces are used to make a very popular fruit paste called *membrillo* in Spain, *marmelada* in Portugal, and *pâté de coing* or *cotignac* in France, which is usually eaten with soft cheese.

Ingredients

1 pound quinces
1/2 cup granulated sugar
2/3 cup black grape juice
2 teaspoons ground allspice
Juice and 2 strips of peel from 1 lemon

To serve: Brazil Nut Shortbread (see page 246)

Method

1. Peel, core, and thinly slice the quinces.

2. Place the quince slices in a large, heavy saucepan with the sugar, grape juice, allspice, lemon peel and juice, and mix thoroughly. Bring to a boil over high heat, reduce the heat to low, and simmer until the fruit is very soft, about 35 minutes.

3. Remove and discard the lemon peel and mash the fruit with a potato masher or fork, leaving a bit of texture. If the mixture is too watery, continue to boil it until all of the liquid has evaporated. Serve warm or cold with Brazil Nut Shortbread.

NOTE: The puree can be served with yogurt, crème fraîche, or cakes.

French Pancakes (Crêpes)

Many classic French recipes, such as crêpes, are now part of the cosmopolitan cook's repertoire. Crêpes are most commonly used in savory dishes, but are equally delicious served with sweet fillings.

Ingredients

$^3/_4$ cup all-purpose flour
Pinch salt
1 egg
1 egg yolk
$1^1/_3$ cups milk, or milk and water mixed
1 tablespoon vegetable oil
Additional oil for cooking

Method

1. Sift the flour and salt together into a small bowl, then make a "well" in the center, exposing the bottom of the bowl.

2. Place the egg and egg yolk in the well with a little of the milk.

3. Using a wooden spoon or whisk, mix the eggs and milk, gradually drawing in the flour from the sides.

4. When the mixture reaches the consistency of light cream, beat well and stir in the 1 tablespoon oil.

5. Add the rest of the milk; the consistency should now be that of thin cream. (The batter can also be made by placing all of the ingredients in a blender and blending for a few seconds, taking care not to over-mix.)

6. Cover the bowl and refrigerate for about 30 minutes. (This allows the starch cells to swell, giving a lighter result.)

7. Prepare a crêpe pan or skillet by heating well and brushing with oil. Pancakes are not actually fried in fat—the purpose of the oil is simply to prevent sticking.

8. When the pan is ready, pour in about 1 tablespoon batter and swirl about the pan until evenly spread onto the bottom and up the side.

9. Place the pan over the heat for 1 minute, then use a spatula and your fingers to turn the pancake over, and cook the other side until brown. (Pancakes should be extremely thin, so if the first one is too thick, add a little extra milk to the batter. The first pancake is unlikely to be perfect, and is often discarded.)

10. Make up all the pancakes, turning them out onto a clean towel or plate.

Crème Anglaise

This custard sauce is an essential part of many puddings, such as charlottes and tarts, but it is equally delicious served on its own.

Ingredients

1¹/3 cups milk

1 vanilla bean, split in half lengthwise

2 egg yolks

1 tablespoon granulated sugar

4 drops vanilla essence or 1 teaspoon vanilla extract (optional)

Method

1. Bring the milk and split vanilla bean to a boil over medium-high heat

2. Mix the egg yolks and sugar in a bowl. Remove the vanilla bean from the pan and pour the milk over the egg yolk mixture, stirring constantly. Mix well and return to the pan.

3. Stir over low heat until the mixture thickens enough to coat the back of a spoon, 8–10 minutes. Do not boil. Pour into a cold bowl.

4. Add the vanilla essence, if using.

VARIATIONS: To flavor the Crème Anglaise, add any of the following to the milk instead of the vanilla bean.
- grated zest of 1 orange plus 2 tablespoons Grand Marnier.
- 1 (1-inch) piece of gingerroot, peeled and grated, plus 1 teaspoon ground ginger.
- 1 cinnamon stick plus 1/2 teaspoon ground cinnamon.
- 1 tablespoon instant coffee granules.

Or, at the end of the cooking time, you can add the sieved pulp of 4 passion fruit plus 1 tablespoon rum.

Milk Pudding

Milk pudding is made by cooking milk and sugar over low heat until the mixture thickens and becomes toffee-colored. This popular dessert is called *dulce de leche* or *leche quemada* in Spanish-speaking countries, and *doce de leite* in Brazil.

Although easy to make, milk pudding is time consuming to prepare and it needs constant stirring to prevent it from sticking to the bottom of the pan. It can be cooked to various consistencies; at the " spoon" stage it has the consistency of soft-set jam, but it may be cooked until it is solid enough to cut, like a fudge. It can be made by boiling an unopened can of sweetened condensed milk in water for 1¹/2 hours, but the result, even though delicious, does not have the same delicate texture and flavor achieved by the slow-cooking method.

Two versions of milk pudding are given opposite: one is a traditional recipe and the other a short-cut taken from *The Book of Latin American Cooking*, by Elisabeth Lambert Ortiz.

Traditional Milk Pudding

Ingredients

7$^1/_4$ cups whole milk
3 cups granulated sugar
1 teaspoon baking soda

Method

1. Mix the milk, sugar, and soda together in a large, heavy saucepan and bring to a boil over high heat, stirring continuously. Once the milk has boiled, reduce the heat to low and simmer, uncovered, stirring every 5 minutes, until the mixture is reduced by one third, about 1$^1/_2$ hours.

2. Increase the heat to medium and stir constantly with a wooden spoon until the mixture is light toffee-colored and thick enough for you to see the bottom of the pan when the spoon is drawn across it, about 45 minutes to 1 hour.

3. Remove the saucepan from the heat and beat the mixture with a wire whisk until creamy and cool, about 2 minutes. Cover and refrigerate for up to 3 weeks or indefinitely in sterilized jam jars. The mixture can be used as a filling for cakes or served on its own.

NOTE: This recipe is very good for using large quantities of milk and the ratio is 1 cup granulated sugar for each 2$^2/_3$ cups milk. The zest of 1 lime or $^1/_2$ an orange can be added to the milk at the beginning of cooking for a nice flavor. Or, for variety, chopped nuts or raisins soaked in liqueur can be added at the end.

Colombian Milk Pudding

This Colombian recipe is a compromise between the traditional method and the 'boil in the can' one. The result is a creamy milk pudding.

Ingredients

1 can (14 ounces) evaporated milk
1 can (14 ounces) skimmed, sweetened condensed milk

Method

1. Mix the ingredients together in a heavy saucepan and bring to a boil over high heat. Reduce the heat to low and simmer, stirring constantly, until the mixture is thick and toffee-colored, about 25 minutes.

2. Transfer to a bowl and refrigerate until ready to serve. It will keep up to one week in the refrigerator, but indefinitely if poured into sterilized jars while still hot.

NOTE: A traditional way of serving milk pudding is with a thick slice of cheese (mozzarella, Gouda or Edam) and a cup of strong, black coffee.

Apple Sauce

A slight variation on traditional applesauce, this version can be used as an ingredient in other recipes or eaten on its own with yogurt or ice cream.

Ingredients

1 pound cooking apples
Finely grated zest of 1 lime
$1/2$ teaspoon ground allspice
3 tablespoons water
2 teaspoons sugar
1 tablespoon butter

Method

1. Peel, quarter, core, and slice the apples.

2. Place in a heavy saucepan with the lime zest, allspice, water, and sugar. Cover and cook over low heat until the apples are soft.

3. Beat in the butter, cool slightly, and add extra sugar, if required. Serve hot or cold.

Poaching Syrup

This is a basic syrup recipe which can be flavored in many ways and used to poach. Cinnamon sticks, star anise, citrus rind, and herbs such as rosemary and thyme can all be used with tasty results.

Ingredients

1$\frac{1}{3}$ cups granulated sugar
2$\frac{2}{3}$ cups water

Method

1. Place the sugar and water in a large skillet and cook over low heat until the sugar is dissolved. Add any spices or flavorings to taste.

2. Increase the heat to high and bring to a boil without stirring.

3. Boil until the syrup reaches the desired concentration. Use as required.

NOTE: Stirring causes sugar crystals to form on the sides of the pan. Should this happen, dip a clean pastry brush into hot water and use it to brush the side of the pan to dissolve the crystals.

Mango and Passion-fruit Ice-cream   MAKES ABOUT 4 CUPS

Mangoes are commonly used to make ice creams, but passion fruit is more often used for ice lollies. The mixture of both is certain to please Latins and Europeans alike!

Ingredients

3 large, very ripe mangoes, peeled
4 passion fruit, cut in half
$\frac{2}{3}$ cup confectioners' sugar
Juice of 1 lemon
$\frac{1}{3}$ cup granulated sugar
$\frac{1}{2}$ cup water
6 egg yolks
1$\frac{1}{3}$ cups heavy cream

Method

1. Remove the flesh from the mangoes and passion fruit and place in a food processor along with the confectioners' sugar and lemon juice. Process to a purée, press through a sieve, and set aside.

2. Place the granulated sugar and water in a saucepan and cook over low heat until the sugar is completely dissolved. Increase the heat to high and boil to the thread stage (see page 282). Cool 1 minute.

3. Place the egg yolks in a large bowl. Add the sugar syrup and whisk until the mixture is thick and mousse-like. Do not allow the syrup to come into contact with the whisk when adding it to the yolks, or it will solidify.

4. Beat the cream until it forms soft peaks, then fold in the mango purée and the egg yolk mixture. Pour into a freezer container and freeze. When partially frozen, beat again with a whisk and freeze until firm.

Peanut Crunch Ice-cream

Peanut recipes are great favorites in many Latin American countries, especially when they also appeal to the nations' sweet tooth.

Ingredients

$^1/_2$ cup granulated sugar
$^1/_4$ cup water
$^3/_4$ cup unsalted, shelled and toasted peanuts
$1^3/_4$ cups milk
$1^1/_3$ cups heavy cream
3 tablespoons creamy peanut butter
$^2/_3$ cup granulated sugar
6 egg yolks
Few drops of vanilla essence or $^1/_2$ teaspoon
vanilla extract

Method

1. Grease a baking sheet. Place the $^1/_2$ cup granulated sugar in a heavy saucepan with the water and cook over low heat until the sugar is dissolved. When it is dissolved completely, increase the heat to high and boil the liquid until it is caramel-colored. Remove the pan from the heat, add the peanuts, then quickly pour the mixture onto the greased tray and let cool.

2. Combine the milk, cream, peanut butter, and $^2/_3$ cup sugar in a heavy saucepan and bring to a boil.

3. In a large bowl, beat the egg yolks with the vanilla until frothy. Add the scalded milk mixture, whisking constantly. Pour into a shallow dish or 2 ice cube trays. Let cool.

4. Freeze the ice cream until solid but still soft enough to leave an impression when pressed with a finger.

5. When the peanut and caramel crunch is completely cooled, break it into pieces with a rolling pin.

6. Place the ice cream into a cold bowl, break it up, then beat it with an electric mixer or rotary beater until smooth, pale, and creamy. Fold in the peanut and caramel chunks and refreeze. Remove from the freezer 20 minutes before serving.

Guava, Cinnamon and Ginger Ice-cream

Guava is popular in all tropical countries; its delicate flavor and strong aroma make a delicious ice cream.

Ingredients

2 cans (14 ounces each) guava halves in syrup, undrained
1 strip lemon zest
1 teaspoon ground cinnamon
$1/4$ cup confectioners' sugar
1-inch piece of gingerroot, peeled and grated
Juice of 1 lime
$1^{1}/3$ cups heavy cream, lightly whipped

Method

1. Combine all ingredients except the cream in a large saucepan and bring to a boil.

2. Reduce the heat to low, cover, and simmer 20 minutes. Discard the lemon zest. Transfer the mixture to a blender or food processor and process until smooth. Press the mixture through a sieve and let cool.

3. Fold the lightly whipped cream into the guava purée. Taste, and if too sweet, add a few more drops of lime juice. Chill, then freeze. When partially frozen, whisk well and return to the freezer.

NOTE: If fresh guavas are available, use 1 pound. Peel the fruit with a potato peeler, cut in half, and poach gently in sugar syrup (see page 223) with the lemon rind and cinnamon until very soft. Remove the guavas from the syrup and boil the syrup to the thread stage (see page 282). Process the guavas with $1/3$ cup of the syrup and follow the recipe as above.

Coconut Ice-cream

If one ingredient can represent the essence of tropical food, it has to be the coconut. This fruit is used for drinks, ice creams, puddings, savory dishes, biscuits and cakes and is delicious when mixed with other fruits in combinations invariably called 'tropical' or 'exotic.' It is essential to use fresh coconut in this recipe.

Ingredients

$2^{1}/2$ cups finely grated fresh coconut (see page 276)
$2^{2}/3$ cups coconut milk
1 egg
1 egg yolk
$1/2$ cup granulated sugar
$2^{2}/3$ cups heavy cream

Method

1. Heat the fresh coconut with the coconut milk in a small saucepan.

2. Place the egg, yolk, and sugar in the top of a double boiler or a bowl set over, not in, a pan of simmering water and whisk until light and fluffy.

3. When the milk and coconut mixture has nearly come to a boil, pour it over the egg mixture, and whisk well. Let cool.

4. Whip the cream until it forms soft peaks and fold it into the coconut mixture. Transfer it to another bowl, if necessary, and freeze.

5. When partially frozen, rewhisk the ice cream and refreeze.

Cinnamon and Vanilla Ice-cream

Dark brown sugar gives this ice cream a beautiful color, which is enhanced by the distinctive flavors of cinnamon and vanilla—simply irresistible!

Ingredients

1 vanilla bean, split in half lengthwise
$1^1/_3$ cups heavy cream
$1^3/_4$ cups milk
2 tablespoons granulated sugar
3 cinnamon sticks, broken
1 teaspoon ground cinnamon
6 egg yolks
$1^1/_3$ cups packed brown sugar

Method

1. In a large saucepan, mix the vanilla bean, heavy cream, milk, granulated sugar, cinnamon sticks, and ground cinnamon. Bring to a boil, stirring frequently. Remove from the heat, cover, and set aside for 30 minutes.

2. Beat the yolks with the brown sugar until well combined. Gradually add the strained milk mixture. Pour the mixture back into the same pan and cook over low heat, stirring constantly, until the mixture thickens slightly.

3. Pour into a freezer-proof container and chill. Freeze the mixture until solid but still soft enough to yield to pressure when pressed with a finger, about 3 hours.

4. Transfer the ice cream to a cold bowl, break it up, then whisk it, or proces it in a blender or food processor until smooth, pale, and creamy. Refreeze.

5. Remove from the freezer 20 minutes before serving.

Sweetcorn Ice-cream

Corn is used in so many Latin American dishes that it comes as no surprise to find sweet corn ice cream. It has a creamy, rich texture with a fresh, clean flavor of corn.

Ingredients

4 large ears of corn on the cob, uncooked
$1^1/_3$ cups heavy cream
$2^2/_3$ cups milk
6 egg yolks
$^1/_2$ cup granulated sugar
$^1/_2$ teaspoon vanilla essence or 1 teaspoon vanilla extract

Method

1. Scrape the corn kernels from the cobs with a sharp knife. Process the kernels in a blender with the heavy cream and milk until smooth. Pour into a large saucepan, bring to a boil, and set aside to cool completely.

2. Strain the mixture, pressing the kernels with the back of a spoon to extract all of the liquid.

3. Beat the egg yolks and sugar until well blended. Whisk in the milky corn liquid. Return it to the pan and cook over low heat, stirring constantly, until the custard coats the back of the spoon. Do not boil. Add the vanilla essence. Strain the mixture into a shallow tray and allow to cool. Freeze.

4. Once frozen, take the ice cream out of the freezer and allow to soften at room temperature. Process or whisk it to remove the ice crystals.

5. Place the ice cream back in the container and refreeze.

Pineapple Ice-cream

Pineapples have a high acid content, so they freeze better in cream-based ice creams than sorbets.

Ingredients

1 large pineapple
1^3/$_4$ cups water
^{3}/$_4$ cup granulated sugar
4 egg yolks
1^1/$_3$ cups heavy cream, lightly whipped
3 tablespoons light rum

Method

1. Peel the pineapple, remove the core, and cut the flesh into large chunks.

2. Place the water and sugar into a large skillet and cook over low heat until the sugar has dissolved. Add the pineapple chunks and bring to a boil over high heat. Reduce the heat to low and simmer until the pineapple is cooked, about 30 minutes. Strain the liquid, return it to the pan, and return to a boil. Reserve the pineapple for later use.

3. Boil the liquid to the thread stage (see page 282). Cool for 1 minute. Whisk the egg yolks and gradually pour in the sugar syrup, making sure it does not touch the whisk or it will solidify. Whisk until the mixture is very thick and leaves a ribbon trail. Cool for 2 minutes.

4. Process or blend the pineapple to a purée. Add the purée, whipped cream, and rum to the mousse mixture and mix thoroughly. Pour into a container, chill, then freeze.

5. When partially frozen, transfer the ice cream to a cold bowl, break it up, then whisk until smooth, pale, and creamy. Refreeze.

6. Remove from the freezer 15 minutes before serving.

VARIATION: For a hint of coconut, reduce the heavy cream to ^{3}/$_4$ cup and blend ^{1}/$_2$ cup creamed coconut together with the pineapple chunks.

NOTE: For a more intense pineapple flavor, use pineapple juice instead of water.

Rich Vanilla Ice-cream

This is a basic vanilla ice cream recipe to which fruit purées, chopped nuts, or liqueurs may be added (see variations below).

Ingredients

¼ cup granulated sugar
½ cup water
1 vanilla bean, split in half lengthwise
3 egg yolks
1 ¾ cups heavy or light cream

Method

1. Place the sugar, water, and vanilla bean in a saucepan and cook over low heat until the sugar is dissolved, stirring frequently.

2. When the sugar is completely dissolved, bring the syrup to a boil and cook to the thread stage (see page 282). Allow to cool for 1 minute, then remove the vanilla bean, scrape out the black seeds, and return the bean to the syrup.

3. Whisk the egg yolks until frothy and gradually whisk in the sugar syrup, making sure it does not touch the whisk or it will solidify. Whisk until the mixture is very thick and leaves a ribbon trail. Cool, whisking occasionally.

4. In a large bowl, beat the cream until it forms soft peaks. Fold it into the egg yolk mixture and freeze.

5. When the ice cream is partially frozen, whisk again and return it to the freezer. (If you wish to add other flavorings, do so at this stage, then refreeze.)

VARIATIONS: Almost anything can be added to this basic recipe: try chopped prunes soaked in port, caramelized almonds, passion-fruit purée, or coffee liqueur.

Cakes, Breads, Cookies, and Pastry

CAKES, BREADS, COOKIES, AND PASTRY

Cakes and pastries are very popular throughout Latin America, not as desserts but as mid-morning or afternoon snacks. Many sweet dishes are based on traditional Spanish and Portuguese recipes, and some are still made in identical circumstances. For example, in Spain enormous quantities of egg whites were used in the making of sherry, and the leftover yolks were donated to convents, where they were transformed into cakes and confections. Even though sherry was never produced in the New World, Spanish nuns took the tradition of convent baking with them when they went as missionaries to Mexico and Peru, the two most important countries in colonial times. The tradition continues to this day, with nuns, novices, and orphan girls producing elaborate handmade cakes and sweets—a source of income and pride for the convents involved. Their wedding cakes are also very sought after, not only for their exquisite sugar work, but also because they are believed to bring good fortune to newlyweds.

Brazilian desserts and pastries are invariably very sweet and rich in eggs—a legacy from the Portuguese. While Mexican baking also uses large quantities of sugar and eggs, it shows more Spanish influence in its use of nuts, particularly almonds. With time, most recipes began to incorporate native ingredients, such as chocolate, vanilla, cashew nuts, and peanuts.

Most cakes are simple creations: Swiss rolls filled with milk pudding or guava paste, and sponge cakes made with almonds, walnuts, chocolate, cornmeal, and coconut. Although sweeter than European cakes, they are not as rich and they rarely include buttercream or icing.

Breads, on the other hand, are almost completely European in style. While the indigenous unleavened *tortilla* bread rules the roost in Mexico and Central America, Spanish, Portuguese, and French varieties can be found everywhere else. Bakers also have the European tradition of baking at least twice a day.

Sweet pastries tend to be small turnovers and pies (*empanadas* and *pastelzitos*) rather than open tarts. They are usually filled with fruit or nuts, but the flavoring varies from country to country.

The recipes within this chapter have been chosen for their simplicity, yet all will give you an authentic flavor of Latin American baking.

Coffee, Cocoa and Cinnamon Cake

Cocoa is commonly used in baked goods and puddings in South America. This is a light, not-too-rich cake that goes well with ice creams and fruit compotes, but is also delicious on its own with a cup of coffee.

Ingredients

3/4 cup strong black coffee
2 tablespoons cocoa powder
1 cup granulated sugar
6 tablespoons butter, softened
1/2 teaspoon vanilla extract
2 eggs
1 cup all-purpose flour
1/2 teaspoon baking soda
1 teaspoon baking powder
1 teaspoon ground cinnamon

To serve: confectioners' sugar
Cinnamon and Vanilla Ice Cream (see page 227)

Method

1. Preheat the oven to 400°F. Grease an 8-inch moule-à-manqué or round cake pan and line the bottom with a circle of greased waxed paper. Dust it lightly with sugar and flour.

2. In a small saucepan, mix the coffee, cocoa, and half the granulated sugar and bring to a boil. Reduce the heat and simmer, uncovered, for 10 minutes. Cool completely.

3. Cream the butter and remaining granulated sugar in a mixing bowl until light and fluffy. Stir in the vanilla extract. Add the eggs one at a time, beating well after each addition. Add a little of the flour, if necessary, to prevent the mixture from curdling.

4. Sift the remaining flour with the other dry ingredients twice and combine with the butter mixture. Fold in the coffee and cocoa liquid until the mixture is smooth and well blended.

5. Pour into the prepared cake pan and bake in the center of the oven for 20 minutes. Turn the oven temperature down to 350°F and continue baking for 15 minutes, or until the sides have shrunk away from the pan slightly and the top springs back when pressed lightly with a fingertip. Remove from the oven and allow to cool in the pan.

6. Turn out, dust with confectioners' sugar, and serve.

Chocolate, Orange and Prune Cake

Dried and canned prunes are widely used in South American cuisine. They appear frequently in desserts, stuffings, canapés, petits fours, and cakes.

Ingredients

$2/3$ cup orange juice
$2/3$ cup prunes, pitted and halved
3 eggs, separated
Salt
$3/4$ cup sugar
$1/4$ pound (1 stick) butter, soft but not melted
$3/4$ cup all-purpose flour
2 tablespoons cocoa powder
2 teaspoons baking powder

For the icing:
5 ounces good-quality bittersweet chocolate,
    cut into small pieces
$2/3$ cup heavy cream
1 teaspoon ground cinnamon

To serve: Orange Crème Anglaise (see page 220)
    or Rich Vanilla Ice Cream (see page 229)

Method

1. Preheat the oven to 350°F. Grease a 9-inch cake pan and line the bottom with a circle of waxed paper.

2. In a small saucepan, heat the orange juice, remove from the heat, then add the prunes and let stand 10 minutes to soften.

3. Whisk the egg whites with a pinch of salt until stiff. Still whisking, gradually add the sugar until the mixture is stiff and shiny. Whisk in the egg yolks, then gently mix in the soft butter.

4. Sift together the flour, cocoa powder, and baking powder twice. Using a large metal spoon, carefully fold the flour into the egg mixture.

5. Fold in the prunes and orange juice and turn the mixture into the prepared pan. Bake in the center of the oven for about 30 minutes or until the cake feels firm to the touch. Leave to cool for a few minutes, then run a knife around the sides and turn onto a wire rack to cool completely.

6. To make the icing, gently heat together the chocolate, cream, and cinnamon. Stir until all the chocolate has melted and the mixture is smooth and shiny. Allow to cool and thicken to a coating consistency before pouring over the cake.

7. Allow the icing to harden for at least 2 hours. Serve with chilled Orange Crème Anglaise or Rich Vanilla Ice Cream.

Carrot Cake

The unusual combination of carrots and chocolate works really well in this light cake. It's a favorite with children.

Ingredients

5 carrots, peeled and coarsely chopped
  (1^3/$_4$ cups)
^{2}/$_3$ cup vegetable oil
4 eggs
1 cup plus 2 tablespoons sugar
1^1/$_2$ cups all-purpose flour
Pinch salt
1 tablespoon baking powder
1 teaspoon ground cinnamon
Good pinch ground cloves

For the icing:
^{1}/$_4$ cup sugar
^{1}/$_2$ cup milk
4 tablespoons butter
^{2}/$_3$ cup cocoa powder

Method

1. Preheat the oven to 400°F. Lightly grease a 9-inch square cake pan and line the bottom with a piece of greased waxed paper.

2. In a blender or food processor, blend the carrots, oil, and eggs to a pulp. Add the sugar and mix well.

3. Sift the flour, salt, baking powder, cinnamon, and cloves together. Add to the carrot mixture and blend for a few seconds or until the flour is completely incorporated. Pour into the prepared pan and bake in the center of the oven for 35 minutes or until a sharp knife inserted into the center of the cake comes out clean. Remove from the oven and allow to cool.

4. Combine all the icing ingredients in a small saucepan and boil until syrupy, about 10 minutes. Pour the hot liquid on top of the cake and leave to cool completely.

5. Cut into 3-inch squares and serve.

Light Peanut Oil Cake

This cake uses oil instead of butter and the result is a light cake with good keeping qualities. A more fragrant oil, such as walnut or hazelnut, can be used for a more distinctive flavor.

Ingredients

1$^1/_2$ cups all-purpose flour
2 teaspoons baking powder
4 eggs, separated
1 cup sugar
$^1/_2$ teaspoon vanilla extract
$^1/_4$ cup peanut oil
1 can (5 ounces) evaporated milk

To serve: confectioners' sugar and Quince Purée
  (see page 218)

Method

1. Preheat the oven to 350°F. Grease an 8-inch moule-à-manqué or round cake pan and line the bottom with a circle of greased waxed paper.

2. Sift together the flour and baking powder.

3. In a bowl, beat together the egg yolks, sugar, and vanilla extract until light and fluffy. Incorporate the oil and evaporated milk, then carefully fold in the sifted flour.

4. Whisk the egg whites until they stand in soft peaks, then fold them into the mixture using a large metal spoon. Pour into the prepared pan and bake for about 30 minutes or until a sharp knife or skewer inserted into the center comes out clean. Remove from the oven and cool in the pan for 10 minutes.

5. Turn out the cake and, just before serving, dust it with confectioners' sugar. Serve with Quince Purée.

Walnut and Rice Flour Cake

Walnuts are a versatile ingredient used in many South American cakes, sweets, and puddings. This intensely flavored cake contains no wheat flour.

Ingredients

$^1/_4$ pound (1 stick) butter, at room temperature
7 tablespoons granulated sugar
3 eggs, separated
$^3/_4$ cup rice flour
$^1/_4$ cup ground walnuts
1 teaspoon baking powder
3 drops vanilla extract
2 tablespoons confectioners' sugar

To serve: Pineapple and Star Anise Compote
  (see page 215)

Method

1. Preheat the oven to 400°F. Grease an 8-inch cake pan and line the bottom with a circle of greased waxed paper.

2. Cream the butter and granulated sugar together in a mixing bowl until light and fluffy. Add the egg yolks, one at a time, and beat well.

3. Mix the rice flour, walnuts, and baking powder together. Add to the butter mixture and beat until smooth. Add the vanilla extract.

4. Whisk the egg whites to medium peaks and fold into the mixture using a large metal spoon. Pour into the prepared pan.

5. Bake in the center of the oven for 25 minutes or until the sides have shrunk away from the pan slightly and the top springs back when pressed lightly with a fingertip.

6. Remove from the oven and allow to cool in the pan for 10 minutes, then turn out on to a wire rack and let cool completely.

7. Dust the cake heavily with the confectioners' sugar and serve the Pineapple and Star Anise Compote separately.

VARIATION: When the cake is cold, split it horizontally in 3 layers using a serrated knife, and sandwich the layers together using a half recipe of Colombian Milk Pudding (see page 221). Dust the top of the cake with confectioners' sugar before serving.

Easy Cornmeal, Coconut and Prune Cake

This is an all-in-one recipe that produces a moist and delicious cake.

Ingredients

1 cup flaked coconut
$^3/_4$ cup hot water
$^1/_4$ pound (1 stick) butter, cut into small cubes
$^1/_2$ cup prunes, quartered
$^1/_2$ cup polenta or coarse cornmeal
6 tablespoons self-rising flour
1 teaspoon baking powder
$^3/_4$ cup sugar
3 eggs, beaten
Juice of $^1/_2$ lime

Method

1. Preheat the oven to 350°F . Grease a $8^1/_2$ x $4^1/_2$ x $2^1/_2$-inch loaf pan and line the bottom with greased waxed paper. Dust it lightly with sugar and flour.

2. In a medium bowl, mix together the coconut, hot water, butter, and prunes until the butter has completely melted.

3. In a large bowl, sift the polenta, flour, and baking powder together. Mix in the sugar.

4. Add the coconut mixture, eggs, and lime juice to the flours and mix thoroughly with a wooden spoon until all the ingredients are well combined. Pour into the prepared pan and bake in the middle of the oven for 30 to 35 minutes or until the sides have shrunk away from the pan slightly and the top springs back when pressed lightly with a fingertip. Remove the cake from the oven and allow to cool slightly before turning out on to a plate. Serve warm or cold.

NOTE: This cake is very good the next day, cut into slices, lightly toasted, and buttered.

Spicy Corn Muffins

Using three of the best-loved ingredients in Latin America—corn, chiles, and cilantro—this recipe is quick to make. Although muffins are North American in origin, similar shaped buns are found in many South American countries.

Ingredients

1^1/$_2$ cups sifted all-purpose flour
^{1}/$_2$ cup yellow cornmeal
1 tablespoon baking powder
Pinch salt
^{1}/$_4$ cup chopped fresh cilantro leaves
2 Fresno or jalapeño chiles, seeded and finely chopped (see page 194)
2 tablespoons light brown sugar
6 tablespoons water
3 large eggs
^{1}/$_4$ cup vegetable oil

Method

1. Preheat the oven to 350°F and warm a baking sheet. Line eight (2^1/$_2$-inch) muffin pan cups with paper liners. If using a 12-cup pan, fill the remaining holes with water.

2. Sift the flour, cornmeal, baking powder, and salt together twice and put into a large bowl. Stir in the cilantro, chiles, and sugar.

3. In a small bowl, mix together the water, eggs, and oil. Add this liquid to the dry ingredients and mix, using a round-tipped knife, until well combined. Fill each muffin cup about two-thirds full, then place the pan on the warmed baking sheet. Bake for about 15 to 20 minutes or until a sharp knife inserted into the center comes out clean.

4. Remove from the oven and allow the muffins to cool in the pan for 5 minutes. Serve warm.

VARIATION: For sweet cornmeal muffins, omit the chiles and cilantro, use milk instead of water and add 1 teaspoon ground cinnamon to the flour.

NOTE: This batter can also be baked in a well-greased cake pan or gratin dish and sliced before serving.

Cuban White Bread

This delicious bread is baked in an unusual way, but with great results.

Ingredients

1 cake (.6 ounce) fresh yeast or 1 envelope
  ($^1/_4$ ounce) active dried yeast
1$^1/_4$ cups warm water
1 teaspoon sugar
2 teaspoons salt
3$^1/_4$ cups bread flour
$^1/_4$ cup cornmeal

Method

1. In a small bowl, thoroughly mix the fresh yeast with 2 tablespoons of the warm water and the sugar.

2. Sift the salt and flour into a large bowl. Stir in the active dried yeast, if using.

3. Add the fresh yeast and water to the flour and mix to a sticky dough. Remove the dough to a lightly floured surface and knead for 10 to 15 minutes or until smooth and elastic. Form the dough into a ball.

4. Lightly oil a bowl, put the ball of dough into it and turn to coat with oil. Cover the bowl with plastic wrap. Leave to rise in a warm, draft-free place for 1 to 1$^1/_2$ hours or until doubled in size.

5. Turn the dough onto a lightly floured surface and shape into a round or long loaf. Sprinkle a baking sheet with half the cornmeal and put the shaped bread on top. Allow to rise for 5 minutes.

6. Slash two diagonal lines in the top of the dough with a sharp knife, brush the whole loaf with water and sprinkle the remaining cornmeal on top. Place in a cold oven. Set the oven to 400°F and place a roasting pan filled with hot water at the bottom of the oven.

7. Bake until the bread is crusty and the bottom sounds hollow when tapped. Transfer to a wire rack to cool slightly and serve warm or cold.

Corn Bread

There are numerous recipes for corn bread as it is very popular throughout Latin America. It can be made using cornmeal or polenta and, when available, fresh corn kernels are also added to the mixture. Corn bread is best served warm or straight from the oven.

Ingredients

1³/₄ cups milk
2 tablespoons butter
1 teaspoon salt
1 teaspoon sugar
¹/₂ teaspoon chili powder
¹/₂ teaspoon paprika
6 tablespoons instant polenta or cornmeal
1¹/₂ teaspoons baking powder
3 eggs
1 can (12 ounces) sweet corn, drained and
   coarsely chopped

Method

1. Preheat the oven to 375°F. Grease a 2-quart shallow baking dish.

2. In a large saucepan, mix together the milk, butter, salt, sugar, chili powder, and paprika and bring to scalding point.

3. Sift together the cornmeal and baking powder.

4. Remove the milk from the heat and slowly add the cornmeal, stirring with a wooden spoon to prevent lumps forming. Add the eggs and sweet corn and mix thoroughly. Pour the mixture into the prepared dish and bake for about 30 minutes or until lightly brown and set.

VARIATIONS:

- Finely chop 1 onion and 1 red bell pepper and sweat in 2 tablespoons olive oil until nearly soft, about 10 minutes. Add to the mixture at step 4.

- Scrape the kernels from 2 ears of corn and use instead of the canned sweet corn.

- Shred ³/₄ cup of Cheddar or Red Leicester cheese and add to the mixture at step 4.

- Very quick cornbread: In a bowl or food processor, mix together ³/₄ cup cornmeal, 6 tablespoons melted butter, ¹/₂ teaspoon salt, 1 teaspoon sugar, 1 teaspoon aniseed, 2 teaspoons baking powder and ³/₄ cup milk. Pour into a greased 9-inch square cake pan and bake for about 40 minutes at 375°F, or until a sharp knife or skewer inserted into the center comes out clean.

- Richer cornbread: Use 1¹/₄ cups buttermilk mixed with ²/₃ cup sour cream instead of the milk and follow the recipe as above.

Sun-dried Banana and Walnut Bread

Latin American baking is similar to that of Spain and France—lots of white crusty bread but almost no brown breads. However, the ever-growing number of vegetarians and health-conscious people is changing things, so in recent years it has become easier to find whole-grain bread, although mainly in health food shops.

Ingredients

5 ounces dried banana chips, coarsely chopped
$^2/_3$ cup sugar
$1^1/_3$ cups oats
$^2/_3$ cup whole wheat flour
$^1/_4$ cup all-purpose flour
2 teaspoons baking powder
$^1/_2$ teaspoon salt
$^1/_2$ teaspoon baking soda
$^2/_3$ cup orange juice concentrate
1 egg
2 tablespoons vegetable oil
$1^1/_4$ cups walnuts, coarsely chopped

Method

1. Preheat the oven to 350°F. Brush a
    $8^1/_2$ x $4^1/_2$ x $2^1/_2$-inch loaf pan with oil.

2. Put the chopped bananas in a small bowl,
    cover with boiling water and set aside for
    10 minutes. Drain the bananas and discard
    the water.

3. In a large bowl, combine the sugar, oats,
    both flours, baking powder, salt, and baking
    soda.

4. Mix the orange juice, egg, and oil together
    and add to the dry ingredients. Mix in the
    bananas and walnuts. Pour the mixture into
    the prepared pan and bake in the preheated
    oven until the edges begin to brown and a
    skewer inserted in the center comes out
    clean, about 1 hour. Cool in the pan for
    15 minutes, then turn onto a rack to cool
    completely.

Polenta

Polenta is eaten in many Latin American countries. Being filling and cheap, it is basically a poor man's food and is normally served with saucy dishes, such as Chicken and Okra Casserole (see page 68). It is very rarely fried and can be eaten cold with milk and sugar as a dessert.

Ingredients

2 quarts water
2 teaspoons salt
1¼ cups coarse cornmeal or polenta
Oil

Method

1. Put the water and salt into a large saucepan and bring to a boil.

2. Remove from the heat and sprinkle in the cornmeal, whisking quickly to avoid lumps.

3. Return the pan to low heat and cover it to prevent spattering.

4. Continue cooking until the polenta is thick, approximately 20 to 25 minutes, stirring often to prevent sticking and burning. Serve hot, piled high on a plate.

NOTE: The water can be substituted by chicken or beef stock to give the polenta a savory flavor.

Brazil Nut Shortbread

Delicious on its own with a cup of coffee or hot chocolate, this shortbread recipe is easy to make and keeps for a long time. Cookies are very popular in Latin American countries, with arrowroot, coconut, cocoa, peanut, and cream cookies being some of the favorites.

Ingredients

$^1/_2$ cup Brazil nuts
$^1/_4$ pound (1 stick) butter
6 tablespoons sugar
$^3/_4$ cup all-purpose flour
3 tablespoons rice flour
$^1/_2$ teaspoon ground cinnamon

Method

1. Preheat the oven to 325°F.

2. Grind the Brazil nuts finely in a food processor.

3. Beat the butter until soft, add the sugar and mix thoroughly.

4. Sift in the flours, cinnamon, and Brazil nuts and work to a smooth dough.

5. Place a 6-inch flan ring on a baking sheet and press the shortbread dough into a neat circle inside it. Remove the flan ring and flatten the dough slightly with a rolling pin. Crimp the edges and prick thoroughly with a fork.

6. Mark the shortbread into 8 wedges, sprinkle slightly with a little extra sugar and bake for 40 minutes until a pale biscuit color. Remove from the oven, recut the wedges and leave to cool for 2 minutes. Lift on to a cooling rack and cool completely. Store in an airtight container.

NOTE: If a food processor is not available, chop the nuts finely.

Toasted Cassava Meal

Cassava or manioc meal plays the part of bread in a Brazilian meal, where it is sprinkled over juicy dishes to soak up the liquid. It has a bland taste, so for special occasions it is fried in butter and a variety of ingredients are added to it. Cassava meal is also known as *gari* in Indian food stores.

Ingredients

6 tablespoons butter
2 cups cassava meal
Salt and freshly ground pepper

Method

1. In a skillet, over medium heat, melt the butter. Stir in the cassava meal and cook, stirring constantly, until golden brown and dry. This will take about 10 minutes. Season to taste with salt and pepper and serve hot or cold.

VARIATIONS:
*   Festive cassava: Add 1 medium onion to the butter and cook until soft. Mix $1/3$ cup raisins and 11 green olives (pitted and halved) with the cassava meal and fry for 10 minutes. Serve hot.

*   With eggs: Cook 1 small chopped onion in the butter, add 2 beaten eggs and cook for 1 minute. Add 5 tablespoons of cassava meal and cook, stirring frequently, for 8 minutes, or until the meal becomes golden. Season with salt and pepper and stir in 2 tablespoons chopped fresh parsley leaves. Serve hot or cold.

Hazelnut and Lemon Cookies

A legacy from the Spanish kitchen, these cookies are easy to make and delicious.

Ingredients

$^2/_3$ cup ground hazelnuts
6 tablespoons sugar
6 tablespoons all-purpose flour
Grated zest and juice of 1 lemon
1 egg

Method

1. Preheat the oven to 350°F. Lightly grease a baking sheet.

2. In a bowl, mix the ground hazelnuts with the sugar and add the flour and lemon zest.

3. Beat the egg and lemon juice together and add to the mixture.

4. Place teaspoonfuls on the greased baking sheet and bake in the preheated oven until the cookies are brown and crisp. Transfer to a wire rack to cool.

Triple Chocolate Cinnamon Cookies

From North America to Argentina, cinnamon is the all-time favorite spice for sweets and baking. Here it is combined with the much-loved walnut and chocolate.

Ingredients

3 tablespoons all-purpose flour
$^1/_3$ cup cocoa powder
$1^1/_2$ teaspoons ground cinnamon
$^1/_4$ teaspoon baking powder
Pinch salt
6 tablespoons unsalted butter, softened
$^1/_2$ cup sugar
3 eggs
8 ounces unsweetened chocolate, melted and cooled
$1^1/_4$ cups walnuts, coarsely chopped
6 ounces milk chocolate, finely chopped

Method

1. Preheat the oven to 350°F. Lightly grease 1 or 2 baking sheets.

2. Sift together the flour, cocoa, cinnamon, baking powder, and salt.

3. In a large bowl, beat the butter, sugar, and eggs until smooth. Stir in the melted chocolate and mix well. Add the flour mixture and mix thoroughly. Finally, stir in the nuts and chopped milk chocolate.

4. Drop tablespoons of the mixture onto greased baking sheets and bake until the cookies look dry and cracked but feel soft when lightly pressed, about 11 minutes.

5. Transfer to a wire rack to cool.

Ginger Tuiles

Ginger is used in savory dishes on the northeast coast of Brazil, but the rest of the country uses it mostly in sweets, cookies, and baking.

Ingredients

1 tablespoon butter, melted, for greasing
$^1/_4$ cup unsalted butter, softened
6 tablespoons sugar
Pinch salt
$^1/_2$ teaspoon ground ginger
1 egg white, room temperature
6 tablespoons all-purpose flour, sifted
2 tablespoons finely chopped crystallized ginger

Method

1. Preheat the oven to 375°F. Brush two baking sheets heavily with the melted butter, dust lightly with flour and put in the freezer.

2. Warm a heatproof bowl in the oven for 5 minutes. In the warmed bowl mix the softened butter, sugar, salt, and ground ginger with a whisk until thoroughly combined.

3. Gently mix in the egg white and flour. Chill for 30 minutes before using.

4. Spread teaspoonfuls, well apart, on the chilled baking sheets. Sprinkle with the chopped ginger and bake in the oven until pale brown, 5 to 6 minutes.

5. Shape the tuiles by bending them around an oiled rolling pin or the handle of a large wooden spoon.

6. When cold, store in an airtight container.

NOTE: Parchment paper can be used instead of brushing the baking sheet with butter.

Fresh Herb Pastry

Latin Americans are very fond of savory pastries such as empanadas, and flavoring the pastry itself is also very popular.

Ingredients

1²/₃ cups all-purpose flour
Pinch salt
¹/₂ teaspoon cayenne pepper
¹/₄ pound (1 stick) butter, chopped
2 tablespoons lard or shortening
1 tablespoon finely chopped fresh oregano
   leaves
2 tablespoons finely chopped fresh parsley
   leaves
5 tablespoons very cold water

Method

1. Sift the flour with the salt and cayenne pepper.

2. Rub in the butter and lard until the mixture resembles bread crumbs. Stir in the herbs and mix well.

3. Add the cold water and mix to a firm dough, first with a knife, then with one hand. It may be necessary to add more water, but the pastry should not be too damp.

4. Wrap and chill for 30 minutes before using.

Sweet Rich Shortcrust Pastry

Sweet tarts made with this type of pastry are found in the southern countries of South America, where the food has a stronger European influence.

Ingredients

1²/₃ cups all-purpose flour
Pinch salt
¹/₄ pound (1 stick) butter, chopped
1 tablespoon sugar
1 egg yolk
3 tablespoons very cold water

Method

1. Sift the flour with the salt.

2. Rub in the butter until the mixture resembles coarse bread crumbs. Stir in the sugar.

3. Mix the egg yolk with the water, then add to the mixture. Mix to a firm dough, first with a knife, then with one hand. It may be necessary to add more water, but the pastry should not be too damp.

4. Wrap and chill for 30 minutes before using.

VARIATION: To make a plain rich shortcrust, omit the sugar.

Puff Pastry

Although more often bought frozen than made at home, puff pastry is really quite easy to make.

Ingredients

1²/₃ cups all-purpose flour
Pinch salt
2 tablespoons shortening
²/₃ cup very cold water
²/₃ to 1 cup butter

Method

1. If you have never made puff pastry before, use the smaller amount of butter: this will give a standard puff pastry. If you have some experience, more butter will produce a lighter, very rich pastry.

2. Sift the flour with a pinch of salt. Rub in the shortening. Add the water and mix with a knife to a doughy consistency. Turn the dough onto the table and knead quickly until just smooth. Wrap and leave to relax in the refrigerator for 30 minutes.

3. Lightly flour the work surface or a board and roll the dough into a rectangle about 12 x 4 inches.

4. Tap the butter lightly with a floured rolling-pin to form a flattened block measuring about 3 x 3 inches. Place the butter on the rectangle of pastry. Fold the third of the pastry closest to you over the butter then bring down the top third. Press the sides together with the rolling pin to prevent the butter escaping. Give the pastry a 90° counterclockwise turn so that the folded edge is on your left.

5. Tap the pastry with the rolling pin to flatten the butter a little, then roll out quickly and lightly until the pastry is three times as long as it is wide. Fold it very evenly in three as before and press the edges firmly with the rolling pin. Turn the pastry counterclockwise so the folded edge is on your left. Roll out again to form a rectangle as before.

6. The pastry has now had two rolls and folds, or 'turns' as they are called. Leave to rest in a cool place for 30 minutes or so. The rolling and folding must be repeated twice more, the pastry again rested, and then again given two more 'turns'. This makes a total of six. If the butter is still very streaky, roll and fold the pastry once more. Use as required.

Pastelzitos

Pastelzitos are small savory pastries that are popular throughout Latin America. This recipe comes from Ecuador, but the Chinese in Brazil had a reputation for making the lightest and nicest pastelzitos.

Ingredients

For the pastry:
1²/₃ cups all-purpose flour
¹/₂ teaspoon salt
¹/₂ teaspoon baking powder
4 tablespoons butter, cut into cubes
5 drops lemon juice
¹/₄ cup water
Vegetable oil for frying

For the filling:
1 recipe Picadillo (see page 92)

Method

1. Sift the flour, salt, and baking powder into a large bowl. Rub in the butter until the mixture resembles coarse bread crumbs.

2. Mix the lemon juice into the water and add enough to the flour to form a soft but not sticky dough.

3. Knead until elastic, about 3 minutes. Cover and rest for 30 minutes.

4. Divide the dough into 12 equal parts. On a floured surface, roll each piece of dough into a 5-inch circle. Put 2 teaspoons of Picadillo in the center of each circle, brush the edges with water and press together to form a semicircle. Seal the ends well.

5. Heat the oil in a large skillet until a crumb will sizzle vigorously in it. Fry the pastelzitos until golden brown and crisp. Drain on paper towels. Serve at once.

VARIATIONS:

- Sweet corn: Mix an 8¹/₂-ounce can of drained sweet corn with ²/₃ cup sour cream; season well with salt and freshly ground black pepper and follow the recipe as above.

- Hearts of palm: Slice the hearts of palm from a 14-ounce can and mix with ¹/₂ cup shredded Cheddar and ¹/₄ cup heavy cream. Season with salt and freshly ground black pepper and follow the recipe as above.

- Cheese: Mix ¹/₂ cup shredded Cheddar with ¹/₂ cup grated Parmesan and ¹/₂ teaspoon paprika. No salt is needed since both cheeses are quite salty. Follow the recipe as above.

NOTE: The lemon juice is sometimes substituted by a few drops of white rum or vodka. It is believed to give the pastry a crisp, light texture when fried.

Drinks

DRINKS

Latin America produces a variety of alcoholic drinks, ranging from home-brewed *chiche* to spirits such as *tequila*, *cachaca*, and *pisco* as well as excellent wines from Chile and Argentina. Very good beer is also produced and consumed in great quantities throughout the continent.

This chapter includes recipes for classic cocktails such as margaritas, describes the traditional way of drinking tequila, and provides guidelines on how to match wine with chile-flavored dishes. The most popular non-alcoholic drink in Latin America is undoubtedly coffee, followed by chocolate, and maté tea. The history of all these drinks makes fascinating reading, and the recipes using them make delicious drinking.

Wine

by Elizabeth Morcom

South America has been producing wine since the arrival of the Spanish *conquistadores* in the 16th century. European vines were first planted in Mexico and spread rapidly southwards. After Europe, South America produces more wine than any other continent. Although Chilean wine enjoys the most international acclaim, Argentina and Brazil produce greater quantities —to satisfy a huge home consumption. Wine is also made in Uruguay, Peru, Bolivia, and even a little in Colombia, Ecuador, and Venezuela. In Central America, Mexico is an important producer.

ARGENTINA AND BRAZIL

In the past, poor grape varieties predominated, yielding indifferent wines. Although major investment in wine is still comparatively new, premium grape varieties are now being planted in these two major wine-producing countries and their wineries updated, with exciting prospects for the future, especially in Argentina. The vineyards there are mainly in the western province of Mendoza, in the foothills of the Andes, and just a short hop over the mountains from Chile's wine areas. The vineyards of Brazil are mainly in the south of the country, bordering Uruguay. Although Spain and Portugal have influenced the past development of wine in these countries, the grape varieties now being planted are definitely "international" and, as in many New World countries, a truly individual wine "identity" is largely lacking. Argentina has the aromatic, white torrontes grape variety with its grapy, muscat aromas, but chardonnay and semillon are now common too. The malbeci—a less well-known Bordeaux grape variety, also found in Cahors but not much elsewhere—used to be widely planted for red

wines and is a good match for the local beef, but better-known cabernet and merlot are now exciting more interest. Brazil has greater problems than Argentina in producing good-quality wine, but it too is making progress with classic, premium varietals, and investment from abroad is considerable.

CHILE

Of the main producers, Chile has made the speediest progress and is already making world-class wines. Most of the vineyards are in the Central Valley to the south of the capital, Santiago, where the climate is almost ideal for wine making. Plantings of classic, premium grape varieties, such as Sauvignon, Chardonnay and Sémillon, Cabernet, Merlot and, to a lesser extent, Pinot Noir, have been extensive, and interest from foreign investors, including owners of Bordeaux Château, has been keen. Chilean wines for export are increasingly well made: characterful, clean, and fruity. Most are made for drinking within two or three years. Above all, they provide an excellent value for the money.

MEXICO

Mexico is Latin America's fourth most important producer of wine, with vineyards mainly in the north part of the country. The climate is not ideal, but premium grape varieties have now been planted, largely along Californian lines, and there has been some foreign investment, especially in brandy and sparkling wine production.

MATCHING WINE WITH LATIN AMERICAN FOOD

As it is with colors, so it is with food and wine—certain combinations, such as fish and tannic red wine, do not work well, while others, such as lamb and claret, work like a dream. However, there are no hard and fast rules; much comes down to personal choice. The secret is to try to pair like with like, which is what I have attempted to do in my wine recommendations for the recipes in this book. Ideally, there should be no clash and no domination of flavors. Both wine and food should show each other off to best advantage.

Intensity of flavor is as important as the type of flavor and, of course, there is quality; an "everyday" dish should not be paired with an expensive, top-class wine and vice versa. Color association also plays its part: pale dishes are often more successfully matched with white wines and rich, dark dishes with reds.

As in any cuisine, there are "problem" ingredients, such as vinegar, avocado, egg, chocolate, and, of course, spices such as chile, but a successful match can usually be found. The position of a particular dish within a meal can also affect wine choice. Because our senses become gradually dulled during the course of a meal, lighter wines are usually served before fuller-bodied wines, whites before reds, dry wines before sweet, and younger wines before older wines.

WINES AND CHILES

Just as there are many varieties of grape, so there are different varieties of chile, with different aromas and flavors. These can often coincide. Fresh jalapeños or serranos, for example, can have herbal, green olive, or vegetal characteristics, as do many wines. Dried chiles, on the other hand, have smoky, tobacco, or chocolate overtones, which are also found in red wines such as Pinot Noirs, with their ripe fruit and earthy, sometimes smoky flavor, and reds aged in American oak, such as Rioja and many New World Cabernets. (Avoid those with harsh, mouth-drying tannins, which tend to intensify the heat of chiles.)

Although dry white wines may be overwhelmed by hotter chiles, those with citrus flavors, such as Chardonnays and Sémillons, seem to work well with milder chile dishes, especially those containing fish. Distinctive Sauvignons, such as those from New Zealand, can be perfect matches for dishes with green and red peppers as well as chile.

When it comes to hot and very hot chiles, a wine is needed which will match the flavors of the dish and sooth the heat. Spirits help, but often a rounded, full-bodied, fruity red or a mouth-filling, smooth, off-dry white, such as a Chenin Blanc, Gewürztraminer, or Riesling will work well. Sparkling wine is often a good choice too. A delicate, dry white would be overwhelmed by very hot chiles, even if it quenches the thirst. Lager works only as a thirst quencher and heat soother—it does little to harmonize with other flavors. A carefully chosen wine should cope with the heat of the chile and complement the flavors of the dish.

Spirits and Cocktails

This section describes the more well-known alcoholic drinks made of native ingredients in Latin American countries.

Cachaça is a Brazilian rum made from sugar cane. It is considered 'the drink of the poor', but is used extensively in many mixed drinks and is the main ingredient of *caipirinha*, the national drink of Brazil. It is also drunk on its own in small glass cups.

Chicha is an Indian fermented beer-like drink made from maize according to centuries-old tradition: a pot is filled with chewed corn kernels and left to ferment for three days. Once strained, the liquid has a cloudy appearance and sour taste. Chicha is popular in Mexico and all the Andean countries of South America.

Pisco is a Peruvian type of brandy made from distilled muscat wine. It is also very popular in Bolivia and Chile.

Pulque, from Mexico, is another fermented beer-type of drink. It is made from the sap of the maguey or century plant.

Tequila is a Mexican distilled drink made from the *Agave azul tequilana*, a relative of the maguey plant. The roots of the plant are ground, mixed with water, fermented, and distilled twice, resulting in a colorless drink. Tequila can also be aged and will then have a light straw color. One of the traditional ways of drinking tequila is with lime and salt. In one hand, a good pinch of salt is put in the space between the thumb and index finger, and half a lime is held with the same hand. With the glass in the other hand, the salt is licked, all the tequila is swallowed at once, and then the lime juice is sucked. The lime can be substituted by an orange slice or a lime-rubbed slice of cucumber.

Fruit Drinks

Fruit is the dessert *par excellence* in Latin American countries and fresh fruit juices are consumed in great quantities. Fruit bars are as common in Brazil as pubs are in England, and serve mainly made-to-order fruit drinks. Freshly squeezed orange juice or milk are used as the bases for a variety of drinks, the most common ones being avocado, milk, lime juice, and sugar blended to a thick milk shake consistency, and papaya shake, using orange juice or milk. The combinations are endless and the *batidas* or *vitaminas*, as they are called, are frequently drunk as a mid-morning or afternoon snack.

Margarita   SERVES 4

This classic Mexican drink is made with tequila.

Ingredients

1 slice lime
Salt in a saucer
$1/4$ cup lime juice
$2/3$ cup tequila
$1/4$ cup Triple Sec
Crushed ice

Method

1. Chill 4 tumblers or cocktail glasses in the freezer for 10 minutes.

2. Moisten the rim of the glasses with the slice of lime and dip into the saucer of salt until lightly frosted.

3. In a cocktail shaker or blender, combine the remaining ingredients until well blended. Pour into the prepared glasses and serve.

Pisco Sour

This is a very popular drink in Peru, Bolivia, and Chile. The egg white is added to create a foam.

SERVES 4

Ingredients

1$^1/_4$ cups pisco (see page 259)
4 teaspoons granulated sugar
Juice of 1 lime
4 ice cubes, crushed
1 egg white

Method

1. Chill 4 tumblers or cocktail glasses in the freezer for 10 minutes.

2. In a bowl, mix together the pisco, sugar, and lime juice. Transfer to a cocktail shaker, add the egg white, and shake vigorously 9 or 10 times.

3. Strain into the chilled glasses and serve.

Coconut Punch

Drinks using milk are very popular in Brazil. This one is made using thick coconut milk and lime. The *cachaçsa* can be substituted by white rum.

SERVES 4

Ingredients

1 can (14 ounces) thick coconut milk
Juice of 2 limes
$^1/_4$ cup granulated sugar
$^1/_2$ cup *cachaça* or white rum
6 ice cubes, crushed

Method

1. Place all of the ingredients in a food processor or blender and process for 1 minute. Pour into chilled tumblers or cocktail glasses and serve at once.

VARIATIONS: To make a fruity coconut punch, add any of the following before processing it:
- the pulp of 3 passion fruits.
- 2 fresh guavas, peeled and seeded.
- $^1/_2$ fresh mango, peeled and the flesh cut into cubes.
- $^1/_2$ fresh pineapple, peeled, cored, and cut into cubes.

Caipirinha

The national drink of Brazil is traditionally made straight in the glass with *cachaçsa*, but can also be made with vodka.

SERVES 4

Ingredients

4 limes, washed and cut into chunks
4 tablespoons granulated sugar
1 cup *cachaça*
8 ice cubes, crushed

Method

1. Divide the limes and sugar among 4 tumblers. Using a spoon, mix the limes and sugar together, crushing the limes to extract the juice and oil from the skin.

2. Divide the *cachaça* and crushed ice among the glasses, stir well, and serve.

Sangrita

This is a drink from Mexico which is made with tequila, orange and tomato juice, and chile sauce.

SERVES 4

Ingredients

$^1/_4$ cup fresh orange juice
Juice of 1 lime
$1^1/_3$ cups tomato juice
$^3/_4$ cup tequila
2 teaspoons hot chile sauce
Pinch salt

Method

1. Chill 4 tumblers in the freezer for 10 minutes.

2. Mix together all of the ingredients and pour into the chilled tumblers. Serve as an apéritif.

Yugeno

This is a Peruvian drink made with pisco and orange juice.

SERVES 4

Ingredients

$^3/_4$ cup fresh orange juice
$^3/_4$ cup pisco (see page 259)
8 ice cubes, crushed

Method

1. Chill 4 tumblers or cocktail glasses.

2. Mix together the orange juice, pisco, and ice, pour into the chilled glasses, and serve at once.

Avocado, Lime and Milk Batida

Strange as it may sound, this is a delicious and very nutritious drink.

SERVES 4 TO 6

Ingredients

2 ripe avocados
$4^1/_4$ cups very cold milk
Juice of 1 lime
3 tablespoons granulated sugar (to taste)

Method

1. Blend all of the ingredients except the sugar in a food processor or blender. Add sugar to taste and serve at once.

VARIATION: Substitute the avocados with 3 large, ripe bananas.

NOTE: Very frequently 3 tablespoons fine oats will be added to the banana or avocado batida, making it a complete and delicious meal.

Papaya and Orange Batida

This is a particularly good recipe for using over-ripe papayas.

SERVES 4

Ingredients

2 small, very ripe papayas, peeled, seeded, and diced
4 cups freshly squeezed orange juice
Juice of $1/2$ lime
Granulated sugar

Method

1. Combine all the ingredients except the sugar in a blender or food processor. Add sugar to taste and serve at once.

NOTE: The orange juice can be substituted by cold milk; both versions are very popular.

Mixed Fruit Batida

Any fruit, or even leftover fruit salad, can be used for this batida, and the orange juice can be substituted by milk.

SERVES 4

Ingredients

1 banana, peeled and sliced
$1/2$ pineapple, peeled and cut into large cubes
$1/2$ papaya, peeled and cut into cubes
4 cups orange juice
Squeeze of lime juice

Method

1. Mix all of the ingredients together in a food processor or blender and process to a smooth drink. Serve at once.

VARIATION: To make this drink into a healthy meal, add a few tablespoons yogurt.

Tropical Limeade

This unusual drink is delicious; a dash of rum can be added for an extra kick.

SERVES 4

Ingredients

5 limes, thoroughly washed and sliced
Handful of ice cubes
4 cups very cold water
$1/4$ cup granulated sugar (to taste)
4 mint leaves

Method

1. Mix all of the ingredients together in a food processor or blender until the ice is completely crushed and the limes become a pulp. Press through a strainer and serve immediately.

NOTE: This drink can also be made using half lemons and half limes, although the lemon skins are more bitter.

Coffee

Although coffee is African (Ethiopian) in origin, Latin America is the world's largest producer today. Coffee was introduced to the Caribbean in the 18th century by the French and plantations quickly spread throughout Central and South America. By this time, coffee drinking was already an established habit in Europe, especially in England, Paris, and Vienna, where coffee houses had flourished since the mid-17th century.

Coffee grows best in the regions situated between the tropics of Cancer and Capricorn, hence its large production in African and Latin American countries. It is a labor-intensive crop, and in most countries the picking is still done by hand. There are three main varieties of coffee.

Arabica is considered the best of the three varieties and represents 70 percent of the world's production. It makes a rich, smooth, and aromatic coffee with the lowest caffeine level.

Robusta has a rougher, more intense flavor and has almost double the caffeine content of Arabica. It is a much cheaper bean and is normally used to make instant coffee and cheaper coffee blends.

Liberica is produced in large quantities, but it has a very insignificant taste.

There are many types of coffee, mostly named after their country of origin. The best known are Colombian, Costa Rican, Brazil Santos, Guatemalan, Jamaican, Kenyan, and Mocha, all being of the Arabica variety. As with grapes, the soil, altitude, and weather play an important part in determining the taste and aroma of coffee beans. The other important factors are the roasting and blending. Roasting develops the aroma, flavor, and body of the coffee beans and determines the delicacy or richness of a brew. The most common types of roasting are as follows:

Light or pale roast has a delicate, yet full taste and is the most suitable to drink with milk.

Medium roast has a stronger flavor and aroma, but no bitterness. It is good with or without milk and makes a good after-meal coffee.

Dark roast has a strong flavor and aroma, a deep color, and is best served black.

Continental roast has a very strong, bitter taste. It is used mainly with cheap beans, since most of the beans' oils are destroyed during roasting. It is drunk black in small cups and is definitely an acquired taste.

Since the taste for coffee differs so much from country to country, roasting and blending are traditionally undertaken by the importers rather than the producers. All coffee beans have qualities that are remedied or enhanced by mixing them with other types of beans, and to achieve a good blend, up to eight types are sometimes used. The perfect balance is achieved when flavor, body, and aroma are in complete harmony. It is, of course, a matter of personal taste, but modern consumers are extremely discerning in their choice.

To achieve a good brew it is important to have the correctly ground coffee for the method used:

Percolators—coarse grind

Cafetière—medium grind

Espresso pots and machines—espresso grind

Filter—fine grind

Ideally, the coffee should be ground just before being used in order to preserve all its qualities.

The volatile molecules present in the coffee are responsible for its flavor; richness escapes when the beans are exposed to air.

Vacuum-packed ground coffee retains most of the qualities of freshly ground coffee, but once opened, the packet should be tightly sealed or kept in an airtight container in the refrigerator, where it will hold its freshness for about one week. Storing whole beans in the same way will keep them fresh for up to three weeks. Coffee, ground or whole, freezes well if stored inside an airtight container; the beans can then be ground from frozen and used at once.

Instant coffee is usually made with poorer quality Arabica beans from Brazil and intensively produced Robusta beans from Africa. A strong brew of freshly roasted and ground coffee is made. This brew is then spray-dried, leaving behind the coffee powder. The heat needed to evaporate the water destroys the coffee's natural oils, the result being a drink that resembles coffee, but does not have the characteristic taste or aroma of freshly made ground coffee.

Instant freeze-dried coffee retains more freshly made coffee qualities and is the best of the instant coffees. A strong brew is made, then frozen and ground into particles. The water is then removed with a very small amount of heat, which leaves the fresh coffee taste almost intact.

Decaffeinated coffee is made by 'washing' the caffeine off the coffee beans using water or an organic solvent (methylene chloride). Neither method alters the coffee's final taste, but the water process is usually preferred to the chemical one. There are a few rules to follow to get the most out of freshly ground coffee:

1. If not brewed enough, the result will be weak and tasteless coffee. If brewed for too long, the coffee will taste bitter and the fragrance will be destroyed. To make weak coffee, it is better to make a normal brew and then dilute it with water; to make strong coffee, increase the amount of coffee, not the brewing time.

2. Coffee-making equipment should be clean and free of any residue, as the oils left in the pot will turn rancid and make the new brew taste bitter.

3. Water should be fresh and cold to start with and brought almost to the boiling point.

4. The distinctive coffee fragrance is released only while the coffee is hot, so warm the pot and cups with hot water to prolong the coffee's wonderful aroma.

5. The longer the water is in contact with the coffee, the less ground coffee is needed; Cafetières therefore need less coffee than filters. As a general rule, one rounded tablespoon of ground coffee per coffee cup is used, but it varies according to the method of making and personal taste.

6. Avoid buying coffee in bulk or beans stored in open bins; when exposed to air over a period of time they lose most of their delicious smell.

COFFEE DRINKING IN LATIN AMERICA

Almost all Latin Americans, including children, start the day with a large cup of strong coffee diluted with hot milk and almost invariably sweetened. In Mexico, brown sugar, cinnamon, and cloves are added to the breakfast *café con leche*. For the rest of the day, small cups of strong black coffee are consumed at regular intervals. It is said that an average Latino will drink about 20 of these small cups a day, while real addicts may drink as many as 40 cups. Towards the end of the afternoon, a small piece of cake or some sweets will be eaten with the coffee. Black coffee drinking goes on until the end of the evening and is believed by many people to promote a good night's sleep! Until recently, most people had never heard of decaffeinated coffee.

In most households, coffee is made ready-sweetened. Water and sugar are brought to a boil, ground coffee is added, and the brew is passed through a paper or cloth filter straight into a warmed coffee pot or insulated pitcher.

Instant coffee is mostly used in countries that do not produce coffee themselves, such as Chile and Argentina. In coffee-producing nations, even poor landworkers or *peons* grow enough coffee in their back gardens to supply their family needs, and use traditional methods of roasting and grinding. In Brazil, the unstable economy sometimes makes the price of coffee prohibitive for most of the population, but people are prepared to give up all other foodstuffs in order to have their beloved coffee.

Chocolate

Until recently, cocoa, the seed of the fruit of the cacao tree, was believed to be a native of the rainforest regin of South America. However, new evidence shows that it originated in Mexico and spread to Central America long before the arrival of the Spaniards. *Chocolatl*, as it was called by the Aztecs, was a very important part of the economy and the beans were used as currency. The drink made from cocoa, a sort of hot chocolate made with water and flavored with honey, chile, allspice, and vanilla, was reserved for the aristocracy and apparently prohibited to women. It was not much different from the chocolate drunk in Mexico today.

After the Conquest, foodstuffs brought back from Mexico and Peru, such as tomatoes, potatoes, peppers, and corn, began to be cultivated in the Mediterranean area. Cocoa was the only crop that could not be transplanted to Europe, since it needed a tropical climate in which to grow. Most of the producing areas were Spanish colonies, so Spain kept the monopoly on production and consumption for more than 100 years.

Between 1600 and 1660, chocolate drinking became an established habit throughout Europe, although it was superseded by tea in England and Russia—a pattern that persists to this day. When it was the main breakfast drink, however, great pains were taken to get it just right. Spices, sugar, cream, and milk were all added, producing a drink not much different from what the Aztecs drank. The French food writer Anthelme Brillat-Savarin, in his book *The Physiology of Taste* (1825), gives his recipe for perfect hot chocolate, and the painstaking attention to detail shows its importance in a society already introduced to coffee and tea.

A cocoa tree is small and will produce about 20 pods in each harvest. Each pod weighs about 1 pound and contains 20–40 seeds or beans. The beans are the size of almonds and need to go through a long process before they are transformed into something palatable. When removed from the pod, the seeds have a white pulp covering them which drains away after they have fermented for a few days. They are then dried naturally in the sun or by artificial means. When completely dry, the beans are roasted, cracked, and ground. The process used for grinding melts down the cocoa butter, which constitutes 50 per cent of the beans. The butter cools to a solid brown block, called 'mass', which is the raw material for all chocolate products. Cocoa is made by removing 70–80 per cent of the butter from the 'mass.'

For 300 years after being brought to Europe, chocolate was always thought of as a drink. It wasn't until the 19th century and the invention by Rodolphe Lindt of a process called 'conching,' which enhances the texture and taste of chocolate, that it also became a confectionery. Conching is a very costly process and the chocolate found today in many Latin American countries is still made without it. The result is a less rich, coarser chocolate, where gritty bits of sugar, spices, and sometimes almonds can still be tasted.

Mexican Coffee

This is a sweetened after-dinner coffee flavored with allspice.

SERVES 4

Ingredients

$2^2/_3$ cups water
3 tablespoons granulated sugar
1 teaspoon ground allspice
2 tablespoons ground coffee

Method

1. Bring the water, sugar, and allspice to a boil in a medium saucepan. Add the coffee, mix thoroughly, and let stand 5 minutes.

2. Strain into a warmed coffee pot or cups and serve.

Brazilian Black Coffee

This is a pleasant way of preparing an after-lunch or after-dinner coffee with a hint of cocoa.

SERVES 4

Ingredients

$2^2/_3$ cups water
2 tablespoons granulated sugar
1 teaspoon cocoa powder
2 tablespoons ground coffee

Method

1. Bring the water and sugar to a boil in a medium saucepan. Meanwhile, warm up a coffee pot or small coffee cups.

2. Mix the cocoa with the ground coffee and add to the water as soon as it comes to a boil. Remove from the heat, let stand 4 minutes, and strain into the cups or pot. Serve at once.

NOTE: If using a cafetière, add the cocoa to the coffee and pour the hot water on top. If using a filter, follow the first method.

Mexican Hot Chocolate

If Mexican chocolate is not available, this recipe makes a very good, rich substitute.

SERVES 4

Ingredients

8 ounces dark chocolate, chopped
1 tablespoon water
$^1/_2$ teaspoon ground cinnamon
2 tablespoons granulated sugar
Pinch of ground cloves
$^1/_4$ cup ground almonds
4 cups milk
Few drops vanilla essence or 1 teaspoon vanilla
   extract

Method

1. Melt the chocolate with the water, cinnamon, sugar, and cloves over low heat, stirring frequently.

2. In a small saucepan, bring the almonds and milk to a boil.

3. Remove the melted chocolate mixture from the heat and stir in half of the milk.

4. Return the saucepan to the heat and slowly add the remaining milk, whisking continuously, to form a froth. Add the vanilla essence and more sugar to taste and serve at once.

NOTE: A quicker way to make this is to place the chocolate and half of the milk mixture in a blender; with the motor running, add the remaining milk slowly until all is well blended and frothy.

268

Champurrado

Champurrado is a drink from Guatemala made with chocolate, coffee, and milk and thickened with coarse polenta or cornmeal. This is a quicker version which uses cocoa instead of chocolate.

SERVES 4

Ingredients

$2^2/_3$ cups milk
$^2/_3$ cup black coffee
$^1/_4$ cup cocoa powder
$^1/_4$ cup polenta or cornmeal
2 tablespoons granulated sugar
2 teaspoons ground cinnamon
$^1/_2$ teaspoon ground cloves
Few drops vanilla essence or 1 teaspoon vanilla
   extract

Method

1. Mix all of the ingredients except the vanilla, in a food processor or blender and pour into a heavy saucepan.

2. Whisking continuously, cook over medium heat for 20 minutes or until slightly thickened. Add the vanilla essence and additional sugar to taste, and serve at once.

Menu Suggestions

1. Sweet potato, corn, and green chile soup

   Beef stew in dried chile sauce

   Grilled pineapple skewers with coconut ice cream

2. Peanut soup

   Duck with Rice and Mint

   Tropical fruit salad with cinnamon crème Chantilly

3. Avocado, papaya, and grapefruit salad

   Turkey escalopes with chile cream sauce

   Cinnamon and vanilla ice cream with hazelnut and lemon cookies

4. Sweet corn Velouté with salsa cruda

   Fresh tuna steamed in fruit juice

   Peruvian coffee chocolate pots

5. Zucchini and green bean salad

   Salt cod cakes with three pepper salsa

   Mango and passion fruit ice cream

6. Tortilla salad with watercress and chile dressing

   Lamb brochettes with mango and avocado salsa

   Mexican bread pudding

7. Hearts of palm flan with herb pastry

   Grilled snapper with mango chile sauce

   Flambé bananas with vanilla ice cream

8. Chilled hearts of palm and avocado soup

   Pork chops with pineapple and lime salsa

   Triple chocolate and cinnamon Buscuits with Rich Vanilla Ice Cream

9. Ceviche

   Garlic-roasted chicken with sweet potatoes

   Lime and lemon mousse with pistachio praline

10. Two-bean chili with vegetables

    Mexican rice

    Fresh mangoes and pineapples

11. Brazilian meat and black bean stew

    "Burnt" Coconut Crème Caramel

12. Avocado and Red Pimiento Salad with Chile Dressing

Layered polenta and vegetable pie

"Burnt" coconut crème caramel

13. Chickpea soufflé cakes with red pepper mayonnaise

Vegetable stew with almonds and dried chiles

Tropical fruit salad

14. Creamy chicken gratin

Brazil nut shortbread with pineapple and star anise compote

15. Crab gratin

Turkey blanquette with coconut milk and chiles

Mango and passion fruit ice cream

16. Taco fiesta

Fresh papaya with lime juice

17. Guacamole with Potato and Cheese Cakes with Peanut Sauce

Baked stuffed trout

Nut and coffee tart with coffee cream

18. Herb potato and eggplant roulade with spicy tomato sauce

Marinated vegetable salad

Crunchy banana dessert

Glossary

GLOSSARY

Acaraje A typical Afro-Brazilian food, *acaraje* are black-eyed pea dumplings fried in dendea oil; they may be served on their own or filled with a variety of spicy stuffings.

Aji The generic name for chiles in Peru, Bolivia, Ecuador, and other South American countries.

Allspice Also called Jamaican pepper, allspice is native to tropical America. It resembles large brown peppercorns and tastes like a mixture of cloves, cinnamon, and nutmeg. Best bought whole and ground when needed, allspice is widely used in Caribbean and Central American cooking. Jamaica is the world's largest producer.

Annatto or **Achiote** Also called *urucu*, annatto is a food coloring made from the small, bright red seeds of an evergreen tree found in the Caribbean and throughout South America. The powder made from the seeds is used in all sorts of dishes, sweet and savory, and is also used to color cooking oil. The seeds are exported to England, where they are used for coloring Leicester and Red Cheshire cheeses.

Antichudos A typical Peruvian food, sold in the streets as a snack. Chunks of ox heart are skewered, marinated in spicy vinegar sauce, and grilled. They are usually very spicy.

Arrowroot A fine flour made from the dried roots of a tropical plant. It is mainly used to make biscuits and as a thickening agent.

Atole or **Pozol** A Mayan dish of ground maize spiced with chiles that is eaten for breakfast; a sort of spicy porridge.

Avocado A fruit native to tropical America. Its name is a corruption of the local word *ahucatl*. There are three main varieties: West Indian, Guatemalan, and Mexican. Also known as the alligator pear, the avocado is second only to olives in containing the highest percentage of fat, 79 percent of which is monounsaturated.

Avocados are a good source of vitamins A, B, and C and a moderate source of potassium; they contain no cholesterol.

Bacalao or **Bacalhau** Dried salted cod.

Bahian cooking Bahia is a state on the northeast coast of Brazil, where the African influence on people and cuisine predominates. The mixture of West African ingredients, dishes and culture with that of the native Indians and the Portuguese has resulted in a unique and diverse cuisine.

Bain-marie A baking pan half-filled with hot water in which terrines, custards, etc. stand while cooking. The food is protected from direct fierce heat and cooks in a gentle, steamy atmosphere. Also a large container that will hold a number of pans standing in hot water, used to keep soups, sauces, etc. hot without further cooking.

Bake blind To bake a pastry shell while empty. In order to prevent the sides falling in or the base bubbling up, the pastry is usually lined with paper and filled with 'blind beans' (see below).

Baste To spoon over liquid (sometimes stock, sometimes fat) during cooking to prevent drying out and to promote flavor.

Batida A generic term in Brazil for blended cocktail drinks, alcoholic or not.

Blanch Originally, to whiten by boiling, e.g. briefly to boil sweetbreads or brains to remove traces of blood, or to boil almonds to make the brown skin easy to remove, leaving the nuts white. Now commonly used to mean parboiling, as in blanching vegetables when they are parboiled prior to freezing, or precooked so that they have only to be reheated before serving.

Blind beans Dried beans, peas, rice, or pasta used to fill pastry shells temporarily during baking.

Braise To bake or stew slowly on a bed of vegetables in a covered pan.

Brazil nut Also known as Para or cream nuts, Brazils come from one of the largest trees in the Amazon forest. They are easy to open if chilled for 10 minutes, and easier to slice if boiled shelled for 5 minutes and allowed to cool.

Burrito A flour tortilla used as a wrapper for a variety of fillings.

Cacao A bean, native to South America, which grows on a tall tree that grows wild in the rain forests along the Orinoco and Amazon rivers. The seeds are the size of almonds and have to be fermented and treated in order to become cocoa and chocolate. Cacao is now cultivated in most tropical regions of the world and is a major source of income for many developing countries (see page 266).

Cachaça A Brazilian colorless rum made from sugar cane, used extensively in mixed drinks or drunk on its own.

Caipirinha The national drink of Brazil, made with limes blended with cachaça or rum, ice, and sugar.

Cancha Toasted corn.

Caramel Sugar cooked to a toffee.

Caruru An Afro-Brazilian stew made with shrimp, okra, and fish.

Cashew A fruit indigenous to Brazil. Eaten ripe, it is delicate and delicious, but it is mainly used to make concentrated juice. It is hard to find outside the producing countries. Better known are the nuts attached to the fruits. The Portuguese introduced them to warm areas of the world, including Goa in India, which is today the biggest producer of cashew nuts.

Cassareep A syrup made from the boiled-down juice of cassava or manioc, used extensively in Caribbean cooking.

Cassava or **Manioc** Also called *yuca*, this tuber is native to Brazil, but was taken to Africa in the 16th century, where it became a staple starch. There are two main varieties, one of which is poisonous until washed. There are many by-products of cassava, including tapioca, cassava meal, and cassareep.

Cassava meal or **Manioc meal** A seasoning served throughout Latin America. *Farinha de mandioca*, as it is known in Portuguese, may be eaten plain, sprinkled on juicy food to soak up the liquid, or lightly toasted in butter and mixed with herbs, sultanas, sweet corn, etc. Together with the basic tomato salsa, it stays on the dining table for every meal and is particularly good with beans.

Chancho A South American term for pig or pork.

Charqui Originally dried llama meat, but today it may also be donkey and mule meat. It is eaten mainly in Andean countries.

Chicha A fermented, beerlike drink made from maize; it has a cloudy appearance and sour taste. Very popular in the Andean countries of South America, particularly Peru and Bolivia.

Chilaquiles A casserole made with fried stale tortillas layered with vegetables and covered with a chili sauce or stock.

Chiles These are hot members of the Capsicum family, of which all peppers are part. There are hundreds of varieties of chile, and as a general rule, the smaller the chile the hotter it will be. Green chiles also tend to be hotter than the red variety, and dried chiles are just as hot as fresh ones. (See also pages 192–201.)

Chimichangas Uncooked flour tortillas that are filled, then fried.

Chorizo A spicy sausage made with pork, garlic, and red chili powder. Originally from Spain, it is found throughout Latin America.

Chunos Also known as *papa seca*, these are freeze-dried potatoes, made by an ancient technique invented by the Andean Indians. The same method is still used today (see page 19).

Churrasco A barbecued meat feast, usually prepared outdoors, with a variety of meat cuts. A tradition in Argentina, southern Brazil, and Uruguay.

Churros A deep-fried, long, doughnutlike pastry, filled with *doce de leite* and tossed in sugar and cinnamon. They are eaten in Chile, Argentina, Brazil, and other South American countries.

Cilantro An herb, originally from the Mediterranean, which is the most commonly used herb in Latin American cuisine. Its unique flavor is slowly destroyed by heat, so add half the amount stated in any recipe at the beginning of cooking and mix in the remainder just before serving. The seeds of this herb are called coriander and are ground as a spice. The herb is also called fresh coriander or Chinese parsley.

Coconut The fruit of the coco-palm. It has a brown fibrous husk covering thick white flesh and a hollow core containing coconut water. The flesh and its various products play an important part in the cuisines of many countries, being used in both sweet and savory dishes. The various forms of coconut may be bought ready-prepared from supermarkets, but it is relatively easy to make them yourself from fresh coconuts (see below).

Fresh Coconut

When buying fresh coconut, choose those that feel heavy and when shaken appear to have plenty of liquid inside. The 'eyes'—three dark round spots on top of the coconut—should be clean of mold and moisture.

Method

1. With a skewer or screwdriver pierce the 'eyes' and drain the cloudy liquid into a bowl or cup. (Coconut water, as this liquid is called, is usually drunk cold or mixed with alcohol. Coconut milk is the liquid extracted from pressing grated coconut flesh that has been mixed with water or milk for at least 30 minutes.)

2. To break the shell, cover the coconut with a tea towel and hit it with a hammer. Alternatively, put the whole nut into a preheated oven, 400°F, for 5 minutes. The heat makes the shell easier to break and leaves the flesh free once the nut is cracked.

3. Coconut flesh has a thin dark skin on the outside that must be removed. Use a potato peeler or sharp knife to peel it off.

4. Using a metal grater or the appropriate blade on a food processor, grate the flesh to the desired coarseness.

To make coconut milk

1. Place the grated coconut in a food processor or blender and cover with hot water or hot milk. Blend well and leave to cool. Strain through a fine sieve or a muslin cloth, making sure to extract all the liquid from the pulp.

NOTE: Follow the same instructions to make coconut milk from flaked coconut. If using creamed coconut, follow the instructions on the packet.

Comal A pottery griddle used to cook tortillas.

Cream To beat ingredients together, such as butter and sugar, when making a sponge cake.

Crêpes Thin French pancakes.

Cuy An Andean rodent, this guinea pig is found mainly in Peru and Bolivia, where it is the biggest source of protein in the diet.

Deglaze To loosen and liquefy the fat, sediment and browned juices stuck at the bottom of a skillet or saucepan by adding liquid (usually stock, water, or wine) and stirring while boiling.

Dendea oil Oil extracted from the fruit of the oil palm; it varies in color from yellow to deep orange and red and gives a distinctive taste to Bahian food. It is widely used in Brazil, and also in West Africa, where it is called red palm oil. An acquired taste, it can be substituted by adding a little paprika to the cooking oil of any Bahian dish.

Devein To remove the fine black vein in the flesh of shrimp. First peel the shrimp, then use a small sharp knife to cut a slit along the back and lift the vein out. Rinse the prepared shrimp under running water and dry on paper towels before using.

Doce de leite Milk boiled with sugar until it becomes a thick, golden-brown paste with a light caramel taste. A staple sweet in all Latin American countries, it can be eaten on its own or used as filling for cakes, pies, churros, etc. The consistency varies from soft set to a hard paste, and coconuts, nuts, or prunes can be added to it. It is also called *dulce de leche, leche quemada*, or *manjar* (see page 220).

Dried shrimps Very small pink shrimps with a strong flavor and smell of seafood. They are used as a seasoning in many African-Bahian dishes from Brazil, and are also used in Chinese and southeast Asian cooking. They can be bought in oriental food shops.

Egg wash Beaten raw egg, sometimes with salt, used for glazing pastry to give a shine when baked.

Empanadas Small savory pasties or turnovers made by wrapping a white flour dough around a filling of meat, chicken, cheese, hearts of palm, or sweet corn, depending on the region in which they are made. They are called empadas or empadinhas in Brazil and are very popular in Chile, Argentina, Uruguay, and other South American countries.

Enchiladas Tortillas dipped in a thin red or green tomato sauce and quickly fried. They are then rolled up like a taco with a cheese or meat filling and the remaining sauce is poured over before serving.

Epazote A perennial herb, also known as ambrosia in English. It is used as a flavoring in Mexican cooking, especially with beans. It has a strong and bitter flavor and is hard to find outside Mexico.

Escabeche Term used to describe foods marinated or pickled in vinegar. Of Arab origins, this method of preserving food was introduced to Latin America by the Spanish.

Escalope A thin slice of meat, sometimes beaten out flat to make it thinner and larger.

Farinha de mandioca See Cassava meal.

Farofas A typical Brazilian dish made with cassava meal fried in butter and a variety of added ingredients, such as eggs, olives, raisins, cheese, prunes, bacon, chopped meat, carrots, and other vegetables. It is served with meat, fish, or poultry dishes and can also be used as a stuffing.

Feijoada completa The national dish of Brazil (see page 90).

Flamber To set alcohol alight. Usually to burn off the alcohol, but frequently simply for dramatic effect.

Flan Crème caramel of Spanish origins found in all Latin American countries. It is served plain or flavored with coconut, cinnamon, almonds, cheese, chocolate, lemon, coffee, or fruit (see page 216).

Fold To mix with a gentle lifting motion, rather than to stir vigorously. The aim is to avoid beating out air while mixing.

Frijoles Beans.

Glaze To cover with a thin layer of melted jam (for fruit flans) or syrup (for rum baba), butter, or oil.

Granadilla A type of passion fruit.

Gratiner To brown under a broiler after the surface of the dish has been sprinkled with bread crumbs and butter and, sometimes, cheese. Dishes finished like this are sometimes called *gratinee* or *au gratin*.

Guacamole Mexican sauce or dip made with mashed avocado mixed with tomato, chopped onions, cilantro, and chile. It is served with almost any Mexican dish, especially tortillas and refried beans (see page 185).

Guarana The seed of a jungle plant used to make the most popular soft drink in Brazil. It has a tangy, fruity flavor. The seed has a small amount of caffeine and is used in the pharmaceutical industry to make herbal "pep" pills.

Guava Yellow to greenish, very fragrant tropical fruit, the size of a large plum. It has a soft skin covering reddish or white flesh, in the center of which is a cavity containing pulp and small, hard seeds. Guavas are very delicate and should be eaten soon after purchase, either peeled or unpeeled. They are used to make compotes, fruit pastes, and jams, and are very popular in tropical countries.

Guinea pig See Cuy.

Hearts of palm Also called palmito, these are the tender shoots of certain palm trees. They are about 3 inches long and 1 inch in diameter. They have a delicate flavor and are served simply with vinaigrette or used in salads, cold soups, and little turnovers. Even in tropical countries fresh palm hearts are difficult to find, so canned ones are acceptable. Those sent for export, however, tend to be smaller and have less flavor. In Brazil palm hearts are sold in glass jars so the quality can be checked before buying.

Humitas Sometimes wrongly called tamales, humitas are small pies made with fresh corn dough, wrapped in corn husks and steamed. The fillings vary from country to country, the most common ones being pork, chicken, sausage, cheese, and peanuts. They are popular in Peru, central Brazil, and Andean countries.

Infuse To steep or heat gently to extract flavor, as when infusing milk with onion slices.

Julienne Vegetables or citrus rind cut in thin matchstick shapes or very fine shreds.

Locro A thick soup, almost a stew, made of different vegetables, although potatoes are the most commonly used. Found traditionally in Andean countries, such as Ecuador, Bolivia, and Peru.

Macerate To soak food in a syrup or liquid to allow flavors to mix.

Maguey A large "century plant" from the arid areas of Mexico. It plays an important part in Mexican culture: its sap is used to make the popular alcoholic drink pulque, the leaves yield a strong, coarse fiber, which is used to make mats and ropes, and the roots can be eaten as a vegetable.

Maize Corn. There are many varieties of corn,

with colors ranging from black to white and purple to yellow; the kernels also vary in hardness and size.

Manioc See Cassava.

Margarita A Mexican cocktail made with tequila, lime juice, sugar, and a dash of triple sec (see page 259).

Marinade The liquid used for marinating. Usually contains oil, onion, bay leaf, and vinegar or wine.

Marinate To soak meat, fish, or vegetables before or after cooking in acidulated liquid containing flavorings and herbs.

Masa harina Flour used to make tortillas and tamales. It is made by heating corn kernels with lime juice, which makes the skins come off easily. The kernels are then dried and ground. Masa harina can be white, yellow, or other colors, according to the type of corn used, and can vary in coarseness, although it is usually made to the correct texture for tortillas.

Matambre An Argentinian beef dish, the name of which means "kill hunger."

Mate or **Yerba mate** A tea made from the dried leaves of a shrub that grows wild in the southern countries of South America. Very popular in Argentina, Paraguay, Uruguay, and Chile, mate is drunk by gauchos (South American cowboys) in preference to coffee.

Mole **sauce** A traditional thick, savory sauce from Mexico. Chiles, fresh, dried, or smoked, are the fundamental ingredient. The most famous *mole* is *mole poblano*, which is made with three types of dried chiles and bitter chocolate (see page 75).

Moqueca A fish stew from Bahia, Brazil, frequently flavored with chiles and dendea oil. It can also be made with shrimp (see page 129).

Moule-à-manqué French cake pan with sloping sides. The resulting cake has a wider base than top, and is about 1-inch high.

Mulato chiles See chile chart, page 199.

Nopales The young pads of the prickly pear cactus. These have their spines removed and are then used mainly in Mexican salads. Nopales canned in brine, vinegar, or water are known as nopalitos and are available from shops specializing in Mexican food.

Okra Of African origin, this edible seed pod is found in the cuisines of the Caribbean and Brazil, where African slaves were brought to work on the sugar plantations. Buy bright green, firm pods that snap at the tip and do not bend. Wash and dry thoroughly, then trim off both ends of the pods, or they will become slimy when cooked. They can be boiled, fried, or cooked in hot oil, and the addition of a little lemon juice or vinegar will prevent them losing their bright color.

Palm oil See Dendea oil.

Papas secas Dried potatoes (see Chunos).

Papaya A tropical fruit, also known as pawpaw. It has an elongated pear shape, is green and hard outside when unripe and yellow orange and soft when ripe. Cut in half when ripe, the fruit has a deep apricot-colored flesh with lots of small, round black seeds that are scooped out and discarded. The flesh is sweet and aromatic, making it a favorite breakfast fruit in the tropics. It varies enormously in size, from 20 pound giants to the small variety found in supermarkets. Unripe papaya is used for a variety of dishes, including stews, sweets, chutneys, and compotes; the ripe fruit is eaten fresh with lime juice or used to make fruit salads and drinks (see page 256).

Pasilla Dried chile from Mexico (see chile chart, page 199).

Passion fruit Fruit native to South America, where there are many different varieties: purple, yellow, bell-apple, sweet calabash, and granadilla are all used mainly for making juices, ice creams and confections. The fruit's name comes from its flower, which is supposed to resemble all the elements of Christ's passion.

Peanuts Also known as groundnuts or monkey nuts, peanuts are peas rather than nuts and have a high protein and iron content. Native to Brazil, they grow in tropical and subtropical areas of the world and have many uses. In South America, peanut oil is extensively used, and peanuts appear in both savory and sweet dishes.

Pibil Chicken steamed in a closed clay pot, a typical dish from the Yucatan region of Mexico.

Pibre A type of sea urchin, found on the Chilean coast.

Pimiento One of the mildest members of the pepper and chile family and very similar in appearance to a sweet red bell pepper. Pimientos are usually canned in brine. They are very popular in Mediterranean cuisines.

Pipian Sauce used for slow-cooked stews and similar dishes. It is thickened with ground pumpkin seeds and can be flavored with tomatillos and coriander for a green pipian, or with tomatoes and red chiles for a red version.

Pirão A porridge-type dish made with polenta or cassava meal mixed with enough juice from fish stews to give a soft consistency; served hot.

Pisco Peruvian brandy, which tastes a little like cognac, but is colorless. Very popular in Bolivia and Chile.

Plantain Belonging to the same family as the banana, plantains are larger than common bananas, with a firm and not very sweet flesh. As they ripen, they change from green to yellow and finally black. They can be used at any stage of ripeness, but must always be cooked. They are added to soups and stews as a thickening agent, fried in butter and oil and served as a vegetable or dessert, and steamed or barbecued in their skins. Widely used in Latin American cuisine, particularly in Ecuador, for savory dishes as well as fruit pastes, jams, drinks, cakes, etc.

Praline Almonds cooked in sugar until the mixture caramelizes, then cooled and crushed to a powder. Used for flavoring desserts and ice cream.

Proof To put dough or a yeasted mixture to rise before baking.

Pulque Fermented, beerlike drink from Mexico made from the sap of the maguey or century plant.

Purée Liquidized, sieved, or finely mashed fruit or vegetables.

Quinoa A plant native to the Andes, which produces a small grain very high in protein and easily digested. Called 'mother grain' by the Incas, it was regarded as holy and, together with potatoes, was a staple crop. It is used extensively in Peruvian cuisine, mainly as a thickening agent. It may be bought in health food shops and should be thoroughly rinsed before cooking. It can replace couscous or cracked wheat with great success.

Reduce To reduce the amount of liquid by rapid boiling, causing evaporation and a consequent strengthening of flavor in the remaining liquid.

Refresh To hold boiled vegetables under a cold tap, or to dunk them immediately in cold water to prevent their cooking further in their own steam, and to set the color of green vegetables.

Relax or **Rest** Of pastry: to set aside in a cool place to allow the gluten (which will have expanded during rolling) to contract. This lessens the danger of shrinking in the oven. Of batters: to set aside to allow the starch cells to swell, giving a lighter result when cooked.

Render To melt solid fat (e.g. beef, pork) slowly in the oven.

Salsas Uncooked sauce of freshly chopped ingredients (see page 174).

Scald Of milk: to heat until on the point of boiling, when some movement can be seen at the edges of the pan but there is no overall bubbling.

Seal or **Seize** To brown meat rapidly, usually in fat, for flavor and color.

Season To flavor food, generally with salt and pepper.

Soft ball The term used to describe sugar syrup reduced by boiling to sufficient thickness to form soft balls when dropped into cold water and rubbed between finger and thumb.

Sweat To cook gently, usually in butter or oil, but sometimes in the food's own juices, without frying or browning.

Sweet potatoes There are various types of sweet potatoes, all native to tropical America. The flesh can vary in color from white to deep yellow. They are usually boiled in their skins to prevent the flesh from discoloring and are delicious roasted or baked; they can also be used in soups, candies, and a pudding very much like sweetened chestnut purée.

Tabasco See chile chart, page 197.

Taco A filled, rolled-up tortilla, the Mexican equivalent of a sandwich. Tacos can be eaten soft, or deep-fried with an enormous variety of stuffings (see page 163).

Tamales Mexican steamed pies made with masa harina dough. They may be eaten plain or stuffed with a savory or sweet filling. The uncooked tamales are wrapped in corn husks or banana leaves and steamed (see page 170).

Tapioca See Cassava.

Tequila A popular Mexican drink made from the starchy root stock of a plant called *Agave azul tequilana*. Normally colorless, it can be pale yellow when aged (see page 259).

Timbale A dish cooked in a castle-shaped mold, or a dish served piled up high.

Tomatillos Also called husk tomatoes or Mexican green tomatoes, tomatillos are small tomatoes that are ripe, even when firm and green. They have a tart flavor, can be bought canned and are used extensively in Mexican cuisine. Green gooseberries make a reasonable substitute.

Tortilla Mexican flat bread made from corn or wheat dough (see page 162).

Tortilla chips Also known as tostaditas, these are wedges of corn tortilla fried until crisp. Black or blue corn can be used to make tortillas, which results in dark tortilla chips. Different flavorings, such as chiles, cheese, and herbs, may also be used.

Tostadas Wheat tortillas that are deep-fried or baked into a basket shape, then filled with a variety of savory fillings or fruits.

Tostaditas See Tortilla chips.

To the thread Of sugar boiling: term used to denote the degree of thickness achieved when reducing sugar, i.e. the syrup will form threads if tested between wet finger and thumb. Short thread: about $1/2$ inch; long thread: 2 inches or more.

Turron Popular Mexican sweet paste made with ground almonds or peanuts mixed with sugar.

Vatapa Bahian fish stew containing peanuts, dried shrimps and chiles.

Well A hollow or dip made in a pile or bowlful of flour, exposing the tabletop or the bottom of the bowl, into which other ingredients are placed prior to mixing.

Yerba mate See Mate.

Zest The outer colored skin of an orange or lemon, used to give flavor. It is very thinly pared without any of the bitter white pith.

RESOURCES

Bueno Foods
2001 4th Street S.W.
Albuquerque, New Mexico 87102
Phone (800) 95Chile (952-4453)
Fax (505) 242-1680
Specializing in chiles and Mexican specialty items
National orders accepted
Catalog available

Coyote Cafe General Store
132 West Walter Street
Santa Fe, New Mexico 87501
Phone (800) 866-HOWL or (505) 982-2454
Fax (505) 989-9026
Specializing in beans, chiles (including canned chipotles en adobo), canela, spices, tamarind, corn husks.
National and International orders accepted;
Catalog available

Dean and Deluca
560 Broadway
New York, New York 10012
Phone (212) 431-1691
Fax (212) 226-2003
Specializing in gourmet ingredients
Catalog available

Williams-Sonoma
P.O. Box 7456
San Francisco, California 94120-7456
Phone (800) 541-2233
Fax (702) 360-7152
Specializing in kitchen equipment and specialty foods
Catalog available

Frieda's Finest Produce Specialties
P.O. Box 58488
Los Angeles, California 90058
Phone (800) 241-1771
Fax (714) 816-0273
Catalog available
Internet address: www.friedas.com
Specializing in fresh fruits and vegetables and complimentary items from Latin cuisines, dried fruits and nuts, exotic fruits from around the world, specialty vegetables

Los Chileros de Nuevo Mexico
P.O. Box 6215
Santa Fe, New Mexico 87502
Phone (505) 471-6967
Fax (505) 473-7306
Specializing in gourmet chiles and Southwestern foods

Mo Hotta-Mo Betta
Tim and Wendy Eidson
P.O. Box 4136
San Luis Obispo, California 93403
Phone (800) 462-3220
Fax (800) 618-4454
Internet address: www.mohotta.com
Specializing in scarry and habañero hot sauces, salsas, chiles and soups, pickled products
Catalog and International shipping available

FURTHER READING

Miller, Mark: *The Great Chile Book* (Ten Speed Press, Berkeley, California, 1991).

Ortiz, Elisabeth Lanbert: *The Book of Latin American Cooking*, (Ecco Press, 1994).

Cusick, Heidi Haughy: *Soul and Spice* (Chronicle Books, San Francisco, 1995).

DeWitt, Dave and Gerlach, Nancy: *The Whole Chile Pepper Book* (Little Brown, Boston, 1990).

Younger, Johanna and Fisher, James: *Chiles & Other Peppers*, (Sunset Books Inc. 1994).

Wells, Troth: *The Global Kitchen, Meat Vegetarian Recipes from Africa, Asia and Latin America for Western Kitchens, with Country Information and Food Facts*, (The Crossing Press, 1995).

Cocina Latino Americana, (Editoria Americana, 1988).

Cordova, Regina and Carrasco Emma: *Celebracion: Recipes and Traditions Celebrating Latino Family Life*, (Doubleday and Co. Inc., 1996).

Hill, Nicola: *The Chili and Peppers Cookbook* (Courage Books, Philadelphia, PA, 1995).

DeWitt, David: Hot Spots (Prima Publishing, Rocklin California, 1992).

DeWitt, Dave and Wilan, Mary Jane and Stock, Melissa T.: Hot and Spicy Latin Dishes (Prima Publishing, Rocklin, California, 1995).

Gordon-Smith, Clare: Basic Flavorings: Chiles, (Courage Books, Philadelphia, PA 1996).

Novas, H.: Latin American Cooking Across the USA, (Random House, 1996).

Solomon, Jay: *Great Bowls of Fire!: The World's Spiciest Soups, Chiles, Stews and Hot Pots*, (Prima Publishing, Rocklin, California, 1997).

Naj, Amal: *Peppers: A Story of Hot Pursuits* (Knopf, 1992).

INDEX

almonds:
  toasting 76
  vegetable stew with 135
apple:
  and tomatillo salsa 183
  sauce 222
avocado(s) 262
  batida 266
  guacamole 185
  salad:
    with papaya and grapefruit 54
    with red pimento 48
    with seafood and hearts of palm 55
  salsa 180
    with mango 176
  soup:
    with lime 28
    with hearts of palm 34

banana(s) 104
  and walnut bread 244
  dessert, crunchy 210
  flambé 205
  fried 147
batida 262, 274
beans 150-4
  beans, pork stew with 102
  Brazilian meat and black bean stew
    (feijoada) 90
  drunken 152
  kidney bean salad, mixed 56
  milky coconut 154
  pinto, fried 105
  refried 151
  two-bean chili with vegetables 85
  zucchini and green bean salad 50
beef 22, 63, 82
  ground:
    Picadillo 92
    two-bean chili with vegetables 85
    with apples, olives, and almonds 88
  shredded, spicy 89
  steak, grilled 86
  stew in dried chile sauce 87
  stew, with dried fruit 84
  stock 189
bolinho de bacalhau 115
Brazil nut(s) 275
  shortbread 246
Brazilian black coffee 267
Brazilian meat and black bean stew 90
bread 19, 232, 241-4
  banana and walnut 244
  corn 242
  pudding, Mexican 211
  white, Cuban 241
brochettes, lamb 107
burritos 163, 275

cachaca 259, 275
caipirinha 260, 275
cakes 232-9
  carrot 236
  chocolate, orange, and prune 234
  coffee, cocoa, and cinnamon 233
  cornmeal, coconut and prune 239
  light peanut oil 237
  walnut and rice flour 238
carrot cake 236
caruru 118, 275
cassava meal 275
  toasted 247
casseroles:
  chicken and okra 68
catering quantities 22
cayenne toasts 28
ceviche 38, 52
chalupa 163
champurrado 268
charlotte, pineapple 207
cheese:
  and potato cakes 42
  Mexican rice with 158
  pastelzitos 253
  potato, cheese, and cayenne puffs 136
  see also ricotta
chicha 259, 275
chickpea souffle cakes 43
chicken 22, 62, 63
  and okra casserole 68
  garlic-roasted 64
  gratin, creamy 66
  in chocolate and chile sauce 76
  in tomatillo and nut sauce 70
  mousse, chunky 72
  pipian 135
  sausages, with pepper and chile 67
  stock 188
  thighs in pumpkin seed sauce 69
  wings, spicy 71
  with shrimp and peanut sauce 73
chilaquiles 163, 275
chile(s) 192-201, 275
  chart 195-9
  con carne, two bean, with vegetables 85
  dressings:
    lime 48
    watercress 49
  dried 194, 198-9
    sauce 87, 106
    vegetable stew with 135
  green: sweet potato and corn soup with 29
  oil 200
  paste 180
    dried 182
    veal chops in 94
    yellow 182

preparing 194
  purée, jalapeño 95
salsas:
  chipotle 183
  jalapeño and lime 177
  melon and chile 178
  pineapple and chile 178
sauces:
  Anaheim 128
  cream 78
  with chocolate 75
  with mango, thick 124, 181
serving wine with 258
chimichangas 163, 275
  chorizo 168
chocolate:
  and chile sauce, turkey in 75
  chocolate, orange, and prune cake 234
  créme caramel 216
  drinking 263, 268
  Peruvian coffee chocolate cups 213
  triple chocolate cinnamon cookies 248
chorizo 275
  chimichangas 168
cinnamon:
  and vanilla ice cream 227
  créme anglaise 220
  créme Chantilly 212
cocktails 259, 264-5
cocoa 266
  cocoa, coffee, and cinnamon cake 233
coconut 2 76
  and shrimp torte 40
  cornmeal, coconut, and prune cake 239
  créme caramel, 'burnt' 216
  fish stew with 129
  ice cream 226
  milk 276
    beans in 154
  punch 264
  rice, yellow 157
cod:
  roast with nut sauce 113
  salt:
    Bahian style 121
    cakes 116
coffee 263-5
  and nut tart with coffee cream 206
  black, Brazilian 267
  chocolate cups 213
  coffee, cocoa and cinnamon cake 233
  créme anglaise 220
  Mexican 267
Colombian milk pudding 221
conversion tables 20-1
cookies:
  Brazil nut shortbread 246
  ginger tuiles 250

hazelnut and lemon 248
triple chocolate cinnamon 248
corn 16
    bread 242
    cornmeal, coconut, and prune cake 239
    ice cream 227
    muffins 240
    sweet corn:
        and sweet potato soup 29
        pastelzitos 253
        velouté 29
    tortillas 164
corvina 52, 112
couscous timbales 51
crab:
    and fish soup 33
    and shrimp cake, spicy 45
    baked crab shells 44
    tostadas 167
créme anglaise 220
créme caramel 216
créme Chantilly, cinnamon 212
Creoja sauce 179
crêpes see pancakes
cuban white bread 241

desserts 204-23
dip, peanut, chile, and ricotta cheese 186
doce de leite 221, 277
dried fruit, beef stew with 84
drinks 256-68
duck 22, 63
    with rice and mint 79
    with shrimp and peanut sauce 73
dulce de leche 221

eggplant and herb potato roulade 133
empanadas 277
    ricotta and vegetable 142
enchilada 163, 277
escabeche sauce 184

feijoada 90, 278
fish 22, 112
    and shrimp in ginger and peanut sauce 115
    ceviche 52
    soup:
        with crab 33
        with shrimp 35
    stew with coconut and shrimp sauce 129
    stock 189
frijoles refritos 151
fruit:
    coconut punch 260
    drinks 212, 259
    juice, tuna steamed in 120
    mixed fruit batida 262
    poaching syrup 223

salad, tropical 212
    see also dried fruit

garlic-roasted chicken with sweet potatoes 64
ginger:
    créme anglaise 220
    tuiles 250
glace de viande 189
gorda 163
grapefruit, avocado, and papaya salad 54
green soup with hazelnuts 32
guacamole 185, 278
guasacaca 180
guava(s) 278
    ice cream 226

haddock, baked 126
halibut ceviche 52
hazelnut(s):
    and lemon cookies 248
    green soup with 32
hearts of palm 278
    and avocado soup, chilled 34
    flan, with herb pastry 39
    pastelzitos 253
    salad, with seafood and avocado 55
herb pastry 251

ice cream 204, 223-9
    cinnamon and vanilla 227
    coconut 226
    corn on the cob 227
    guava, cinnamon and ginger 226
    mango and passion fruit 223
    peanut crunch 224
    pineapple 228
    vanilla, rich 229

kale, shredded 145

lamb 22, 63
    braised shoulder in dried chile sauce 106
    brochettes with mango and
        avocado salsa 107
    roast, with mint and fried pinto beans 105
    stew with red peppers 104
leche quemada 221
lemon:
    and hazelnut cookies 248
    and lime mousse 208
lime:
    and avocado soup 28
    and jalapeño salsa 177
    and lemon mousse 208
    and pineapple salsa 101
    and tomato sauce 126
    creoja sauce 179
    lime chile dressing 48

limeade, tropical 262

maize see corn
mango:
    and avocado salsa 176
    and chile sauce 181
    and passion fruit ice cream 223
margarita 259, 279
masa harina 164, 279
mayonnaise 187
    red pepper, spicy 187
meat 63, 82-108
    and black bean stew (feijoada) 90
melon and chile salsa 178
menu suggestions 270-1
Mexican bread pudding 211
Mexican coffee 267
Mexican crêpe gratin 140
Mexican hot chocolate 268
Mexican rice 158
milk pudding 221
minced meat see beef
mole 70, 279
mole poblano 75
moqueca 129, 279
mousse, chunky chicken 72
muffins, cornmeal 240

nopales/nopalitos 38, 279
nut:
    and coffee tart 206
    sauce 113
        with tomatillo 70

oil 112
    chile-flavored 200
okra 279
    and chicken casserole 68
    salad, warm 51
    shrimp with 118
onions, cured 144
orange:
    and papaya batida 262
    chocolate, orange, and prune cake 234
    créme anglaise 220

pancakes (crêpes) 219
    Mexican crêpe gratin 140
    pancake stack pie 91
papaya 279
    and orange batida 262
    and Scotch bonnet salsa 179
    avocado and grapefruit salad with 54
parsley sauce, spiced 86
passion fruit 280
    and mango ice cream 223
    créme anglaise, with rum 220
pastelzitos 253

pastry 251-2
  cornmeal 142
peach charlotte 207
peanut oil cake, light 237
peanut(s) 280
  crunch ice cream 224
  ricotta cheese dip with 186
  sauce 42, 108
    ginger-flavored 116
    and shrimp, chicken with 73
  shrimp and okra with 118
  soup 27
pepper(s):
  and chicken sausages 67
  mayonnaise, spicy 187
  red, lamb stew with 104
  roast pepper and tomato soup 30
  salsa 115, 177
  stuffed 141
Peruvian coffee chocolate cups 213
Peruvian quinoa salad 58
picadillo 92
pies:
  pancake stack 91
  polenta and vegetable 138
  ricotta and vegetable
    empanada 142
pimientos 280
  and avocado salad 48
  sauce, with pumpkin seed, and
    cilantro 122
pineapple:
  and chile salsa 178
  and lime salsa 101
  charlotte 207
  compote, with star anise 215
  ice cream 228
  skewers, grilled 214
pipian 135, 280
pisco 259, 280
  sour 264
pistachio praline 208
plantain 280
poaching syrup 223
polenta 245
  and vegetable pie 138
pollo en mole verde 70
pork 22
  chops with salsa 101
  roast 63
    hot 96
    sweet 100
  shredded 103
  spicy 98
  stew with beans 102
potato(es) 19, 23, 132
  and cheese cakes 42
  and eggplant roulade 133

puffs, with cheese and cayenne 136
poultry 22, 62-79
praline 280
  pistachio 208
prune:
  charlotte 207
  chocolate, orange, and prune
    cake 234
  cornmeal, coconut, and prune
    cake 239
puff pastry 252
pulque 259, 280
pumpkin seed sauce 69
  with pimento and cilantro 122
punch, coconut 260
purées 280
  jalapeño 95
  quince 218
  sweet potato 146

quails' egg, marinated 46
quesadillas 163
quince purée 218
quinoa 280
  salad, Peruvian 50

rabbit with peanut sauce 108
raisin and walnut rice 155
red dried chile paste 182
rice 19, 23, 150, 155-9
  baked red 159
  coconut, yellow 157
  duck with 79
  fried 155
  green 156
  Mexican 158
  soup, tropical-style 34
  walnut and rice flour cake 238
ricotta:
  dip, peanut and chile 186
  and vegetable empanada pie 142
roasting tables 63

salads 23, 38, 46-51, 54-8
  avocado and pimento 48
  avocado, papaya, and grapefruit 54
  fruit, tropical 212
  kidney bean, mixed 56
  okra, warm 51
  quail's egg and zucchini 46
  quinoa, Peruvian 58
  seafood, avocado, and hearts of palm 55
  tortilla 49
  vegetable, marinated 57
  zucchini and green bean 50
salmon tacos 114
salsas 174, 281
  avocado, spicy 180

chipotle chile 183
cruda 176
jalapeño and lime 177
mango and avocado 176
melon and chile 178
pineapple and chile 178
pineapple and lime 101
red pepper 115
roja 180
Scotch bonnet and papaya 179
three pepper 177
tomatillo and apple 183
sangrita 261
sauces:
  Anaheim chile 128
  apple 222
  chile cream 78
  creoja 179
  dried chile 87, 106
  escabeche 184
  lime and tomato 126
  mango and chile 181
  nut, spicy 113
  parsley, spiced 86
  peanut 42, 108
  pumpkin seed 69
  tomatillo and nut 70
  tomato, spicy 181
sausages, chicken, pepper and chile 67
Scotch bonnet and papaya salsa 179
seafood salad, with avocado and hearts of
  palm 55
sesame seeds, toasting 76
shellfish 22, 112
shortbread, Brazil nut 246
shortcrust pastry 251
shrimp:
  shrimp(s) 22
  and coconut torte 40
  and crab cake 45
  and fish in ginger and peanut sauce 116
  and fish soup 35
  and peanut sauce 73
  fish stew with 129
  in pimento, pumpkin seed and cilantro
    sauce 122
  with okra and peanuts 118
snapper:
  grilled 124
  with Anaheim chile sauce 128
sope 163
soup 22, 26-35
spinach:
  green soup with hazelnuts 32
  spirits 259
starters 38-45, 115
steak see beef
stews:

   beef in dried chile sauce 87
   fish 129
   meat and black bean (feijoada) 90
   lamb, with red peppers 104
   pork and beans 102
stocks 188-9
sweet potatoes 281
   garlic-roasted chicken with 64
   purée 146
   soup, with corn and chile 29
sweet corn *see* corn
syrup, poaching 223

taco(s) 163, 281
   fiesta 165
   salmon 114
tamales 170, 281
tart, nut and coffee 206
tequila 259, 281
timbales, couscous 51
toasts, cayenne 28
tomatillo(s) 281
   and apple salsa 183
   and nut sauce 70
tomato:
   and roast pepper soup 30
   sauce 181
      with lime 126
tortilla(s) 162-71, 281
   chips 163, 281
   corn 164
   flour 166
   salad 49
   soup garnish 26
tostadas 163, 281
   crab 167
   sweet 167
tostaditas 163, 282
totopos 163
trout, baked stuffed 125
tuna steamed in fruit juice 120
turkey 22, 62, 63
   blanquette 77
   escalopes with chile cream sauce 78
   gratin, creamy 66
   in chocolate and chile sauce 75

vanilla ice cream 229
   with cinnamon 227
vatapa 116, 282
veal:
   chops in chile paste 94
   roast stuffed breast 95
   stock 188
vegetable(s) 23, 132-47
   and polenta pie 138
   and ricotta pie 142
   rice 155

   root, gratin 134
   salad, marinated 57
   stew with almonds and dried
      chiles 135

walnut:
   and banana bread 244
   and rice flour cake 238
   and raisin rice 155
   créme caramel 216
watercress:
   and chile dressing 49
   green soup with hazelnuts 32
   salad 40
wines 257-8

xinxim de galinha 73

yellow chile paste 182
yellow rice 155
   coconut 157
yugeno 261

zucchini and green bean salad 50